LOUISIANA

FOLKTALES

Lupin, Bouki, and Other Creole Stories
in French Dialect and English Translation

LOUISIANA FOLKTALES

Lapin, Bouki, and Other Creole Stories
in French Dialect and English Translation

COLLECTED AND EDITED
by Alcée Fortier

INTRODUCTION TO NEW EDITION
by Russell Desmond

University of Louisiana at Lafayette Press
2011

http://ulpress.org

University of Louisiana at Lafayette Press
P.O. Box 40831
Lafayette, LA 70504-0831

ISBN 13 (paperback): 978-1-935754-10-7

Parts one and two, as well as the English translations in part three, were all published as *Louisiana Folk-Tales* (Houghton-Mifflin for the American Folk-lore Society, 1895). The Creole French versions of the tales in part three were originally published in the *Journal of American Folk-lore* (Volume 1-2, 1888-1889) and in the *Publications of the Modern Language Association of America* (Volume 3, 1887). Appendix one was originally published in Alcée Fortier's *Louisiana Studies* (F. F. Hansell & Bro., 1894); appendix two was originally published in *Publications of the Modern Language Association of America* (Volume 3, 1887); appendix three was originally published in the *Journal of American Folk-lore* (Volume 1, 1888); and appendix four was originally published in *Comptes-Rendus de l'Athénée Louisianais* (July 1880).

Library of Congress Cataloging-in-Publication Data

Fortier, Alcée, 1856-1914.
Louisiana folktales : lupin, bouki, and other creole stories in french dialect and english translation / collected and edited by Alcée Fortier ; introduction to new edition by Russell Desmond.
p. cm.
Includes bibliographical references.
ISBN 978-1-935754-10-7 (pbk. : alk. paper)
1. Tales--Louisiana. 2. Creoles--Lousiana--Folklore. I. Title.
GR110.L5F55 2011
398.209763--dc23
2011035072

CONTENTS

INTRODUCTION TO 2011 EDITION

by Russell Desmond

Alcée Fortier's professional accomplishments covered the fields of education, history, literary criticism, linguistics, and the study of folklore. As a lifelong educator, apart from teaching French and other Romance languages for some thirty-six years, he continuously fought for the preservation of the French language in Louisiana, serving for over twenty years as president of L'Athénée Louisianais, an organization designed to promote French language and literature in the state, as well as serving smaller terms as president of such associations as the Public School Alliance of New Orleans, the Alliance Franco-Louisiane, and the Fédération de l'Alliance Francaise aux Etats Unis et Canada. He also served as president of the Louisiana Historical Society for nearly twenty years. In this field, he is mostly remembered for his multi-volume *History of Louisiana* (1904), which, however useful or enjoyable, broke no new ground. His bits of literary criticism have been largely forgotten, though he should be remembered as the original editor of a series of popular small, blue-grey French classic texts published by D. C. Heath. As a linguist, Edward Larocque Tinker credited him as being a "master of Spanish, Italian, German, Provencal, Catalan, Romansh [a Swiss dialect], Greek and Latin, as well as of French and English," to which *The Dictionary of Louisiana Biography* adds his knowledge of Portuguese and Sanskrit. His first paper before the Modern Language Association (an organization over which he also later presided) was on the subject of the Cherokee language, and later papers addressed the French Creole dialect and the language of Louisiana's Acadians. Fortier was an active folklorist who founded the New Orleans (later the Louisiana) Folklore Society and once presided over the American Folklore Society. His articles on Louisiana folklore in the latter organization's journal, combined with his various writings on Louisiana's language and culture (much of which was compiled into the book *Louisiana Studies*) may seem to a current audience to be his most significant writing. Already in 1958 the *Comptes Rendus* of the Athénée Louisianais would note that, "it is generally admitted that his *Louisiana Studies*, published in 1894, constitutes his most important and learned work." Since Fortier's day, the Creole language of Louisiana has received much in-depth study, and that very specialized field in and of itself is not something we feel the need to pursue here.[1] The Creole

---

1. Recent studies include *Dictionary of Louisiana French* by Albert Valdman, senior editor (University Press of Mississippi, 2010); *French and Creole in Louisiana* by Albert Valdman, editor (Plenum, 1997); *Dictionary of Louisiana Creole* by Valdman et al. (Indiana University, 1998); and *If I Could Turn My Tongue Like That: The Creole Language of Pointe Coupee Parish, Louisiana* by Thomas Klingler (Louisiana State University Press, 2003).

folktales he transcribed, however, are of a continuing interest to the general public, and, therefore, with the intent of providing them a larger readership, they are reprinted here in Fortier's original bilingual Creole/English versions. Supplementing this text are his original notes and one earlier tale as transcribed in both Creole and French by his friend (and mentor, as a founding member of L'Athénée Louisianais and student of Louisiana language and folklore), Dr. Alfred Mercier.

There has been much speculation and confusion regarding both the origin and the original publication of some of these folktales, specifically those involving the character whom Fortier called Compair Lapin, but who is known to the English-speaking world, thanks to Joel Chandler Harris, as B'rer Rabbit. In the preface to his book, *Uncle Remus* (1880), Harris commented on the controversy already raging over the origin of the B'rer Rabbit stories, some of which he had published in the *Atlanta Constitution* the previous year,

> Professor J. F. Powell, of the Smithsonian Institution, says the Negro borrowed them from the North American Indians, but Mr. Herbert Smith finds them among the South American Indians, one from India, and one from the far east—Siam. In 1881 T. F. Crane discussed their European, Amazonian and African parallels.

> In 1893 Adolf Gerber could state:

> B'rer Rabbit is the most famous hero in the whole realm of animal tales . . . if Mr. Jacobs be right, he stands in the story of the "Wonderful Tar Baby" for no less a personage than the great founder of the Buddhistic religion himself. . . . On the Bahama Islands, an elephant devises the tar baby; in Canada, a Frenchman forms it. In Brazil, an old woman or man makes a wax baby, and puts it either in a tree or on the ground. A monkey gets stuck on it, like B'rer Rabbit in this country (*Journal of American Folklore*, vol. 23, p. 247-251).

Gerber finds variants of the Harris stories in such European sources as the *Disciplina Clericalis* translated by Petrus Alfonsi from the Arabic in the twelve century, the *Roman de Renart*, Renhart Fuchs, the fables of Odo of Sherington, and the *Fabulae Extravagantes* (Caxton's translation of which is in Jacob's *Aesop*). By the end of the century a veritable war between folklorists had ensued, with one side claiming the origin of the stories was in Europe and Africa, and the other in India. There is no telling just how much ink has been spilled in this 125-year-old quest to attain the exact origin of something as chimerical as a simple folktale. More important, for our purposes, is its literary journey.

It is clear that Joel Chandler Harris was unfamiliar with Alcée Fortier's work. Indeed, Harris' first published article featuring B'rer Rabbit material predated Fortier's first piece with such material by eight years, and his first Uncle Remus book preceded Fortier's book publication of the tales by some fifteen years. Could Harris have otherwise obtained this material from the French-speaking Louisiana community? This is hardly possible. He visited New Orleans twice. First, as a teenager, he served as private secretary to the editor of the short-lived *Crescent Monthly* for six months in 1866-67. His biographer suggests that Harris' reaction to the very foreignness of the city ensured that the only lesson he gained from his first New Orleans visit was to hurry home and not leave Georgia for long ever again. And we can only doubt the French language proficiency of a seventeen-year old illegitimate "anglo" from Georgia with little formal education. Although much later (1893) he would be credited as the translator of a book called *Evening Tales* (from the French of Frédéric Ortoli), it is known that this work was really done by his French-Canadian wife, whom he met in Florida well after his first New Orleans visit and married in 1873. His second visit to the Crescent City was after he had achieved fame with his Uncle Remus stories, in 1882, when he went to New Orleans to meet Mark Twain to discuss doing a joint lecture tour (he also met George Washington Cable and Lafcadio Hearn at this time).

Did Fortier, then, get his material from Harris? This is also inconceivable. In his notes to the tale "Piti Bonhomme Godron," Fortier acknowleges Harris' contribution to the field when he says, "in our Louisiana tales, Compair Lapin, as in Uncle Remus, is the great deceiver, while Compair Bouki is always imposed upon, as was poor Isengrin, the wolf" (cf. *Le Roman de Renart*). He thus carefully distinguishes the origin of his "Louisiana tales" from those of Uncle Remus' creator, but implies their common origin in African-American folklore.

Interestingly, the first printed English language appearance of the North American versions of these stories were transcribed by neither Fortier nor Harris. In later remarks, Harris maintained that it was when he read the tale of the tar baby and other "Buh Rabbit" stories retold in an article in *Lippincott's Magazine* by William Owens that he first recognized their literary merit, and how this inspired him to draw upon his own remembrances of the same folktales he had heard as a youth, undoubtedly when, as a teenager in the early 1860s, he was an apprentice to the publisher of *The Countryman*, a journal printed on the Turnwold Plantation in Putnam County, Georgia. The truth of the matter is that these stories were already prevalent in the English-speaking South well before Harris published any of them, as Owens had revealed:

> Travellers and missionaries tell us that . . . the same wild stories of Buh Rabbit, Buh Wolf, and other *Buhs* that are so charming to the ears of American children, are to be heard to this day in Africa, differing only in the drapery needed to the change of scene ("The Folklore of the Southern Negroes," *Lippincott's Magazine*, December 1877).

Harris had already created the Uncle Remus character and used him in several dialect sketches he had published in the *Atlanta Constitution* the previous year (1876) as a mouth-piece for commentary on the post-Civil War South. Soon Uncle Remus became the teller of the tales he had heard told by the slaves Old Harbert and George Terrell on the Georgia plantation (cf. "The Story of Mr. Rabbit and Mr. Fox as Told by Uncle Remus," *Atlanta Constitution*, July 20, 1879). And so B'rer Rabbit stepped onto the stage of English-language literary history.

The literary origin of the Louisiana French Creole versions of the stories is a bit more obscure. In the bibliography of his book *Gombo: The Creole Dialect of Louisiana* (1936), Edward Larocque Tinker states that the St. John the Baptist Parish weekly, *Le Meschacébé*, published seven African fables and Creole songs in dialect between 1858 and 1877. He also mentions Dr. Alfred Mercier (under the pseudonym "Vié Jack") as the transcriber of two of the tales in that journal (June 24 and July 15, 1876). One of the Mercier stories was reprinted at the end of his "Etude sur la Langue Créole en Louisiane" in the journal of the Athénée Louisianais (July 1, 1880), which is reproduced in its entirety as Appendix Four of this volume. Lafcadio Hearn had noted in the *New Orleans Times-Democrat* of June 13, 1886 that the French literary journal *Mélusine* had begun printing samples of Creole folklore from Guyana, one of which, a story about "Compere Tigre et Compere Bouki," he recalled seeing printed in the *Opelousas Courier* in Louisianian dialect some years previously. He himself considered but never completed a project "to collect the Creole legends, traditions, and songs of Louisiana" (1878 letter to Krehbiel), but he did later publish a book-length anthology of Creole proverbs, *Gombo Zhèbes* (1885), of which about fifty are from New Orleans. In his introduction to the book he admits that his source for most of the New Orleans material, including the notes, was his friend Henry Williams, and that he found the remaining Caribbean and Guayanan material in previously published sources. In *Lafcadio Hearn's American Days* (1924), Tinker states that it was Hearn's friend, New Orleans native Leona Queyrouze, who had coached him in his Louisiana Creole proverbs and pronunciation. It is also known that he consulted with other members of the local francophone community such as Dr. Alfred Mercier and his older brother, Armand, as well as his erstwhile friend, the abbé Adrien Rouquette, extensively on the subject of the Creole language. Hearn himself then provided the written text and coaching for his friend George Washington Cable, who wrote several pieces about Creole songs and music for *Century Magazine* (February and April 1886). Of these Fortier commented:

> Mr. Cable, in his extract, has joined two verses into one, and destroyed the rhyme . . . It would be easy to correct the hundred and one errors in Mr. Cable's articles on the slave songs, but this would lead me too far; my remarks are merely to show how difficult it is to write the creole patois, without having made a special study of it. . . . In the *Guide to New Orleans*, a very interesting book published by Mr. W. H. Coleman we find also several pretty negro songs [compiled by Hearn and Cable], but so completely disfigured by errors in the text that it is difficult for a stranger to understand.

It must be admitted that Fortier, one of the defenders of the white Creole aristocracy, took advantage of every occasion to attack Cable for the version of Creole society he had portrayed in his novels. But that controversy does not directly concern us here. Suffice it to say that it is well known that Hearn and Cable were much more forward-looking than the prejudiced Fortier in their concern for the rights of African-Americans who were so maligned in the society of the Old South of which Fortier was very much a representative (Fortier's grandfather, Valcour Aime, is credited as having been the first to refine sugar in Louisiana; with his fortune he built the legendary plantation of Le Petit Versailles with its sumptuous and exotic gardens). And thus we are presented with the great irony that a very prejudiced man like Fortier, who was so callous and indifferent to the civil and social rights of the African-Americans who surrounded him his entire life, should produce, as the most scholarly and original work of his whole career, studies which preserve and analyze the language and culture of the very people whose rights he had so neglected. Unlike Hearn or Cable, Fortier was no mere amateur enthusiast of the subject, learning only from previously published sources or from those members of the indigenous francophone community patient enough to share their knowledge of the subject with him. While Hearn was undoubtedly a brilliant student of the French language and its literature as well as of the black French Creole language and culture, he, like Cable, was not in the same league as the professional linguist Fortier, who was a native French speaker from Louisiana, born and raised on his grandfather's plantation surrounded by Creole-speaking slaves. And, however condescending or paternalistic Fortier's remarks concerning the "negro" seem to us today, the quality of his work is undeniable. He treated his subject with all of the patience and thoroughness of the finest scholarship, with an attention ultimately born of a kind of admiration and affection, whether conscious or not. In a 1906 article on sugar plantations and their culture, Fortier reminisced how, for over forty years since the Civil War,

> . . . every year I am visited in New Orleans by my old nurse who comes from the country to visit her "boy." She always says, upon arriving, in her dialect, "Mo vini oua mo garçon. . . ." And she tells my children the wonderful stories of *Bouki* and *Lapin*, the Isengrin and the Fox of the folk tales of Louisiana ("Les planteurs sucriers de l'Ancien Régime en Louisiane," reprinted in *Comptes Rendus de L'Athénée Louisianais*, November 1950).

Both Harris and Fortier were careful to credit the origin of their tales to their true authors. Harris, though a simple journalist, not a linguist or folklorist, clarified that he did not want to print "fiction" and wanted his readers to realize the stories' sources in authentic African-American folklore. Fortier detailed the source of almost all of his tales. Of the nineteen involving Compair Lapin, five were from "Dorlis Aguillard, colored man, 157 Thalia Street, New Orleans;" four from "Julia, little negress, 7 Prytania Street, New Orleans;" four from various other sources, four go uncredited, and two are from "an old negro at *La Vacherie*, St. James Parish," the site of the plantation where Fortier had been raised and of the St. James Sugar Refinery which was also on his grandfather's property.

Since Fortier's day the study of folklore has continued to grow enormously. Other versions of the Louisiana Compair Lapin stories have appeared in *Louisiana Creole Dialect* by James F. Broussard (Louisiana State University Press, 1942); "Les contes populaires de la Louisiane" by Calvin Claudel (*Comptes Rendus de l'Athénée Louisianais*, March 1955); *Folk Tales from French Louisiana* by Corinne L. Saucier (Louisiana State University Press, 1962); "Playing Dead Thrice: Louisiana Animal Tale," by Raleigh Morgan, Jr. (*Revue de Louisiane/Louisiana Review* vol. 4, no. 1, Summer 1975); *Ecrits Louisianais du Dix-Neuvième Siècle: Nouvelles, Contes et Fables* edited by Gerard Labarre St. Martin and Jacqueline K. Voorhies (Louisiana State University Press, 1979); *Anthologie: Littérature française de la Louisiane* edited by Mathé Allain and Barry Ancelet (National Materials Development Center for French, 1981); *Cadjins et créoles en Louisiane* by Patrick Griolet (Payot, 1986); *Cajun and Creole Folktales* by Barry Jean Ancelet (University Press of Mississippi, 1994); *Swapping Stories* by Carl Lindahl, Maida Owens, and C. Renée Harvison (University Press of Mississippi, 1997); and, in an illustrated children's version, *Contes populaires cadiens* by Celiua Soper (Pelican,

1997). Of the numerous French-language publications featuring similarly-themed stories from the Caribbean, Guyana, and Africa, one may take note of *Les Aventures de Leuk-le-Lièvre* by Léopold Sedar Senghor and Abdoulaye Sadji (Nouvelles Editions Africaines, 1975; originally published by Edicef, 1953); *Contes créoles* by Jean Juravier (Présence Africaine, 1985); *Contes du temps de l'antan* by Patrick Chamoiseau (Hatier, 1988); and *Contes créoles des Amériques* by Rafaël Confiant (Stock, 1995). The latter collection also features five "lapin et bouki" stories from Louisiana.

Alcée Fortier's Writings on Creole Language and Folklore

"The French Language in Louisiana and the Negro French Dialect," *Publications of the Modern Language Association of America*, volume 1, 1884-5.

"Bits of Louisiana Folklore," *Publications of the Modern Language Association of America*, volume 3, 1887.

"Customs and Superstitions in Louisiana," *The Journal of American Folk-lore*, volume 1, 1888.

"Louisiana Nursery Tales," *The Journal of American Folk-lore*, volume 2, 1889.

Louisiana Studies: Literature, Customs and Dialects, History and Education (F. B. Hansell & Bros., New Orleans, 1894).

Louisiana Folk-Tales (Houghton-Mifflin for the American Folk-lore Society, 1895).

"Contes louisianais en patois créole," *Comptes-Rendus de l'Athenee Louisianais*, September 1900.

PREFACE.

It is with pleasure that the writer presents to folk-lorists his "Louisiana Folk-Tales." He has devoted several years to collecting his material and preparing it for publication, and he hopes that his book will be considered a useful contribution to the science of Folk-Lore. No attempt was made to make a comparative study of the tales, and they are presented to folk-lorists as material for comparison. Andrew Lang said that the collector should himself eliminate the personal equation while writing his tales and not leave this task to his reader. Such has been the constant aim of the writer and of the persons who kindly assisted him in his work, and this collection is the result of honest and conscientious efforts to give to the public genuine folk-tales.

The tales are given first in the Creole dialect, then in a faithful but not literal translation, as it is desirable to preserve the interest of the story. The study of the Creole dialect is of importance and interest, and the tales have been carefully written in Louisiana dialect, in order that the material may be of use to the philologist.

In the Appendix are reproduced fourteen stories already published in 1888 in the "Transactions of the Modern Language Association of America," and in the "Journal of American Folk-Lore," to the end that the reader may have in one volume a complete collection of Louisiana Folk-Tales.

The writer wishes to acknowledge his obligations and present his thanks to his nieces, Misses Désirée and Marguerite Roman, and to Mr. Zénon De Moruelle, who have assisted him in his collection. One of his most valued assistants has been Mrs. Widow V. Choppin, of St. James Parish, recently deceased. Thanks are also due to the Secretary of The American Folk-Lore Society, for suggestions in the preparation of this work.

ALCÉE FORTIER.

NEW ORLEANS, August 11, 1894.

INTRODUCTION.

I. THE TALES.

It is very difficult to make a complete collection of the negro tales, as the young generation knows nothing about them, and most of the old people pretend to have forgotten them. It is a strange fact that the old negroes do not like to relate those tales with which they enchanted their little masters before the war. It was with great trouble that I succeeded in getting the following stories.

While reading these tales, one must bear in mind that most of them were related to children by childlike people ; this accounts for their *naïveté*. The Louisiana folk-tales were brought over to this country by Europeans and Africans, and it is interesting to note what changes have been made in some well-known tales by a race rude and ignorant, but not devoid of imagination and poetical feeling. It is important to give the variants of popular tales principally to indicate the different characteristics of the human race. The study of folk-lore is interesting to the anthropologist and psychologist. Both may follow the workings of man's mind, of man's feeling, through a number of countries and in primitive people. If we take any popular tale, we shall always find some difference in the impression created on the audience. That impression reacts on the story itself and modifies it to a great extent. The plot of a popular tale seems to be the common heritage of a number of countries which may have derived it from the same source, but the motives are often inspired by local customs.

In Louisiana we have three kinds of tales : the animal tales, of which some are, without doubt, of African origin ; fairy tales or märchen, probably from India ; and tales and songs, real *vaudevilles*, where the song is more important than the plot. In this connection a negro dancing song or *ronde* may be mentioned as illustrating the way in which the tale with a song is related. In the *ronde* accompanying the tale one man sings these almost meaningless words : "Crapaud entré on nid bourdon, et lapé chanter : 'Yapé piqué moin, yapé mordé moin ; Doune, ah ! doune goule ! Doune, ah ! doune goule!'" "A frog enters into a hornets' nest and he is singing: 'They are stinging me, they are biting me: Doune, ah! doune goule! Doune ah! doune goule!'" While singing he writhes in a horrible manner and gesticulates wildly, rubbing his shoulders against all the persons present, who sing with him the refrain and dance to the tune of a most primitive music.

II. THE CREOLE DIALECT.

The dialect spoken by the negroes in Lower Louisiana and known by philologists as the Creole dialect is an interesting subject for study. It is not merely a corruption of French, that is to say, French badly spoken, it is a real idiom with a morphology and grammar of its own. It is curious to see how the ignorant African slave transformed his master's language into a speech concise and simple, and at the same time soft and musical. The tendency was, of course, to abbreviate as much as possible, both in the form of the words and in the construction of the sentence. The word *arrêté* becomes *rété; appelé, pélé;* all parts of speech, not absolutely necessary to the meaning, are thrown out of the sentence. There is hardly any distinction of gender, and the verb is simplified to a wonderful degree. The sounds of the French words vary considerably in the dialect; the principal changes being the frequency in the dialect of the nasal sound *in* and of *é.* The process of agglutination is very common, as in *larie, in dézo,* a street, a bone.

The first story of the collection will be used as a basis for the explanation of a few peculiarities of the Creole dialect. For a more complete treatment of the subject, see my " Louisiana Studies," Hansell, New Orleans, 1894.

NOTES.

1. *Néléphant,* example of agglutination, from *un éléphant;* plural *des néléphant.*

2. *jou* for *jour,* last consonant generally omitted in the dialect.

3. *compair,* the spelling generally adopted for *compère* in writing the dialect.

4. *té apé voyagé,* the imperfect, *était après voyager.* The tenses of the verb are formed from that construction, *après* contracted into *apé* with *té (été)* or *gaingnin (gagner* for *avoir).*

5. *ensembe, pou, toujou,* for *ensemble, pour, toujours.*

6. *yé rivé,* the perfect for *té rivé* (étaient arrivés). *Yé* is personal pronoun plural. The other forms are *mo, to, li, nous, vous.*

7. *bord lamer;* the *de* for the genitive does not exist; as in Old French, the Creole patois says: *fille (le) roi.*

8. *quichoge,* a curious transformation of *quelque chose.*

9. *ben drole, ben* for *bien; drole, o* pronounced like *o* in *robe;* the *ô* does not exist.

10. *étonné yé,* personal pronouns, objects, are *moin, toi, li, nou, vous, yé.*

11. *yé rété,* present indicative, contracted from *yé apé rété, yapé rété.*

12. *yé na,* for *il y a,* impersonal.

13. *ladjeule,* one word, from *la gueule.*

14. *anon,* for *allons, l* changed into *n.*

15. *vancé, couté,* abbreviations of *avancé, écouté.*

16. *mo commère,* possessive adjectives are *mo, to, so, nous, vous, yé,* for both genders and numbers.

17. *na tchué yé,* future for *nous va tchué yé.*

18. *anon couri,* for *allons couri,* strengthens the expression.

19. *ta oua,* future for *to va oua.*

20. *ma rangé,* future for *mo va rangé.*

21. *mapé couri,* present indicative for *mo apé* (après) *couri.*

22. *to si capon, to béte ;* notice conciseness through omission of verb.

23. *li porté, li caché,* preterit, *lui porta, lui cacha.*

24. *ti service, ti* for *petit.*

25. *va sorti,* future for *vous va sorti.*

26. *paré* for *prêt.*

27. *zami,* agglutination of *s* of *mes amis.*

28. *haler* for *tirer,* found often in Acadian dialect.

29. *mo vini,* past tense for *je suis venu.*

30. *pasqué,* softening and abbreviation of *parce que.*

31. *tchombo,* from *tiens bon,* hold fast.

32. *en haut so côté,* on his side ; *en haut* contracted into *on* and used for *sur* and *de.*

33. *plis mié ;* note double superlative, common in the patois.

34. *escousse,* metathesis for *secousse.*

35. *dolo,* one word, from *de l'eau.*

36. *Qui ça ça yé ?* What is the matter ? French, *qu'est-ce ?* A curious expression.

37. *au lieur,* for *au lieu.*

38. *comme ça,* meaningless expression used continually by the negro narrator.

39. *qua oua li,* future for *qui va le voir.*

40. *chivreil* or *chévreil ; i* or *é* often used indifferently ; *u* and *e* are very rare.

41. *ga,* for *garde,* a good example of the abbreviation so common in the Creole dialect.

PART ONE:
Animal Tales.

I.

NÉLÉPHANT[1] AVEC BALEINE.

Ein jou[2] Compair Lapin et Compair[3] Bouki té apé voyagé[4] ensembe.[5] Compair Lapin souvent té ménin li pou[5] fait paillasse avec
li et pi en méme temps Compair Lapin té toujou[5] au courant toute
sorte nouvelle qué Compair Bouki té raconté li. Quand yé rivé[6] au
bord[7] la mer yé oua ein quichoge[8] qui té ben drole.[9] Ça té si tellement étonné[10] yé qué yé rété[11] pou tendé et guetté. C'était ein
néléphant avec baleine qui té apé causé ensemble.

— To oua, dit Bouki, c'est dé plis gros bétes qué yé[12] na dans
moune et c'est yé qui plis fort que les otes zanimaux.

— Paix to ladjeule,[13] dit Compair Lapin, anon[14] vancé[15] et pi
couté,[15] mo oulé connin ça yé apé dit.

Yé vancé proche. Néléphant dit baleine comme ça : — Mo commère,[16] comme c'est vous qui plus gros et plis fort dans la mer et
moin qui plis gros et plis fort en haut la terre, faut nous fait la loi,
et tout ça yé qui révolté na tchué yé.

— Oui, oui, Compair Néléphant, gardé la terre et moin mo va
gardé la mer.

— Tó tendé, dit Bouki, anon couri,[18] pasqué na sorti sale si yé oua
nous zotes apé couté yé conversation.

— Ah ouache, dit Compair Lapin, mo fout pas mal yé, mo plis
malin qué yé. Ta oua[19] comme ma rangé[20] yé tout les dé tout a
l'haire.

— Non, dit Compair Bouki, mo pair, mapé couri.[21]

— Eh ben, couri, d'abord to si capon,[22] bon a rien. Parti vite
mo lasse tendé toi a force to béte.[22]

Ça fait Compair Lapin couri cherché ein la corde qui té longue et
ben fort et pi li porté[23] so tambour et li caché[23] li dans grand zèbe.
Li prend la corde dans eine boute et pi li proché coté Néléphant
et li dit : — Michié, vous qui si bon et si fort, vous doite ben rende
moin ein ti service,[24] va sorti[25] moin dans grand tracas et péché moin
perde l'argent.

Néléphant té content tendé ein si joli compliment et li dit Compair Lapin : — Tout ça to oulé ma fait li pou toi, mo toujours paré[26]
pou obligé tout mo zami.[27]

— Oui, dit Compair Lapin, mo gagnin ein lavache qui bourbé au
ras la mer, vous connin mo pas assez fort pou halé[28] li. Mo vini[29]
coté vous pou vous idé moin ; prend la corde dans vous latrompe, ma
couri marré lavache et quand va tendé moin batte tambour va haler

I.

THE ELEPHANT AND THE WHALE.

One day Compair Lapin and Compair Bouki were going on a journey together. Compair Lapin often took Bouki with him to make fun of him, and to hear all the news which Bouki knew. When they reached the seashore, they saw something which was very strange, and which astonished them so much that they stopped to watch and listen. It was an elephant and a whale which were conversing together.

"You see," said Bouki, "they are the two largest beasts in the world, and the strongest of all animals."

"Hush up," said Lapin, "let us go nearer and listen. I want to hear what they are saying."

The elephant said to the whale: "Commère Baleine, as you are the largest and strongest in the sea, and I am the largest and strongest on land, we must rule over all beasts; and all those who will revolt against us we shall kill them, you hear, commère."

"Yes, compair; keep the land and I shall keep the sea."

"You hear," said Bouki, "let us go, because it will be bad for us if they hear that we are listening to their conversation."

"Oh! I don't care," said Lapin; "I am more cunning than they; you will see how I am going to fix them."

"No," said Bouki, "I am afraid, I must go."

"Well, go, if you are so good for nothing and cowardly; go quickly, I am tired of you; you are too foolish."

Compair Lapin went to get a very long and strong rope, then he got his drum and hid it in the grass. He took one end of the rope, and went to the elephant: "Mister, you who are so good and so strong. I wish you would render me a service; you would relieve me of a great trouble and prevent me from losing my money."

The elephant was glad to hear such a fine compliment, and he said: "Compair, I shall do for you everything you want. I am always ready to help my friends."

"Well," said Lapin, "I have a cow which is stuck in the mud on the coast; you know that I am not strong enough to pull her out; I come for you to help me. Take this rope in your trunk. I shall tie it to the cow, and when you hear me beat the drum, pull hard on

fort en haut la corde. Mo dit vous ça pasqué³⁰ la vache bourbé fond dans la boue.

— C'est bon, dit Néléphant, mo garanti toi ma sorti lavache la ou ben la corde a cassé.

Alors Compair Lapin prend l'ote boute la corde la, li couri au bord la mer, li fait Baleine ein joli compliment, li mandé li même service la pou débourbé so lavache qui té pris au ras ein bayou dans bois. Compair Lapin gagnin la bouche si tellement doux que personne pas capab réfisé li arien. Baleine fait ni eine ni dé, li prend la corde la dans so ladjeule et li dit Compair Lapin : — Quand mo va tendé tambour ma halé.

— Oui, dit Compair Lapin, commencé halé doucement et pi plis fort en plis fort.

— To pas besoin pair, dit Baleine, ma sorti to lavache quand même Djabe apé tchombo³¹ li.

— Tant mié, dit Compair Lapin, tout a l'haire na ri, et pi li batte so tambour.

Néléphant prend halé, halé, la corde la té raide comme ein barre fer, li té apé craqué. Baleine la en haut so coté³² li aussi té apé halé, halé. A la fin li té apé couri au ras la terre pasqué Néléphant té boucou plis mié³³ placé pou halé. Quand Baleine oua li té apé monté en haut la terre, cré mille tonnerre li batte so la tcheu raide et pi li piqué au large. Li fait ein escousse³⁴ si tellement raide que li té trainin Néléphant au ras dolo.³⁵ Néléphant dit comme ça : — Aie, mais qui ça ça yé³⁶ tout ça, c'est ein lavache qui joliment fort pou trainin moin comme ça. Rété ein pé, laissé moi accroupi moin et mette mo dé pié dévant dans la boue. La, mo a genoux asteur." Et li commencé tortillé la corde la avec so la trompe. Li tordé la corde la et a la fin li réissi halé Baleine au ras la terre. Ça té étonné li, au lieurein³⁷ lavache c'était so commère Baleine. Alors li dit çomme ça :³⁸ — Mais, mais, qui ça yé, mo commère ? Mo té crai c'était lavache Compair Lapin mo té apé débourbé.

— Aïe ! dit Baleine, Lapin dit moin même quichogela, mo croi ben li té oulé fout nous zotes.

— Alors li gagnin pou payé ça, dit Néléphant, mo défende li mangé ein brin zèbe en haut la terre pasqué li moqué nous zotes.

— Moin aussite, dit Baleine, mo défende li boi ein goutte dolo dans la mer, faut nous surveillé li et prémier qua oua li,³⁹ faut pas nous raté li.

Compair Lapin, qui té apé couté, dit Compair Bouki : — Li temps nous parti, fait chaud pou nous zotes.

— To oua, dit Bouki, to mette nous zotes dans grand tracas. Jamais ma couri avec toi nille part.

— Oh ! paix to ladjeule, dit Lapin, mo pas fini avec yé, rété ein pé, ta oua comment mo va rangé yé.

the rope. I tell you that because the cow is stuck deep in the mud."

" That is all right," said the elephant. " I guarantee you I shall pull the cow out, or the rope will break."

Compair Lapin took the other end of the rope and ran towards the sea. He paid a pretty compliment to the whale, and asked her to render him the same service about the cow, which was stuck in a bayou in the woods. Compair Lapin's mouth was so honeyed that no one could refuse him anything. The whale took hold of the rope and said : " When I shall hear the drum beat I shall pull."

" Yes," said Lapin, "begin pulling gently, and then more and more."

" You need not be afraid," said the whale; " I shall pull out the cow, even if the Devil were holding her."

" That is good," said Lapin ; " we are going to laugh." And he beat his drum.

The elephant began to pull so hard that the rope was like a bar of iron. The whale, on her side, was pulling and pulling, and yet she was coming nearer to the land, as she was not so well situated to pull as the elephant. When she saw that she was mounting on land, she beat her tail furiously and plunged headlong into the sea. The shock was so great that the elephant was dragged to the sea. " What, said he, what is the matter ? that cow must be wonderfully strong to drag me so. Let me kneel with my front feet in the mud." Then he twisted the rope round his trunk in such a manner that he pulled the whale again to the shore. He was very much astonished to see his friend the whale. " What is the matter," said he. " I thought it was Compair Lapin's cow I was pulling."

" Lapin told me the same thing. I believe he is making fun of us."

" He must pay for that," said the elephant. " I forbid him to eat a blade of grass on land because he laughed at us."

" And I will not allow him to drink a drop of water in the sea. We must watch for him, and the first one that sees him must not miss him."

Compair Lapin said to Bouki : " It is growing hot for us ; it is time to leave."

" You see," said Bouki, "you are always bringing us into trouble."

" Oh ! hush up, I am not through with them yet ; you will see how I shall fix them."

— Ça fait yé couri yé chimin, chaquène gagnin so coté. Quand Compair Lapin rivé dans ein bois li trouvé ein ti chivreil [40] qui té mouri, a force chien té massacré li li té plein bobo et dans plein place so poil té tombé.   Compair Lapin corché li et li metté so la peau en haut so dos; li vlopé li ben la dans, ça fait li té sembe ein ti chivreil. Alors li prend boité en haut trois pattes et pi li passé proche coté. Néléphant qui dit li : — Mais pove piti chivreil, qui ça to gagnin ?

— Oh ! oui, mapé souffri boucou, vous oua c'est Compair Lapin qui poisonin moin et pi li voyé so malédiction en haut moin, jiste pasqué mo té oulé comme vous té dit péché li mangé zèbe.   Prend ga [41] pou vous, Michié Néléphant, Compair Lapin engagé avec Djabe, la servi vous mal si vous pas fait tention.

Alors Néléphant té pair, li dit : — Ti chivreil, ta dit Compair Lapin moin c'est so meilleir zami, dit li mangé zèbe tant li oulé. Pas blié, non, et fais li compliment pou moin.

Ti chivreil la passé so chimin et quand li rivé au bord la mer Baleine dit li : — Mais pove ti chivreil, tapé boité, qui ça ça yé ? mo croi to boucou malade.

— Oh oui, mapé souffri boucou, c'est Compair Lapin qui metté moin dans nétat la, prend ga pou vous, commère Baleine.   Li aussite li té pair, ça fait li dit : — Ti chivreil, mo pas oulé gagné zaffaire avec Djabe, ten prie, dis Compair Lapin boi tout dolo li oulé, mo va laissé li tranquille.

Ça fait Compair Lapin continié so chimin, et quand li rivé au ras Compair Bouki li oté la peau la et li dit comme ça : — To oua ben que mo plis malin qué yé et mo capab fout yé tout temps et yé dé ensemble.   La ou moin mo va passé ein lote va trouvé li pris.

— Vous ben raison, dit Compair Bouki.

II.

COMPAIR TAUREAU ET JEAN MALIN.

Quand Jean Malin té piti li té norphelin et li té pas connin où couri ou ça pou fait. Ein jou li oua ein riche madame qui té apé passé dans so bel carrosse.   Li mandé madame la pou prend li.   Comme madame la oua qué li té ein joli ti garçon et li té gagnin boucou l'esprit li mandé Jean Malin qui l'age li té gagnin.   Jean Malin té pas capab dit li jiste, mais li réponde madame la qué li té tendé so moman dit comme ça li té né quand péchers té en flairs même l'année qué la neige té tombé.   Ça fait madame la prend li dans so bel carrosse et ménin li dans so la maison pou fait so commission et servi a tabe.

They went on their way and after a while they separated. When Compair Lapin arrived in the wood, he found a little dead deer. The dogs had bitten him so that the hair had fallen off his skin in many places. Lapin took off the deer's skin and put it on his back. He looked exactly like a wounded deer. He passed limping by the elephant, who said to him: "Poor little deer, how sick you look."

"Oh! yes, I am suffering very much; you see it is Compair Lapin who poisoned me and put his curse on me, because I wanted to prevent him from eating grass, as you had ordered me. Take care, Mr. Elephant, Compair Lapin has made a bargain with the Devil; he will be hard on you, if you don't take care."

The elephant was very much frightened. He said, "Little deer, you will tell Compair Lapin that I am his best friend; let him eat as much grass as he wants and present my compliments to him."

The deer met a little later the whale in the sea. "But poor little deer, why are you limping so; you seem to be very sick."

"Oh! yes, it is Compair Lapin who did that. Take care, Commère Baleine." The whale also was frightened, and said: "I want to have nothing to do with the Devil; please tell Compair Lapin to drink as much water as he wants."

The deer went on his way, and when he met Compair Bouki he took off the deer's skin and said: "You see that I am more cunning than all of them, and that I can make fun of them all the time. Where I shall pass another will be caught."

"You are right indeed" said Compair Bouki.

II.

COMPAIR TAUREAU AND JEAN MALIN.

When Jean Malin was small he became an orphan, and he did not know where to go or what to do. One day he saw a rich lady who was passing in her beautiful carriage, and he asked her to take him with her. As the lady saw that he was a pretty little boy and that he appeared to be very smart, she asked him how old he was. Jean Malin could not say, but he answered the lady that he had heard his mother say that he was born when the peach-trees were in bloom the year the snow fell. The lady took him in her fine carriage to her house, to be her messenger boy and to wait at table. The little fellow soon

Ti bougue la prend l'aimin madame la autant qué so défint moman
et méme li té jaloux ein michié riche qui té vini rende visite tous les
jous pou marier avec madame la.

Mais i faut mo dit vouzotes qué michié la c'était ein taureau qui
té connin tourné n'homme dans jou pou vini fait l'amour madame la, et
pi les soirs li té tournin taureau encore pou couri manzé zherbe dans
parc. Jean Malin té rémarqué qué quand michié la té au ras madame
so l'amoureuse n'avait pas taureau dans la plaine, et quand taureau
té dans parc michié l'amouré té pas la. — I faut mo guetter, dit
Jean Malin, yé na quichoge qui ben drole, qué mo pas comprende.
Jean guetté, guetté, mais li té gagnin ben soin pas laissé taureau
la oua li. Ein jou, bo matin quand Jean Malin té couri cherché di
bois pou limin di fé, li oua Compair Taureau dans parc qui té a
genoux et pi li té apé dit : — Bouhour, madjam, fat madjam, djam,
djam, djara, djara, et pi tout d'ein coup taureau tourné n'homme et
li prend marché vini coté so madame. Ah ! mo dit vouzotes Jean
Malin té pair, li té tremblé comme quand moune fraite.

Ça fait méme jou la n'amouré la té déjénin avec madame la et ti
Jean Malin qui té apé servi a tabe té couri tantot ein coté tantot ein
lote. Li té comme ein papillon a force li té pair. Quand yé mandé
li ein l'assiette li donnin di pain ou ben ein fourcette. Madame la
babillé li et pi quand so l'amouré té parti li dit Jean Malin li sré renvoyé li si li té pas fait mié et pi madame la té oulé connin qui ça
Jean Malin té gagnin.

— Oui, mo connin to pas l'aimin mo l'amouré, cofaire ? Qui ça
li fait toi ?

— Eh ben, mo va dit vous, maitresse, pou vrai mo pair et si vous
té connin ça moin mo connin, vous té pair aussite et vous té pas
quitté n'homme la vini dans vous la maison.

— Qui ça yé, mo oulé to dit moin tout suite ou ben mo va taillé
toi et metté toi dihors pou la gniappe.

Alors Jean Malin prende crié et pi li dit madame la : — Vous va
connin qué vous l'amouré c'est gros taureau la qui dans parc et qué
li connin changé en n'homme et tournin taureau encore pou couri
manger zherbe.

Ah la ! di fé té manqué prend a force madame la té colaire, li té
oulé bimmé Jean Malin, mais pove ti garçon la dit : — Maitresse,
couté moin, quand vous l'amouré a vini encore si mo pas prouvé
vous tout ça mo dit vous c'est la vérité, alors va renvoyé moin et fait
ça vous oulé avec moin.

— C'est bon, dit madame la, na oua ça, mais rappelé toi to va payer
ben cher tous to menteries.

Quéque jours après ça, michié l'amouré vini ; li té faraud. Jean
Malin té pensé en li méme : — Jordi na oua la farce, pas quéli té

began to love the lady as if she were his mother, and he was jealous of a rich gentleman who came to court the lady every day and wished to marry her.

But I must tell you that the gentleman was a bull who could change himself into a man in the daytime, to come and court the lady, and in the evening he became a bull again to go and eat grass in the park. Jean Malin had noticed that when the gentleman was near his lady love there was no bull in the prairie, and when the bull was in the prairie there was no lover in the parlor. "I will have to watch," said Jean Malin, "there is something strange which I don't understand." He watched, watched, but he took good care not to let Compair Taureau see him. One day, early in the morning, when Jean Malin went to get some wood to light his fire, he saw Compair Taureau on his knees, and saying: "Bouhour, Madjam, fat Madjam, djam, djam, djara, djara," and then, all at once, the bull became a man, and went to see his lady. Ah! I tell you, Jean Malin was afraid, he shivered as if he was very cold.

That very morning the lover took breakfast with the lady and Jean Malin waited on them. He ran sometimes on one side, sometimes on the other, as a butterfly, he was so frightened. When they asked him for a plate, he gave bread on a fork, and the lady scolded him. She told him, when the lover left, that she would send him away if he did not do better, and she wanted to know what was the matter with him.

"I know you don't like my lover, but why? What did he do to you? He always treated you well."

"Well, I will tell you, mistress. I am afraid; and if you knew what I know you would be afraid also, and you would not let that man enter your house."

"What is the matter? Tell me immediately or I shall whip you, and put you out for *la gniappe*."

Jean Malin began to cry, and he said to the lady: "Know then that your lover is the great bull which is in the park, and that he can change himself into a man and become a bull again to go and eat grass."

The lady was very angry and wanted to beat Jean Malin; but he said: "Mistress, listen to me. When your lover will come again, if I don't prove to you that all I say is true, you can send me away and do what you please with me."

"All right," said the lady; "but remember that you will pay dear for all your lies."

A few days after that the lover came. He was dressed in great style, and Jean Malin said to himself: "I will see the fun to-day,"

connin qui paroles li té doit dit pou fait michié l'amouré la vini
taureau encore.

Pendant yé té apé dinin madame la té apé gardé Jean Malin pou
oua ça li sré fait.   Dans méme moment qué l'amouré la prend la
main madame la pou bo so joli doigts Jean Malin qui té apé vidé divin
dans so gobelet dit comme ça méme paroles la yé li té tendé taureau
la dit pou tournin n'homme.   Li té pas fini dit so dernier mot, cré
mille tonnerres ! si jamais vous tendé vacarme, c'était jou la.   Chapeau, quilottes, linettes, n'habit michié la, tout so butin tombe par
terre, et l'amouré la tournin taureau dans la salle a manger ; li quilbité
la table, cassé la vaisselle avec gobelets et bouteilles ; li défoncé la
porte vitrée pou chapper et pi li prend galpé dans la plaine.

— Eh ben, vous content asteur ? dit Jean Malin.

Madame la dit : — Oui, Jean Malin, to té raison, to sauvé moin,
mo va gardé toi toujou comme mo prope piti, pasqué to rende moin
ein grand service.

Vouzote croit c'est tout ?   Ah ben non, vouzote allé oua comment
Jean Malin sorti clair avec Compair Taureau qui té fait serment li
sré tripé ti bougue la qui té trahi li.   Jean Malin té toujou pair, li
té gardé partout avant li té fait ein pas, pou pas Compair Taureau té
surprende li.   Ça fait ein jou Jean Malin té couri coté Compair Lapin
pou mandé li ein conseil, li conté li comment li té dans ein grand
n'embarras.

Alors Compair Lapin dit li comme ça : — Couté ben tout ça mo va
dit toi : couri dans bois, to va chercher ein nique hibou qui gagnin
dézef ; ta prend trois dans nique la ein vendredi après soleil couché
et pi to va porté yé coté moin pou mo drogué yé.   Après ça ta fait
ça to oulé avec Compair Taureau.

Alors Jean Malin trouvé trois dézef hibou et li porté yé coté Compair Lapin qui fait so grigris avec di lait ein femelle cabri noir et pi
li donnin yé Jean Malin et li dit li ça pou fait avec dézef la yé. — Va,
asteur, mo garantis toi, Compair Taureau a chagrin quand la fini
avec toi.

Quand Jean Malin té apé tournin coté so maitresse li prend rac-
courci pou pas contré Taureau, pasqué li té gagnin ein ti méfiance
malgré Compair Lapin té assiré li li té pas bésoin pair.   Dans méme
moment la li tendé Compair Taureau apé béglé et gratté la terre et
voyé la poussière en haut so dos. — Mo fout pas mal toi, dit Jean
Malin, "viens, ta oua comme mo va rangé toi.   Aussitot Compair
Taureau oua Jean Malin apé vini li foncé dret en haut li.   Yavé ein
nabe auras la et Jean Malin grimpé, li té pensé c'était plis sire.
Leste comme ein cureuil dans ein ti moment li té dans la téte nabe
là.   Li té temps, Compair Taureau rivé proche en méme temps.

— Han, han, mo gagnin toi a la fin, to va bligé descende ou ben
crever en haut la.

because he knew what to say to make the lover become a bull
again.

While they were dining the lady kept looking at Jean Malin to see
what he would do. When the gentleman took the pretty fingers
of the lady to kiss them, Jean Malin, who was pouring wine into her
glass, said the words he had heard the bull utter. Well, if ever you
heard a big noise it was on that day: the hat, the trousers, the spec-
cles, the coat, all the clothes of the gentleman fell on the floor, and
he was changed into a bull in the dining-room. He upset the table,
broke the plates, the dishes, the glasses, the bottles; he broke down
the glass door to escape, and ran into the prairie.

"Well, are you satisfied?" said Jean Malin.

"Yes," said the lady; "you rendered me a great service, and I
shall always treat you as my son."

You believe that this is all? Oh no. You will see how Jean Malin
got along with the bull which had sworn to kill the fellow that had
betrayed him. The boy was always afraid, and whenever he went
out he would look around to see if the bull was not there. One day
he went to see Compair Lapin, to ask his advice, and told him in
what a bad fix he was.

Compair Lapin said: "Listen to what I am going to tell you. Go
into the woods and look for an owl's nest. Take three eggs on
a Friday at sunset and bring them to me for me to charm them.
Then you will do all you want with Compair Taureau."

Jean Malin found the three owl's eggs and carried them to Compair Lapin, who made his *grigris* on them with the milk of a black
goat, and told Jean Malin what to do.

When Jean Malin was going back to the house of his mistress, he
looked around for the bull, for he felt a little anxious, in spite of
what Compair Lapin had said. There was the bull, bellowing and
looking furious. "Come," said Jean Malin, "you will see how I am
going to fix you." Compair Taureau galloped straight at him, and
Jean Malin climbed up a tree, for he thought it was more prudent.
In one minute, like a squirrel, he was at the top of the tree and the
bull stood underneath.

"Now I have you at last: you will have to come down," and he
began to strike at the tree with his horns.

Li prend donnin coup corne après nabe la et Jean Malin té pas rire tout temps la. Oui, taureau la té colère quand li oua li té pas capabe fait Jean Malin descende. Li metté li a genoux et pi li dit so paroles yé pou tournin n'homme. Li paraite alors comme ein n'homme avec ein la hache dans so la main.

— Descende, descende, pas quitté moin coupé nabe la pasqué mo va fini toi, ti coquin.

— Biché, biché, Compair Taureau, mo oulé oua ça vous capabe fait.

Alors taureau la biché : *gip, gop ; gip, gop.* Vouzote té capabe tendé la hache la résonné et nabe la té tremblé. Alors Jean Malin dit : — Li temps. Li voyé ein dézef hibou en haut n'épaule Compair Taureau, so bras avec la hache tombé par terre. N'homme la ramassé la hache la avec la main qui resté : *gip, gop ; gip, gop,* li apé biché toujou.

— Anon oua, dit Jean Malin. Li voyé dézième dézef la en haut l'ote bras, li aussi li tombé avec la hache comme premier la. N'homme la baissé, li prend la hache la avec so dents : *gip, gop ; gip, gop,* li apé biché toujou.

— Han, han, dit Jean Malin, asteur to compte clair. Li voyé troisième dézef la en haut la téte n'homme la — la téte tombé par terre. Bras yé avec jambes yé et pi so corps prend tortillé comme ein serpent dans di fé. Alors Jean Malin descende et pi li dit : — I faut to tournin taureau encore pasqué nous bésoin toi. Alors li dit paroles yé, la téte et pi bras sauté après corps la et n'homme la tournin taureau encore. Li prend galpé dans dans la plaine jisqua li té tombé, a force li té lasse. Dipis jour la li jamais tracassé Jean Malin qui té gagnin ein meillaire drogue qué li.

III.

COMPAIR LAPIN ET VER DE TERRE.

Tout moune connin qué tous les ans au mois de mai lapin gagnin ein maladie ; c'est ein ver de terre qui mordé li dans so cou en bas so machoire et sicé so disang comme pou de bois. Ça rende li faible, faible, et pendant ein mois ver la tchombo li bien et resté croché dans so cou anvant li tomber. Lapin yé croi quand yé couché dans grand zèbe que dé ver sorti dans la terre et grimpé en haut yé. Ça fait yé pair tout qualité dé vers, et si yé oua ein c'est assez pou fait yé galpé tout la journin comme si yavait ein bande chiens darrière yé. Si mo dit vous zotes tout ça c'est pou raconter vous ein zaffaire qué Compair Lapin té gagnin avec ver de terre.

Jean Malin laughed at him, and the bull was so angry that he knelt down and said the words to become a man. He immediately was changed into a man with an axe in his hand.

"Come down! don't let me cut the tree; for I will kill you, little rogue."

"Cut, Compair Taureau; I want to see what you can do."

The bull struck with his axe: "gip, gop." You might have seen the tree tremble at every blow. Then Jean Malin threw one of the owl's eggs on Compair Taureau's shoulder, and his arm fell down on the ground with the axe. The man picked up the axe with his other hand, and "gip, gop," on the tree.

Jean Malin threw the second egg on the remaining arm of the man, and the arm fell on the ground. He picked up the axe with his teeth, "gip, gop," again.

"Now," said Jean Malin, "I will finish you." He threw his third egg on the man's head, and the head fell on the ground. The arms, the legs, the head, the body of the man, began to wriggle like a snake in the fire. Then Jean Malin said: "I want you to become a bull again." He said the magic words, and the head and the arms jumped to the body, and the man became a bull again and galloped away in great haste. From that time he never worried Jean Malin again, for his *grigris* had not been as strong as that of Compair Lapin.

III.

COMPAIR LAPIN AND THE EARTHWORM.

Everybody knows that every year in the month of May Compair Lapin is sick; it is an earthworm which is in his neck, biting him and sucking his blood like a leech. That makes him weak, weak, and for a month the worm holds on to him, hooked in his neck, before it falls. Rabbits believe that when they lie down in the grass the worms come out of the grass and climb on them. They are, therefore, very much afraid of worms, and if they see one, they run as if they had a pack of hounds after them. If I tell you that it is because I want to relate to you a story about Compair Lapin and the worm.

Ein jour, c'était dans printemps, tout ti zozos té apé chanté, papillon té apé voltizé et pi posé en haut flairs ; té semblé comme si tout zanimaux té apé mercié Bon Djé. Jis ein piti ver de terre qui té apé crié et babillé, li apé dit li té si piti, pas gagnin pattes ni la main, ni zaile et li bligé resté dans so trou ; ti zozo, lézard et méme froumi té tracassé li et manzé so piti. Si sélement Bon Djé té fait li gros et fort comme lote zanimaux, li seré content, pasqué li seré capabe défende li méme, mais li té sans défense et bligé resté dans so trou. Li crié boucou et pi li dit li seré content si li té pou Diabe. Li té pas fini dit tout ça quand li oua Diabe au ras li.

— Eh bien, mo tendé tout ça to dit et mo vini mandé toi qui ça to oulé, mo va accordé toi li et to sera pou moin quand ta mouri.

— Ça mo oulé, mais mo oulé la force, mo oulé vini gros, gros, pou mo capab bimin nimporte qui qua vini bété moin ou tracassé moin. C'est tout, jis ça, mo va content.

— C'est bon, dit Diabe, laissé moin couri, dans ein ti moment to va content.

Aussitot Diabe la parti ver de terre trouvé li méme gros et fort, ça té vini tout d'ein coup, et so trou ou li té coutime resté vini grand et fond comme ein pi. Cré matin ! a force ver de terre té content li té apé ri et chanté. Dans méme moment la Compair Lapin trouvé passé tout proche. Yapa arien dans moune qui té fait li plis pair qué ça. Li prend galpé jisqua li té lasse. Quand li rété, li soufflé :

—Fouiff ! jamais mo té pair comme ça ; si mo pas mouri, jamais mo gagnin pou dormi encore tant gros ver de terre la a resté dans pays icite. Si mo té pas si béte couri vanté moin mo té capab bimin néléphant mo seré couri oua li. Mo connin li colère après moin, c'est Bouki qui couri répété li ça ; mais pététe si mo parlé avec li bien, ma capab rangé tout ça. Mapé couri oua li, pététe ma seyé fait yé batte ou bien contré ensemble, mo pense ça va fait ein joli bataille et pététe mo va débarrassé tout lé dé a la fois. Encore ver de terre la dit moin quand mo passé qué li té gagné pou réglé mo compte. Oh ! non, mo pas capab vive comme ça, qui ça ma fait Bon Djé, Seigneur. Faut mo couri oua néléphant, mo laimin mié risqué li, pasqué si mo parlé avec li bien, pététe mo gagnin la chance gagnin mo procès. Laissé moin rangé dans mo la téte ça malé dit li pou fait li content.

Alors Compair Lapin prend marché jisqua li contré néléphant ; li salié li et fait li ein joli compliment. Néléphant réponde li poliment et mandé li comment ça va.

— Oh ! mo bien malade, dit Compair Lapin, ein lote fois ma vini pou sayé mo la force avec vous, pasqué mo croi mo capab bimin vous.

— To tein sotte, réponde néléphant, couri, mo pas oulé fait toi mal, mo gagnin pitié on toi.

It was a day in spring, the little birds were singing, the butterflies were flying about from one flower to another. It seemed as if all animals were rendering thanks to God for his kindness to them. A little earthworm was the only one which was crying and complaining. He said he was so small, he had neither feet, nor hands, nor wings, and was obliged to remain in his hole. The little birds, the lizards, and even the ants were troubling him and eating his little ones. If God would make him big and strong, like other animals, then he would be contented, because he would be able to defend himself, while now he was helpless in his hole. He cried and cried and said that he would be glad if he belonged to the Devil. Hardly had he spoken when he saw the Devil at his side.

"Well, I heard all you said; tell me what you want; I shall grant it to you, and you will belong to me when you die."

"What I want? — Yes. — I want strength, I want to become big, big, and beat everybody who will come to trouble and bother me. Give me only that and I shall be satisfied."

"That is all right," said the Devil; "let me go, in a short while you will be contented."

As soon as the Devil had gone, the worm found himself strong and big. The change had come suddenly, and his hole had become large and as deep as a well. The worm was so glad that he began to laugh and to sing. At that very moment Lapin passed, and he was terribly frightened. He ran until he was unable to go any farther, and, when he stopped, he whistled, "fouif." "Never," said he, "was I more frightened. I shall never sleep again as long as that big earthworm will remain in this country. If I had not been so foolish as to boast that I could beat the elephant, I should go to him. It is Bouki who told on me; but perhaps if I speak to him I shall be able to fix up matters. I must try to make them meet and fight, and perhaps I shall get rid of both at the same time. It would be a pretty fight. Let me go and see the elephant, or I won't be able to sleep to-night. Besides, the earthworm said that he would fix me. I can't live that way. Good gracious! what am I to do? Let me arrange in my head what I am going to tell the elephant in order to please him."

He went on until he met the elephant. He bowed very politely, and the elephant did likewise, and asked him how he was.

"Oh! I am very sick," said Compair Lapin; "another time I shall come to try my strength with you; I think I can beat you."

"You are a fool," said the elephant. "Go away, I don't want to harm you; I take pity on you."

— Ma fait vous ein pari mo capab bimin vous.

— C'est bon, quand ta oulé.

— Plis tard, sélement mo conin vous bon, mo té vini mandé vous ein piti service.

— C'est bon, qui ça yé ?

— C'eté pou aidé moin, donne moin ein coup de main pou charrier di bois pou bati mo cabane.

— Anon tout suite, si to oulé.

Compair Lapin, qui té porté so la hache, biché ein gros nabe. Quand li tombé par terre, li dit néléphant prend gros boute coté la quilasse. — Moin mo va soulever branche derrière et na va porté li dans place ou mo gagnin pou fait mo cabane.

Néléphant chargé nabe en haut so l'épaule sans garder derrière et Compair Lapin monté dans branche yé et pi li assite et quitté néléphant trainé tout. Quand cila té lasse li té rété pou posé ein pé. Compair Lapin sauté par terre et pi li vini divant pou encouragé néléphant et li dit : — Mais, compair, vous déja lasse ? Mais c'est pas arien ça, gardé moin qui forcé autant qué vous, mo pas senti la fatigue.

— Foutrou, ça lourd comme Diabe, dit néléphant, anon parti.

— C'est ein pé plus loin.

Gros béte la chargé li méme encore avec gros di bois la et pi parti. Lapin apé fait semblant poussé dans branche ; quand li oua néléphant pas apé gardé derrière, li sauté dans branche encore et pi li bien assite et li dit : — Plis loin, encore plis loin, passé a droite, passé a gauche.

A la fin néléphant rivé au ras trou ver de terre, — La, c'est bon, metté li la. — Néléphant jété nabe la droit en haut trou ver de terre qui té apé dromi. Alors ver de terre sorti, li poussé nabe la comme ein la paille et pi li prend insilté néléphant. Lapin pendant temps la té caché dans ein place ou li capab oua et tendé tout. Néléphant perdi patience, li fout ver de terre ein coup avec so la trompe. Alors ver de terre sauté en haut néléphant et yé prend batte.

Yé batte comme ça pendant dé zeures jisqua yé té proche mouri. A la fin ver de terre couri caché au fond dans so trou et néléphant couché par terre pou mouri a force li té massacré. Compair Lapin asteur monté en haut néléphant et li fini bimin li. Li halé so zoreille, li fout li des tapes et li dit comme ça : — Mo té pas dit vous mo seré bimin vous ?

— Oui, oui, dit néléphant, mo gagnin assez, Compair Lapin, mapé mouri.

Alors Compair Lapin quitté li et pi li prend ein gros baton et li entré dans trou ver de terre. Li cassé so la téte, li fini tchué li.

— Comme ça, li dit, mo débarrassé tout les dé.

" I bet you," said Compair Lapin, " that I can beat you."

" All right, whenever you want."

" A little later ; but as I know that you are good, I had come to ask you a favor."

" What is it ? "

" It is to help me, to give me a hand to carry lumber to build my cabin."

" Let us go right off, if you want."

Compair Lapin, who had carried his axe with him, cut down a big tree, and said to the elephant : " Take it by the big end. I shall raise the branches, and we shall carry the tree to the place where I wish to build my cabin."

The elephant put the tree on his shoulder without looking behind him, and Compair Lapin climbed into the branches, and let the elephant do all the work. When the latter was tired he would stop to rest a little, and Compair Lapin would jump down and run up to the elephant to encourage him. " How is that, compair, you are already tired ; but that is nothing. Look at me, who have been working as much as you. I don't feel tired."

" What ! that is mightily heavy," said the elephant.

" Let us go," said Lapin ; " we have not far to go."

The big animal put the load again on his back and Compair Lapin appeared to be lifting the branches. Whenever the elephant would not be looking Lapin would sit on a branch and say : " A little farther ; go to the right, go to the left."

At last they came to the hole of the earthworm, and Lapin told the elephant to put down the tree. He let it fall right upon the worm who was sleeping. The latter pushed out the tree as if it were a piece of straw, and coming out he began to insult the elephant. Compair Lapin went to hide in a place where he could see and hear all. The elephant lost patience and struck the worm with his trunk.

The worm then climbed up the back of the elephant, and there was a terrible fight for more than two hours, until they were nearly dead. The worm finally hid in his hole and the elephant lay down dying. Compair Lapin mounted upon him, pulled his ears and beat him, and said to him : " Did n't I tell you I would beat you ? "

" Oh ! yes, Compair Lapin ; I have enough ; I am dying."

Lapin then left him, and, going into the worm's hole, he broke his head with a stick. " Now," said he, " I am rid of both of them."

Ein ti moment après li contré compair Bouki et li raconté li comment li fait néléphant avec ver de terre batte jisqua yé té tchué ein a lote. — To oua mo camarade, mo va dit toi, quand dé bougue apé génin toi, faut to fait yé batte et tchué yé entre yé. Ça fait ta toujou sauvé to la peau.

IV.

COMPAIR LAPIN ET COMPAIR L'OURS.

Ein jou Compair l'Ours invité Compair Lapin et Compair Bouki pou dinin chez li. Li dit yé li té acheté di beurre, fromage et biscuit, mais li dit : — Anvant dinin faut vous vini idé moin cassé maïs pou mo choal.

Compair Lapin et Compair Bouki accepté n'invitation Compair l'Ours, et yé tous les trois parti dans champs avant soleil levé.

A nef heures yé oua Compair Lapin dressé so zoreilles. — Ça ça yé, dit Compair l'Ours.

— Mo jamin oua arien qui bétant comme moune chez moin. Yapé pélé moin et dérangé moin dans mo nouvrage.

— Mo pas tendé arien, dit Compair l'Ours.

— C'est pasqué vous et Compair Bouki gagnin si piti zoreilles vous pas capabe tendé. Mo zoreilles yé si longues mo tendé des milles.

Li parti et li révini ein moment après et li dit c'était pou so fame qui té gagnin ein commencement maladie. Li fait méme manége la trois fois dans la journin. A midi li dit so fame té au milieu so maladie ; a trois heures li révini tout triste et dit sélement : — Tout fini.

Compair l'Ours et Compair Bouki plainde li boucou pasqué yé té cré c'était so fame qui té mouri. Au lieu ça chaque fois Compair Lapin té dit li té couri chez so fame li couri chez Compair l'Ours et manzé ein pé so provision, et quand li dit : — C'est fini, li té fini manzé tout.

A cinq heures trois zamis yé quitté l'ouvrage et couri chez Compair l'Ours. Vous capabe pensé comment Compair l'Ours té colère quand li oua so provision té disparaite. Tout suite li accusé Compair Lapin, mais li jiré c'était pas li.

— Ma connin tout suite, nouzotes trois va couché en haut la planche la qui dans do l'eau dans soleil et voleur la va malade sire. Compair Lapin, qui te fronté comme tout, dit oui, pasqué li compté couché dans l'ombre Compair l'Ours qui té boucou plis gros qué li. Compair Bouki dit oui aussi.

A little later Compair Lapin met Compair Bouki and told him how he had made the elephant and the earthworm fight until they had killed one another. "You see, my friend, when two fellows are in your way, you must make them fight, then you will always save your skin."

IV.

COMPAIR LAPIN AND COMPAIR L'OURS.

One day Compair l'Ours invited Compair Lapin and Compair Bouki to dine with him. He told them he had bought butter, cheese, and biscuits, but he said: "Before dinner you must come to help me break some corn for my horse."

Compair Lapin and Compair Bouki accepted the invitation of Compair l'Ours, and all three went into the field before daybreak.

At nine o'clock they saw Compair Lapin prick up his ears. "What is the matter?" said Compair l'Ours.

"I never saw anything so annoying as the people at my house. They are calling me and disturbing me in my work."

"I don't hear anything," said Compair l'Ours.

"It is because you and Compair Bouki have such small ears that you can't hear. My ears are so long that I hear miles away."

He went away and came back a moment later, saying it was for his wife who was beginning to be sick. He did the same thing three times during the day. At noon he said his wife was in the middle of her sickness, at three o'clock he came back very sad, and said merely: "All is finished."

Compair l'Ours and Compair Bouki pitied him very much because they thought it was his wife who was dead. Instead of that, each time Compair Lapin had said he was going to his wife's house he went to the house of Compair l'Ours and ate a little of his provisions, and when he said: "It is finished," he had finished eating all.

At five o'clock the three friends left their work and went to the house of Compair l'Ours. You may imagine how Compair l'Ours was angry when he saw that all his provisions had disappeared. Immediately he accused Compair Lapin, but he swore it was not he.

"I shall know right off; all three of us will go and lie down on that plank which is in the water in the sun, and the thief will surely be sick." Compair Lapin, who was very impudent, said yes, because he expected to lie down in the shade by the side of Compair l'Ours, who was much larger than he. Compair Bouki said yes also.

Yé couri coté la planche la, et Compair Lapin té pas content quand li oua c'était ein *stage* bateau et li sré pas capabe collé contre Compair l'Ours pou trappé so l'ombre. Yé couché en haut la planche loin l'ein de l'ote, et pas plitot yé té la qué Compair Lapin té ben malade a cause do l'eau et soleil et li commencé réjété tout ça li té manzé.

— Ah mo trapé toi, mo compair, dit Compair l'Ours. To va payer moin ça et mo va pende toi.

— Pende moin si to oulé, ça pas fait moin arien, dit Compair Lapin, mais si to oulé mo va donnin toi ein bon moyen. Fais ein trou dans la muraille, passez la corde ladans ; toi et Compair Bouki vous pas dans soleil pou tirer la corde la et pende moin. Tout temps vous sra apé pende moin ma crié, et quand mo sra pas crié ça sra signe mo pas gagnin la voix et mo sra mouri.

Compair l'Ours fait ça Compair Lapin té dit et taché li, mais quand Compair l'Ours et Compair Bouki té dans la maison, li détaché li méme et pende so patte yé. Compair l'Ours tiré la corde la, Compair Lapin crié fort, pi si faibe qué Compair l'Ours et Compair Bouki té cré li té mouri et yé couri oua lote coté. Yé jiste oua la poussière Compair Lapin tapé fait et yé tendé so la voix qui tapé dit : — Vous oua mo plis *smart* qué vous, et mo remercié vous pou bon dinin la mo fait chez vous.

V.

L'IRLANDAIS ET CRAPAUDS.

Ein fois yavait ein l'Irlandais sou qui tapé révini village et té passé coté ein piti la rivière ou yé té gagnin boucou crapauds. Li tendé crapauds yé qui tapé dit : — Brum, brum, brum. Ah ! dit l'Irlandais la, tapé dit : — Rum, rum, rum, tolé mo rum, mo va donnin toi ein pé, mais faut to promette moin rende moin mo *jug*. Mais di moin, est-ce que do l'eau la fond ?

— Jou, jou, jou, dit crapauds yé. — Oh ! dit l'Irlandais la ça pas ben fond. — Tien, voila mo *rum.* Li jété so *jug* dans do l'eau et li tende ein bon moment, pi li dit : — Anon, Michié, voyé moin mo *jug*, li tard ; faut mo retournin chez moin ; yapé tende moin. Mais crapauds pas voyé arien. Alors l'Irlandais jété li méme dans do l'eau qui té très haut et té vini jisqua so cou.

— Sacré menteurs, dit l'Irlandais la, — vous dit moin do l'eau la sré vini jisqua mo ginoux et li jisqua mo cou.

Comme li té sou li neyé li méme.

They went to the plank, and Compair Lapin was not pleased when he saw that it was the stage of a boat, and he would not be able to stick to Compair l'Ours to be in the shade. They lay down on the plank, at a distance from one another, and no sooner were they there when Compair Lapin felt very sick on account of the water and the sun, and he began to throw up all that he had eaten.

"Ah! I have caught you, comrade," said Compair l'Ours. "You will pay for that, and I am going to hang you."

"Hang me if you wish, I don't care," said Compair Lapin; "but if you want I shall give you a good way. Make a hole in the wall, pass the rope through it, you and Compair Bouki will not be in the sun to pull the rope and hang me. While you will be hanging me I shall cry, and when I shall not cry it will be a sign I have no voice left and I shall be dead."

Compair l'Ours did what Compair Lapin had said and tied him, but when Compair l'Ours and Compair Bouki were in the house, he untied himself and hung by his feet. Compair l'Ours pulled on the rope, Compair Lapin cried loud, then so low that Compair l'Ours and Compair Bouki thought he was dead, and they went to see on the other side of the wall. They only saw the dust Compair Lapin was making, and they heard his voice saying: "You see I am smarter than you, and I thank you for the good dinner I had at your house."

V.

THE IRISHMAN AND THE FROGS.

Once upon a time there was a drunken Irishman who was returning to his village and who passed by a little river where were many frogs. He heard the frogs say: "Brum, brum, brum!" "Ah!" said the Irishman, "you want my rum; I shall give you a little, but you must promise me to give back my jug. But tell me, is the water deep there?"

"Jou, jou, jou!" said the frogs. "Oh!" said the Irishman, "that is not very deep. Here is my rum." He threw his jug into the water and he waited a good while, then he said: "Well, gentlemen, send back my jug; it is late, I must go back home; they are waiting for me." But the frogs did not send back anything. Then the Irishman threw himself into the water that was very deep and came to his neck.

"Confounded liars," said the Irishman, "you told me the water would come to my knees (*genoux*), and it is up to my neck."

As he was drunk, he was drowned.

VI.

COMPAIR LAPIN ET MADAME CARENCRO.

Est-ce que vous connin pouquoi carencro yé chove? Non, et ben mo va dit vous.

Ein fois yavait ein dame Carencro qui té apé couvé dans ein chéne. Li té gagnin ein bon arien mari et té toujou apé mouri faim. Au pied chéne la yavait ein gros trou et dans trou la ein lapin té resté. Compair Lapin té gros et gras et té donnin Mme. Carencro envie manzé li chaque fois li té oua li. Ein jou li profité cin ti moment ou Compair Lapin té apé dromi et li prend la mousse et des briques et bouché trou la. Alors Compair Lapin sré pas capabe sorti et li sré mouri faim.

Quand Compair Lapin réveillé et li oua li méme fermé li sipplié Mme. Carencro laissé li sorti, mais li réponde chaque fois : — Mo faim et faut mo manger la viande en haut to dézos.

Quand Compair Lapin oua que la prière té pas fait arien li paix, mais Mme. Carencro té si content li té prend Compair Lapin que li tapé liché so la lèvre comme li jonglé quel bon dinin la fait. Comme li pas tendé Compair Lapin remué li cré li té mouri touffé et li enlevé la mousse et les briques qui té fermé trou la. Li commencé descende dans trou, mais Compair Lapin fait ein bond et sorti déhors. Quand li té loin li dit comme ça : — To oua, c'est toi qui pris et ma vengé moin.

Li parti et li couri resté chez ein so zamis pasqué li té pair ré-tournin dans chéne la coté Mme. Carencro. Quéque jous après ça Mme. Carencro, qui té blié Compair Lapin, couri promenin avec so piti qui té tous sorti dans yé coquille. Compair Lapin té content et li pensé comment li sré prend rivanche en haut Mme. Carencro. Li couri dans la quisine, li prend ein grand ferblanc plein la braise et la cende chaud, et quand Mme. Carencro et so piti passé coté la garlie li jeté en haut yé tout ça li té gagnin dans ferblanc pou brulé yé. Mais vous connin carencro gagnin la plime épais cepté en haut yé la tête. Ye sécoué vite mais pas assez vite pou pécher la plume en haut yé la tête bruler jisqua la peau.

Voila pouquoi carencros choves, et qué yé jamin manzé dézos lapin.

VI.

COMPAIR LAPIN AND MADAME CARENCRO.

Do you know why buzzards are bald? No. Well, I am going to tell you.

Once upon a time Mme. Carencro was setting upon her nest on an oak-tree. Her husband was a good-for-nothing fellow, and she was always starving. At the foot of the tree there was a big hole in which a rabbit dwelt. Compair Lapin was large and fat, and every time Mme. Carencro saw him she wished to eat him. One day, while Compair Lapin was sleeping, she took some moss and bricks and closed the hole in the tree. Then Compair Lapin would not be able to get out and would die of hunger.

When Compair Lapin woke up and he found out that he was shut up in the hole, he begged Mme. Carencro to let him out, but she replied each time: "I am hungry and I must eat the flesh on your bones."

When Compair Lapin saw that it was of no use to beg, he stopped speaking, but Mme. Carencro was so glad she had caught Compair Lapin that she licked her lips when she thought of the good dinner she would make. As she did not hear Compair Lapin move, she thought he was dead, smothered, and she took away the moss and the bricks which closed the hole. She began to go down the opening, but Compair Lapin made one jump and got out. When he was at some distance he said: "You see, it is you who are caught, and not I."

He ran away and went to stay at the house of one of his friends, because he was afraid to go back into the oak-tree near Mme. Carencro. Some days later Mme. Carencro, who had forgotten Compair Lapin, went to take a walk with her children, who had all come out of their shells. They passed near the house of Compair Lapin's friend. Compair Lapin was glad, and he thought how he could take vengeance on Mme. Carencro. He ran into the kitchen, he took a large tin pan full of burning embers and hot ashes; and when Mme. Carencro and her children passed near the gallery, he threw down on them all that he had in the tin pan, in order to burn them. But you know that buzzards have thick feathers except on the top of their heads. They shook off the embers and ashes, but not quick enough to prevent the feathers on their heads to burn down to the skin.

This is why the buzzards are bald and never eat bones of rabbits.

VII.

COMPAIR LAPIN ET MICHIÉ DINDE.

Tous les soi quand Compair Lapin té révini so louvrage li té traversé ein lacou ou yé té gaingnin ein gros dinde qui tapé dromi on so perchoir, et comme tous lé zotte dinde cila té metté aussite so latéte en bas so zaile pou couri dromi.

Tous les soi Compair Lapin té rété gardé dinde la, et li té mandé li méme ça li té fait avec so latéte. Enfin ein soi li té si quirié li rété en bas perchoir la et li dit : — Bonsoi, Michié Dinde.

— Bonsoi, dit dinde la sans lévé so latéte.
— Est-ce qué vous gaingnin ein latéte, Michié Dinde ?
— Oui, mo gaingnin ein latéte.
— Ou li yé ?
— Mo latéte la.

Compair Lapin té beau chercher li té pas oua latéte Michié Dinde.

Comme li oua dinde la té pas oulé causer avec li ni montré li ou li metté so latéte, li couri chez li et li dit so sère : — Est-ce qué to connin qué pou couri coucher dinde oté yé latéte? Eh ben, mo cré mallé fait méme quichoge, pasqué c'est moins tracas dromi sans latéte, et moune capabe parlé sans latéte, pasqué dinde la parlé avec moin.

Avant so sère té gaingnin temps dit li arien, li prend ein lahache, et li coupé so latéte. So sère sayé tout quichoge pou coller latéte so frère, mais li té pas capabe, pasqué li té tchué li méme.

VIII.

COMPAIR BOUKI ET MACAQUES.

Bouki metté di fé en bas so l'équipage et fait bouilli dolo ladans pendant eine haire. Quand dolo la té bien chaud Bouki sorti déyors et li commencé batte tambour et hélé Macaques yé. Li chanté, li chanté :

> Sam-bombel ! Sam-bombel tam !
> Sam-bombel ! Sam-bombel dam !

Macaques yé tendé et yé dit : — Qui ça? Bouki gaignin quichoge qui bon pou manzé, anon couri, et yé tous parti pou couri chez Bouki. Tan yé té apé galpé, yé té chanté : — Molési, cherguinet,

VII.

COMPAIR LAPIN AND MR. TURKEY.

Every evening when Compair Lapin returned from his work he passed through a yard where there was a large turkey sleeping on its perch, and like all other turkeys that one also had its head under its wing to sleep.

Every evening Compair Lapin stopped to look at the turkey, and he asked himself what it had done with its head. Finally, one evening, he was so curious that he stopped underneath the perch, and said: "Good evening, Mr. Turkey."

"Good evening," said the turkey, without raising its head.

"Do you have a head, Mr. Turkey?"

"Yes, I have a head."

"Where is it?"

"My head is here."

Compair Lapin looked in vain, but he could not see Mr. Turkey's head. As he saw that the turkey did not want to talk to him or show him where was its head, he went to his house and said to his sister: "Do you know that to go to sleep turkeys take off their heads? Well, I believe I shall do the same thing, because it is less trouble to sleep without a head, and one can speak without a head, for the turkey spoke to me."

Before his sister had the time to tell him anything, he took an axe and cut off his head. His sister tried in every way possible to stick it on again, but could not do so, as her brother had killed himself.

VIII.

COMPAIR BOUKI AND THE MONKEYS.

Compair Bouki put fire under his kettle, and when the water was very hot he began to beat his drum and to cry out:

Sam-bombel! Sam-bombel tam!
Sam-bombel! Sam-bombel dam!

The monkeys heard and said: "What? Bouki has something good to eat, let us go," and they ran up to Bouki and sang: "Molési cher-

chourvan! Chéguillé chourvan   Quand Bouki oua yé li té si content li frotté so vente.   Bouki dit Macaques : — Ma lé rentré dans
chaudière la, et quand ma dit mo chuite, oté moin. Bouki sauté
dans chaudière, dans ein piti moment li hélé : — Mo chuite, mo
chuite, oté moin, et macaques halé li déyors.   Quand Bouki té
déyors li dit Macaques : — Astère cé ouzotte tour rentré dans chaudière.   Quand ouzottes va hélé mo chuite ma oté ouzottes.   Macaques yé rentré.   Dolo la té si chaud, si chaud, sitot yé touché li,
yé hélé : — Mo chuite, mo chuite.   Mais Bouki prend so grand
couverti et couvri so chaudière serré, et tan li tapé ri li dit pove
macaques yé : — Si ouzottes té chuite ouzottes té pas capabe dit
ouzottes chuites.   Quand macaques yé té chuites pou méme Bouki
découvri so chaudière.   Asteur ein tout piti macaque, qui té dans
ein piti coin, chapé sans Bouki oua li.   Asteur, Bouki assite, et li
mangé, mangé jouqua li té lasse.   Mais ein jou li fini mangé dernier
macaque et li di : Fo mo trappé lotte macaques.   Li prend so gros
tambour, li couri on haut la garli et li batte, li batte et li chanté :

> Sam-bombel !   Sam-bombel tam !
> Sam-bombel !   Sam-bombel dam !

Et macaques commencé vini, et apé chanté : — Molési, cheriguillé !
Molési, cheriguillé, chourvan !   Quand tous macaques yé té la Bouki
rentré dans dolo chaud qui té dans chaudière, et dit : — Quand ma
dit : Mo chuite, oté moin.   Dans ein ti moment Bouki hélé : — Mo
chuite, mo chuite.   Ah oua, macaques yé prend gros couverti, et
couvri pove Bouki et yé dit li : — Si to té chuite to sré pas hélé.

IX.

MICHIÉ MACAQUE, MARIÉ.

In fois yavé in macaque qui té lainmin in joli jène fille.   Li billé
comme in nomme et li couri oua li.   Mamzelle la recevoir li si bien
qué li ménin so meilleur zami pou oua so namourése.   Popa mamzelle
la mandé zami michié Macaque question on namouré so fille.   Zami
la dit michié Macaque té bon et pi riche, mais li té gaingnin ein
sécret.   Popa la té oulé connin sécret la, mais zami la dit li va dit li
ein lote jou.   Michié Macaque vini fiancé avec Mamzelle la, et soi so
mariage li invité so zami pou souper la.   Zami la té jalou michié
Macaque, et quand soupé té presque fini li commencé chanté.   C'était
ein chanson pou fait macaque dansé, méme si yé pas oulé, alorse
michié Macaque gardé coté so zami et fait li signe rété chanté.   Mais

guinet, chourvan! Chéguillé, chourvan!" Compair Bouki then said to the monkeys: "I shall enter into the kettle, and when I say 'I am cooked,' you must take me out." He jumped into the kettle, and the monkeys pulled him out as soon as he said "I am cooked."

The monkeys, in their turn, jumped into the kettle, and cried out, immediately on touching the water, "We are cooked." Bouki, however, took his big blanket, and covering the kettle, said: "If you were cooked you could not say so." One little monkey alone escaped, and Bouki ate all the others. Some time after this Compair Bouki was hungry again, and he called the monkeys:

Sam-bombel! Sam-bombel tam!
Sam-bombel! Sam-bombel dam!

When the monkeys came, he jumped into the kettle again and said: "I am cooked, I am cooked." The monkeys, however, which had been warned by the little monkey which had escaped the first time, did not pull Bouki out, but said: "If you were cooked you could not say so."

IX.

MR. MONKEY, THE BRIDEGROOM.

There was a monkey which fell in love with a beautiful young girl. He dressed as a man and went to call on her. He was so well received that one day he took his best friend with him to see his lady-love. The young girl's father asked Mr. Monkey's friend some questions about his daughter's lover. The friend said that Mr. Monkey was good and rich, but there was a secret about him. The father wanted to know the secret, but the friend said he would tell him another day. Mr. Monkey was finally engaged to the young lady, and the night of the wedding he invited his friend to the supper. The latter was jealous of Mr. Monkey, and at the end of the supper he began to sing. This was a song that made all monkeys dance,

li continuin chanté et tout d'in coup michié Macaque lévé et li commencé dansé. Li sauté tellement que so la tchié sorti et tout moune oua li té ein macaque. Popa la comprende sécret la et li batte li raide. So zami chappé apé dansé et chanté.

X.

TORTIE.

In michié qui té vive on bord in bayou trappé in gros tortie et li invité tout suitte so zami pou dinin avec li. So ti garçon, quand li té pas la, couri coté lacage tortie la, et tortie commencé sifflé. — Comme to sifflé bien, dit piti la. — Oh! ça, cé pas arien, ouvri la cage la, et ta oua. Garçon la ouvri la cage et tortie sifflé mié qué anvant. Garçon la té enchanté. — Metté moin on la planche et ta oua, dit tortie la. Garçon la fait ça, et tortie dansé et chanté. — Oh! comme to dansé et chanté bien, dit garçon la. — Metté moin on bord bayou, et ta oua, dit tortie. Garçon la ménin li au bord bayou, et tortie la dansé et chanté. Tout d'in coup li disparaite dans dolo et garçon la commence crié. Tortie lévé dans milié bayou et li dit : — Apprende pas fié moune to pas connin.

Garçon la té pair so popa et li metté ein gros la pierre plate dans lacage. Cuisinier la té cré c'était tortie et li metté lapierre dans chaudière. Li té étonnin oua li resté dire si longtemps et li montré li so maite. Li ordonnin metté tortie on la tabe et li prend so couteau la tabe pou coupé li. C'était pas la peine. Li prend couteau découpé, pas la peine. Li prend casse tête, pas la peine. Li prend lahache ; li cassé lassiette, la tabe, mais tortie la resté telle. Li oua alorse c'était ein lapierre, et jisqua asteur li pas comprende comment so tortie té changé en lapierre.

whether they wished to or not, so Mr. Monkey looked at his friend and beckoned him to stop singing. He continued, however, to sing, and all at once Mr. Monkey got up and began to dance. He jumped about so wildly that his tail came out of his clothes, and every one saw that he was a monkey. The father understood the secret, and beat him dreadfully. His friend, however, ran off, dancing and singing.

X.

THE TORTOISE.

A gentleman who was living on the banks of a bayou caught a large tortoise, and went immediately to invite some friends to take dinner with him. His little boy, in his absence, went to the cage where was the tortoise, and the latter began to whistle. "How well you whistle!" said the child. "Oh! that is nothing; open the cage, and you will see." The boy opened the cage, and the tortoise whistled better than ever. The boy was delighted. "Put me down on the floor and you will see," said the tortoise. The boy did so, and the tortoise danced and sang. "Oh! how well you dance and sing!" said the boy. "Put me on the bank of the bayou, and you will see," said the tortoise. The boy took her to the bayou, and the tortoise danced and sang. All at once she disappeared in the water, and the boy began to cry. The tortoise rose in the middle of the bayou and said: "Learn not to trust, hereafter, people whom you do not know."

The boy was afraid of his father, and put a large flat stone into the cage. The cook, thinking it was the tortoise, put the stone into the kettle. She was astonished to see it remain hard so long, and she called her master's attention to it. He ordered the tortoise to be put upon the table, and he took his table knife to cut it. It was in vain. He took the carving-knife, in vain. He took the hatchet, in vain. He took the axe, he broke the dishes, the table, but the tortoise remained intact. He then saw it was a stone, and to this day he has not understood how his tortoise was changed into a stone.

XI.

COMPAIR BOUKI, COMPAIR LAPIN, ET DÉZEF ZOZO.

Compair Bouki et Compair Lapin té voisin.　In jou Compair Bouki dit li méme li té oulé oua ça Compair Lapin té apé tchui tous les soirs dans so cabane.　Li couri coté cabane Compair Lapin et li oua in gros chaudière on difé. — Oh! comme mo gagnin mal aux dents!　Compair Lapin, ça vous gagnin dans chaudière la?

— Ça pas vous zaffaire, Compair Bouki.

— Qui ça qui senti si bon dans chaudière la, Compair Lapin? Oh! comme mo gagnin mal aux dents!

— Cé dézef zozo, Compair Bouki, pas bété moin.

— Oh! comme mo gagnin mal aux dents!　Laissé moin gouté ça vous gagnin la, ça va guéri moin.

Compair Lapin donnin li quéque dézef, et Compair Bouki trouvé yé si bon li té oulé connin ou li té prend yé.　Compair Lapin dit li li sré ménin li avec li lendemin matin.

Compair Bouki couri chez li et li dit so moman li té gagnin in bien bon souper chez Compair Lapin.　So moman dit li ouvri so labouche pou li capable senti qui ça li té mangé.　Li prend alors in ti morceau dibois et gratté on dents Compair Bouki morceau dézef qui té resté la.

— Oh! comme c'est bon, li dit.　Faut to porté moin in pé.

Compair Bouki couri bonne hère lendemin matin avec Compair Lapin, qui montré li ou dézef yé té et dit li pas prende plis qué inne dans chaque nique, pasqué zozo yé sré oua ça.　Compair Bouki quand Lapin té parti, prend tout dézef dans chaque nique.　Quand zozo révini et yé oua tout yé dézef té volé yé té firié et yé fait in plan pou vengé yé méme.　Yavé dans bois in bayou qui té séle place ou zanimo té capable boi.　Zozo yé placé yé méme autour bayou la et yé oua ein bef vini.

— Compair Bef, est-ce que c'est vous qui mangé nous dézef?

— Non, mo zami, mo mangé jisse zerbe.

Choal dit li mangé jisse difoin; Compair Lapin dit li mangé jisse carottes et laitues, mais quand yé mandé Compair Bouki, li réponde comme in béte: — Oui, c'est moin qui mangé vous dézef.

Pas plitot li té parlé qué tous zozo tombé on li; yé crévé so zié et presque metté li en pièces.

XI.

COMPAIR BOUKI, COMPAIR LAPIN, AND THE BIRDS' EGGS.

Compair Bouki and Compair Lapin were neighbors. One day Compair Bouki said to himself that he wished to see what Compair Lapin was cooking every evening in his cabin. He went to Compair Lapin's cabin and saw a big kettle on the fire. "Oh! what a toothache I have! Compair Lapin, what do you have in that kettle?"

"It is not your business, Compair Bouki."

"What smells so good in that kettle, Compair Lapin? Oh! what a toothache I have!"

"It is birds' eggs, Compair Bouki; don't bother me."

"Oh! what a toothache I have! Let me taste what you have here. It will cure me."

Compair Lapin gave him a few eggs, and Compair Bouki found them so good that he wished to know where they were to be found. Compair Lapin told him he would take him with him the next day.

Compair Bouki went home and told his mother that he had a splendid supper at Compair Lapin's. His mother told him to open his mouth that she might smell what it was that he had eaten. She then took a small piece of wood and scraped off the teeth of Compair Bouki the small pieces of eggs that remained there.

"Oh! how good it is," she said; "you must get me some."

Compair Bouki went early the next morning with Compair Lapin, who showed him where the eggs were and told him not to take more than one from each nest, because the birds would perceive it. Compair Bouki, however, as soon as Lapin was gone, took all the eggs from every nest. When the birds returned and saw that all the eggs had been stolen, they were furious, and formed a plan to avenge themselves. There was in the wood a bayou which was the only place where the animals could drink. The birds placed themselves around the bayou and saw an ox coming.

"Compair Bef, was it you who ate our eggs?"

"No, my friends, I eat nothing but grass."

The horse said he ate nothing but hay. Compair Lapin said that he ate nothing but carrots and lettuce; but when they questioned Compair Bouki, he replied foolishly: "Yes, it is I who ate your eggs."

No sooner had he spoken when the birds fell upon him; they put out his eyes and nearly tore him to pieces.

XII.

CHIEN AVEC TIGUE.

In jou in chien acheté cent poules et in coq, et in tigue acheté cent coqs et in poule. Tous les soi chien la té trouvé in panier plein dézef dans so poulailler, et tigue la té trouvé jisse in dézef. Tigue dit chien volé li, et li taché li, li metté li dans in brouette et li parti pou vende li. On chimin li contré in chévreil ; li conté li so zaffaire et li mandé li si li pas raison vende chien la. Chévreil la dit non, alors tigue la tchué li. In pé plis tard li rencontré in lion et li raconté li so lhistoire. Lion la dit tigue té gagnin tort, et tigue la dit : — Vous parlé comme ça pasqué vous connin vous plis fort qué moin.

Quéque temps après ça tigue couri dans bois et li laissé chien la seul quéque temps. Chassère passé et yé mandé chien la ça lapé fait la. Li raconté so lhistoire, et chassère yé mandé li montré yé ou tigue la té. Tigue la té pair comme djabe, et dépi temps la chien jamin pair béte sauvage.

XIII.

FILLÈLE COMPAIR LAPIN.

In fois Compair Lapin té apé travaille pou Compair Bouki. Bouki té acheté in baril dibère et li té caché li dans so lacave. Dé compair yé té apé travaille dans clos ensembe, et tout d'in coup, Lapin lévé so latéte, et li dit : — Yapé pélé moin pou batisé in piti.

Bouki dit : — Couri tout suite, faut pas to fait li attende.

Lapin parti couri et quand li révini, Bouki dit li : — Eh ben, to batisé piti la ? Coman to pélé li ?
— Mo pélé li Commencé.
— Non, ça cé in drole nom.
In pé plis tard, Lapin, lévé so latéte encore et li dit : — Yapé pélé moin encore pou batisé in lotte piti.
— Couri, dit Bouki, to pas capabe dit yé non.
Compair Lapin parti couri encore et li resté plis longtemps qué

XII.

THE DOG AND THE TIGER.

A dog one day bought one hundred hens and one rooster, and a tiger bought one hundred roosters and one hen. Every evening the dog found a basketful of eggs in his chicken-house, and the tiger found only one egg. The tiger accused the dog of robbing him, and, tying him up, he put him in a wheelbarrow and took him along to sell him. On the way he met a deer, and relating his story to him, he asked him if he was not right to sell the dog. The deer said "no," whereupon the tiger killed him. A little later he met a lion, and related his story to him. The lion said the tiger was wrong and the latter replied, "You speak in that way because you know that you are stronger than I."

After some time the tiger went into the woods and left the dog alone for a few minutes. Some hunters passed by, and they asked the dog what he was doing there. He related his story, and the hunters asked him to show them where the tiger was. The tiger was terribly frightened, and from that time dogs have never been afraid of wild beasts.

XIII.

COMPAIR LAPIN'S GODCHILD.

Once upon a time Compair Lapin was working for Compair Bouki. The latter had bought a barrel of butter, and had hidden it in his cellar. The two companions were working one day in the field together, when, all at once, Lapin raised his head, and said: "They are calling me to be godfather to a child."

"Go immediately," replied Bouki; "you must not make them wait."

Lapin ran off, and when he returned, Bouki said to him: "Well, did you baptize the child? How did you call him?"

"I called him 'Begun.'"

"Indeed, that is a strange name."

A little later, Lapin raised his head again, and said: "They are calling me again to be godfather to another child."

"Go," said Bouki; "you cannot tell them no."

Compair Lapin ran off again, and remained away longer than the

premier fois. Quand li révini Compair Bouki dit li : — Coman to pélé piti la fois cila ?

— Mo pélé li La Motchié.

— La Motchié, mais qui nom c'est ça. Mo jamin tendé drole nom comme ça to donnin piti yé to batisé.

In pé pli tard encore, pendant yé tapé travaille, Lapin lévé so latéte et dit : — Eh ben, yapé pélé moin encore pou in lotte piti ; ça bétant, ma jamin fini mo louvrage.

Bouki dit li : — Couri, to pas capabe dit non.

Compair Lapin parti couri et li té pé ri li tout seul.

Quand li révini encore Compair Bouki dit li : — Coman to pélé cila ?

— Oh ! mo pélé li : Tout fini, pasqué mo vé pli batisé piti.

Asteur Compair Bouki dit li méme : — Faut mo régalé mo méme, mapé couri rempli mo bérier avec mo bon dibère. Li vini gardé dans so baril ; pli arien. Lapin té chéché li nette.

— Ça c'est trop fort, dit Bouki, li va payé moin ça. Li trapé Compair Lapin et li taché li et li dit li : — Qui ça ma capabe fait avec toi asteur, ma jété toi dans dolo.

— Ah ! oui, c'est ça mo laimin.

— Non, to trop content, ma jété toi dans difé.

— Ah ! oui, jété moin dans difé.

— Non, to trop content, ma jété toi dans zéronce.

— Oh ! pardon, mo cher Bouki, pas jété moin dans zéronce.

— Oui, c'est la faut to couri.

Compair Bouki lancé Compair Lapin dans zéronce. Asteur, quand Lapin tombé li coupé so la corde avec so dent et li parti galpé et li crié : — Merci, mo bon Compair Bouki, to metté moin jisse la ou mo moman resté.

XIV.

MAMZELLE MOQUÈRE, MICHIÉ MOQUÈRE, ET MICHIÉ HIBOU.

Ein fois Moquère et pi Hibou tapé fait l'amour méme Mamzelle Moquère. Mamzelle Moquère dit yé : Ah bien, ma marié avec cila qui connin resté pli lontan sans mangé. Moin, ma resté en bas nabe la et vouzotte enho li.

Asteur Moquère gardé so namoureuse et li tapé descende nabe et apé chanté :

first time. On his return Bouki said : "How did you call the child this time?"

"I called him 'Half.'"

"Half! But what name is that? I never heard such strange names as those which you give the children baptized by you."

A little later again, while they were working, Lapin raised his head, and said : "There, they are calling me again for another child ; it is very annoying ; I shall never be able to finish my work."

"Go," said Bouki; "you cannot say no."

Lapin ran off, laughing to himself.

When he returned, Bouki said : "What is the name of the child?"

"Oh! I called him 'All Finished,' because I do not want to be godfather to any other child."

Now, Bouki said to himself : "I must have a good dinner; let me fill my butter dish with my good butter." He looked into his barrel, there was nothing in it. Lapin had eaten all the butter.

"Oh! that is too much," said Bouki; "he will pay me for that." He caught Lapin, he tied him with a rope, and said : "Now, what am I going to do with you? I'll throw you in the river."

"Ah! yes, that is what I like."

"No, you are too glad; I'll throw you in the fire."

"Ah! yes, throw me in the fire."

"No, you are too glad; I'll throw you in the briers."

"Oh! I pray you, my dear Bouki, do not throw me in the briers."

"Yes, it is there you must go."

Bouki threw Lapin in the briers. As soon as he fell, he cut the rope with his teeth, and ran away, crying : "Thank you, my good Bouki; you placed me exactly where my mother resides."

XIV.

MISS MOCKINGBIRD, MR. MOCKINGBIRD, AND MR. OWL.

Once upon a time the Mockingbird and the Owl were courting Miss Mockingbird. She said to them : "Well, I shall marry the one who will remain the longer without eating. I shall remain under the tree and you upon it."

Now, the mockingbird looked at his lady-love and flew down to her, singing :

> Chivi ! Chivi ! Ta la la !
> Chivi ! Chivi ! Ta la la !
> Hévé ! Ta la la !

Quand li rendi en bas li fait comme si lapé bo Mamzelle Moquère, et cila té gagnin mangé dans so bec et li tapé donnin li jène nomme Moquère la. Moquère monté dans so nabe encore.

Hibou oua tout, lorse li aussite parti pou descende, et tant li tapé descende li tapé chanté : —

> Coucou ! Ta la la !
> Coucou ! Ta la la !
> Hévé ! Ta la la !

Li rivé en bas, li vini pou bo mamzelle la, mais mamzelle la tournin so latéte et dit li : — Couri, couri, to lézailes fait mo la figure mal. Pove Hibou té pas gagnin arien pou mangé. Li té bo mamzelle la et mamzelle la té donnin li morceau mangé. Hibou descende aussite, mais li té pé commencé bien faim et ça fait so lavoix té vini faibe et triste, et li té pé dit : —

> Coucou ! Ta la la la !
> Coucou ! Ta la la la !
> Hévé ! Ta la la la !

Mamzelle la té pas oulé gardé li ni donnin li mangé. Pove Hibou té gagnin pou monté dans nabe la so vente vide et Moquère té pé fait so vantor apé chanté si fort : —

> Chivi ! Chivi ! Ta la la !
> Chivi ! Chivi ! Ta la la !
> Hévé ! Ta la la !

Pove Hibou apé mouri faim, yé té jiste capabe tendé li chanté a force li té faibe : —

> Coucou ! Ta la !
> Coucou ! Ta la !
> Hévé ! Ta la !

Li rivé en bas, li seyé bo mamzelle la encore, mais mamzelle la dit li : — Oh couri, couri, to grand lézailes fait mo mal, et mamzelle la donnin li in tape qui capoté li par terre at li té si faim qué li mouri, et Michié Moquère parti volé avec so fame.

Chivi! Chivi! Ta la la!
Chivi! Chivi! Ta la la!
Hévé! Ta la la!

When he reached Miss Mockingbird, he did as if he wanted to kiss her, and she gave him some food which she had in her beak. Mr. Mockingbird flew back to his tree.

The Owl in his turn flew towards his lady love, and he sang:

Coucou! Ta la la!
Coucou! Ta la la!
Hévé! Ta la la!

He wished to kiss Miss Mockingbird, but she turned her head aside, and said: "Go away; your wings hurt me." The poor Owl had nothing to eat, while every day the mockingbird flew down, and, kissing the young lady, got something to eat. The Owl came down also from the tree, but he was beginning to be very hungry, and his voice was very weak when he sang:

Coucou! Ta la la la!
Coucou! Ta la la la!
Hévé! Ta la la la!

Miss Mockingbird did not want to look at him or to give him anything to eat, and he had to go back to his tree with an empty stomach. Mr. Mockingbird, on the contrary, grew more boastful every day, and sang in a loud voice:

Chivi! Chivi! Ta la la!
Chivi! Chivi! Ta la la!
Hévé! Ta la la!

The poor Owl was dying of hunger, and one could hardly hear his song:

Coucou! Ta la!
Coucou! Ta la!
Hévé! Ta la!

He tried to kiss Miss Mockingbird, but she said to him: "Go away; your large wings hurt me," and she gave him a slap which threw him down. He was so weak from hunger that he died, and Mr. Mockingbird flew away with his bride.

XV.

MARIAZE COMPAIR LAPIN.

— Tim, tim, bois sec, cré coton, Compair Lapin, c'est ti bonhomme qui connin sauté.

Vous zotes doit rappeler, qué après yé té voyé Compair Lapin dans grands zerbes, comme li té chapé raide et comme li dit c'était la même so moman té fait li. Pour lors donc mo va dit vous qué même jou la Mamzelle Léonine couri joinde li et yé parti voyagé. Yé marché longtemps, pendant au moin ein mois, a la fin yé rivé au bord ein la rivière qui té boucou fond ; courant la té fort, trop fort pou qué yé té passé li a la nage. L'ote coté la rivière la té ein joli place, nabes yé té vert et chargé tout sortes fruits ; en bas nabe yé tout qualité flairs dans moune té la ; quand ein moune té respiré c'est comme si yé té débouché ein fiole lessence dans ein la chambre.

Mamzelle Léonine dit comme ça : — Anon couri vive la, dabord nous pas capabe tournin coté mo popa. La nous va héreux et personne pas allé tracassé nous zotes. Mais comment nous va fait pou traversé lote coté ?

— Rété, dit Compair Lapin, laissé moin jonglé ein ti moment, et pi li prend marché, alors li rivé au ras ein gros di bois sec qui té tombé dans dolo. — Ala nous zaffaire, li dit comme ça. Li coupé ein grand perche et pi li monté en haut di bois la et li dit Léonine suive li. Pove Léonine monté aussite et li té apé tremblé a force li té pair.

— Tchombo bien, ta oua comment na passé, et pi li poussé avec so baton. Di bois la prende descende courant et yé filé raide ; Lapin apé pagaye, pagaye. Yé navigué ein demi journin avant yé té capabe rivé l'ote coté ; courant la té si fort qué di bois té toujou apé couri. Li raclé la terre quand li passé au ras lécore. — Sauté, sauté, dit Compair Lapin. Quand li dit ça li même té déja en haut la terre. A la fin Mamzelle Léonine sauté aussite et yé trouvé traversé. Ça fait yé té content et yé commencé manzé plein bon kichoge yé té gagnin la, et pi yé posé bien.

Yé trouvé ein joli place pou passé la nouitte et lendemin bo matin yé prend promené partout. Comme tout ça yé oua té vaillant, yé pensé yé sré resté la pou vive. Quand yé té chapé, yé té pas capabe porté largent avec yé, ça fait yé trouvé yé a sec. Mais Bon Djé té

XV.

MARRIAGE OF COMPAIR LAPIN.

Tim, tim! Bois sec. Cré coton! Compair Lapin is a little fellow who knows how to jump!

You all must remember, after they had thrown Compair Lapin into the briers, how quickly he had run away, saying that it was in those very thorns that his mother had made him. Now then, I will tell you that on the same day Miss Léonine went to meet him, and they started travelling. They walked a long time, for at least a month; at last they reached the bank of a river which was very deep. The current was strong, too strong for them to swim over. On the other side of the river there was a pretty place: the trees were green and loaded with all kinds of fruits. Under the trees were flowers of every kind that there is in the world. When a person breathed there, it was as if a bottle of essence had been opened in a room.

Miss Léonine said: "Let us go to live there; besides, we cannot return to my father's. There, we shall be happy, and no one will bother us; but how shall we do to cross over to the other side?"

"Stop," said Compair Lapin, "let me think a moment," and then he began to walk and walk, until he saw a large piece of dry wood which had fallen into the water. "That is what I want," said he. He cut a tall pole, and then he mounted on the log and told Léonine to follow him. Poor Miss Léonine mounted also, but she was so much afraid that she was trembling dreadfully.

"Hold on well; you will see how we shall pass;" and he pushed with his stick. The log began to go down the current; they were going like lightning, and Lapin kept on paddling. They sailed for half a day before they were able to reach the other side, for the current was so strong that the log was carried along all the time. At last it passed very near the shore. "Jump, jump," said Compair Lapin, and hardly had he spoken than he was on shore. Miss Léonine finally jumped also, and they found themselves on the other side of the river. They were very glad, and the first thing they did was to eat as much as they could of the good things they found there. Then they took a good rest.

They found a pretty place to pass the night, and the next day, at dawn, they took a good walk. As everything they saw was so fine, they thought they would remain there to live. When they had run away, they had not been able to take any money with them, so they

béni yé, yé té vini dans ein place ou yé té pas bésoin boucou largent. Yavé déja ein bon boute yé té dans place la, yé té tranquille et content et yé té cré yé tout seul, mais tout d'ein coup yé tendé ein tapage, ein remu menage, ein train, comme si tonnerre té apé roulé en haut la terre.

— Qui ça ça, Bon Djé Seigneur, couri gardé, Compair Lapin.

— Moin, non. Comme si mo assez béte pou couri gardé et pététe trapé kichoge mauvais. Vaut mié mo resté tranquille, comme ça arien pas apé rivé moin.

Train la avec di bri la té augmenté toujou. A la fin, yé oua ein procession néléphants qui té apé vini. Comme yé té passé tranquillement sans taquer personne, ça donne Lapin ein pé courage, alors li vancé coté chef néléphants et pi li dit li mandé li la permission resté dans so pays, qué li té sorti dans pays roi Lion, ou yé té oulé tchué li, qué li té bligé chappé avec so fame.

Néléphant la dit li : — Comme ça, c'est bon, to capabe resté ici tant to oulé, mais pas ménin lote zanimo qui connin manzé yé entre yé. Tant ta comporté bien ma va protégé toi et personne pas allé vini chercher toi icite. Vini oua moin souvent et ma seyé fait kichoge pou toi.

Quéque temps après ça Compair Lapin couri oua roi néléphant, et lé roi té si content quand Compair Lapin té expliqué comment lé roi té capabe fait boucou largent qué li nommé Lapin tout suite capitaine so la banque et gardien so bitin.

Quand Compair Lapin oua tout largent li té apé magnin tous les jou, ca proche rende li fou, et comme li té habitoué boi dipi yé té fouillé ein pi dans so pays qué dolo la té soulé moune, li continié so vilain nabitude, chaque fois li té gagnin la chance li té soulé li bien.

Ein soir li té rentré tard bien piqué, li prend babillé avec so fame. Léonine fait ni eine ni dé, li bimin Compair Lapin si tant qué li resté couché pendant trois semaines. Quand li vini gaillard, li mandé so fame pardon, li di li té soul, qué cété dernière fois et pi li bo li. Mais dans so tcheur li gagné vous ein ranquine qué li té pas capabe pardonné Léonine. Li fait serment quitté Léonine mais anvant ça li té gagnin donne li ein famé la trempe.

Ça fait ein soir Léonine té apé dromi Compair Lapin prend ein la corde, li marré so pattes dévant et derrière, et comme ça li té sir so zaffaire et li prend ein bon fouette et li taillé so femme jisqua li té perde connaissance, et pi li quitté li et li parti voyagé, la ou yé sré jamis tendé parlé li, pasqué li té pair Léonine sré tchué li, et li filé loin.

were without a cent. But God had blessed them, for they had come
to a place where they did not need much money. They had already
been there a good while, and they were quiet and contented, and
they thought that they were alone, when one day, they heard, all at
once, a noise, a tumult, as if thunder was rolling on the ground.

"What is that, my lord? Go to see, Compair Lapin."

"I, no, as if I am foolish to go, and then catch something bad.
It is better for me to stay quiet, and, in that way, nothing can
happen to me."

The noise kept on increasing, until they saw approaching a procession of elephants. As they were passing quietly without attacking
any one, it gave Compair Lapin a little courage. He went to the
chief of the elephants and told him that he asked his permission to
remain in his country; he said that he came from the country of
King Lion, who had wanted to kill him, and he had run away with
his wife.

The elephant replied: "That is good; you may remain here as
long as you want, but don't you bring here other animals who know
how to eat one another. As long as you will behave well, I will
protect you, and nobody will come to get you here. Come sometimes to see me, and I will try to do something for you."

Some time after that, Compair Lapin went to see the king of
elephants, and the king was so glad when Compair Lapin explained
to him how he could make a great deal of money, that he named
immediately Compair Lapin captain of his bank and watchman of
his property.

When Compair Lapin saw all the money of the king it almost
turned his head, and as he had taken the habit of drinking since
they had dug in his country a well, of which the water made people
drunk, he continued his bad habit whenever he had the chance.

One evening he came home very drunk, and he began quarrelling
with his wife. Léonine fell upon him and gave him such a beating
that he remained in bed for three weeks. When he got up, he asked
his wife to pardon him; he said that he was drunk, and that he
would never do it again, and he kissed her. In his heart, however,
he could not forgive Léonine. He swore that he would leave her,
but before that he was resolved to give her a terrible beating.

One evening when Léonine was sleeping, Compair Lapin took a
rope and tied her feet before and behind. In that way he was sure
of his business. Then he took a good whip, and he whipped her
until she lost consciousness. Then he left her and went on travelling. He wanted to go to a place where they would never hear
of him any more, because he was afraid that Léonine would kill
him, and he went far.

Quand Léonine réveillé li pélé, li pélé, moune vini oua ça té yé et yé trouvé li bien marré. Alors yé démarré li et Léonine parti tout suite. Li quitté so la maison, li voyagé longtemps jisqua li vini coté même rivière li té traversé avec Compair Lapin en haut ein di bois. Li fait ni éin ni dé li sauté dans dolo. Courant la té si fort ça té souteni li bien. A force débatte, nager, nager, li traversé lote coté. Quand li monté en haut la terre li té bien lasse et té gagnin pou posé ein bon boute et pi li parti pou tournin coté so popa.

Quand so popa oua li li bo li et li caressé li, mais so fille prend crié et li di li comment Compair Lapin té traité li. Quand so popa tendé ça a force li té colère tout ça yé qui té au ras li prende tremblé.

— Vini icite, Compair Renard, ta couri trouvé lé roi néléphant et ta dit li comme ça si li pas voyé moin Compair Lapin icite plis vite qué li capabe ma va couri dans so pays tchué li et tout lote néléphants et tout ça qui yé dans so pays. Parti tout suite.

Compair Renard voyagé longtemps et a la fin rivé dans pays la ou Compair Lapin té caché. Mais li pas oua li, li mandé pou li mais personne té pas capabe donné so nouvelle. Compair Renard couri trouvé lé roi et li dit li ça so tchenne roi té voyé dit li. Néléphant qui haï Lions réponde : — Va dit to maite si li envi mo cassé so la djole li jis seyé vini. Mo pas apé voyé arien ni personne et commencé par foute to camp. Si to oulé ein bon conseil resté coté toi. Si jamais Lion seyé vini, ma donné li ein lagniappe qué pas eine dans vous zotes gagnin pou tournin dans vous zote pays.

Compair Renard pas mandé so restant, li parti mais li té pas boucou envi tourné chez li, li té pair Lion sré tchoué li si li té vini sans Compair Lapin. Li marché plis doucement qué li té capabe et tout di long chemin li oua yé té apé préparé pou fait la guerre. Li pensé que pététe néléphants té oulé couri taqué lions, li continié so chimin, quand li rivé dans ein la plaine li oua Compair Lapin qui té apé galopé en zigzag, tantot ein coté tantot lote et pi li té rété quand li rencontré zanimo, et pi li parlé avéc yé et pi li parti encore aussi raide comme anvant. A la fin yé fini par contré, mais Compair Lapin té pas reconnaite so vié padna.

— Ou tapé couri comme ça, galopé, galopé tout temps ?
— Ah, réponde Compair Lapin, vous pas connin mauvais nouvelle qué Lion déclaré la djerre tous néléphants et ma pé verti tous milets, choals et chameaux yé pou yé fou camp.

When Miss Léonine came back to herself, she called, she called ; they came to see what was the matter, and they found her well tied up. They cut the ropes, and Léonine started immediately. She left her house, she travelled a long time, until she came to the same river which she had crossed with Compair Lapin upon the log. She did not hesitate, but jumped into the water. The current carried her along, and she managed, after a great many efforts, to cross over to the other side. She was very tired, and she had to take some rest ; then she started to return to her father.

When her father saw her, he kissed her and caressed her, but his daughter began to cry, and told him how Compair Lapin had treated her. When King Lion heard that, he was so angry that all who were near him began to tremble.

"Come here, Master Fox ; you shall go to the king of elephants, and tell him, that if he does not send Compair Lapin to me as soon as he can, I shall go to his country to kill him and all the elephants, and all the other animals, and everything which is in his country. Go quick !"

Master Fox travelled a long time, and arrived at last in the country where Compair Lapin was hidden. But he did not see him ; he asked for him, but no one could give him any news of him. Master Fox went to see the king of elephants and told him what King Lion had said. The elephants hate the lions, so the king replied : "Tell your master that if he wishes me to break his jaw-bone, let him come. I shall not send anything or anybody, and first of all, get away from here quick. If you want good advice, I can tell you that you had better remain in your country. If ever Lion tries to come here, I shall receive him in such a manner that no one of you will ever return home."

Master Fox did not wait to hear any more; but he had no great desire to go back to his country, for he thought Lion would kill him if he returned without Compair Lapin. He walked as slowly as he could, and all along the road he saw that they were making preparations for war. He thought that perhaps the elephants were going to attack King Lion. He went on his way, and on arriving at a prairie he saw Compair Lapin, who was running in zigzags, sometimes on one side of the road, sometimes on the other. He stopped whenever he met animals and spoke to them, and then he started again as rapidly as before. At last Master Fox and Compair Lapin met, but the latter did not recognize his old friend.

"Where are you going like that, running all the time ? "

"Ah !" replied Compair Lapin, "you don't know the bad news. Lion has declared war against all elephants, and I want to notify all mules, horses, and camels to get out of the way."

— Mais to méme qui zaffaire to gagnin pou galopé, yé pas apé prend toi pou fait soldat avec toi?

— Non, to croi ça, réponde Compair Lapin, ah bien, to pas connin arien avec tout to malin. Quand n'officier lé roi a vini chercher choals et milets pou la cavalerie pou fait la djerre yé va dit comme ça : Ala ein bougue grand zoreille, c'est ein milet, anon prend li, et quand méme mo réclamé et dit moin c'est ein lapin yé va dit : Oh non, gardé so zoreille, vouzote oua ben c'est ein milet, et mo sra fouti, yé vá enrolé moin et mo va bligé marché. Mais semblé moin mo connin vous, mais si longtemps mo pas oua vous. Bon Djé tendé moin, c'est Renard, mo zami lézotes fois.

— Oui, oui, c'est moin, mo vié. Eh ben, ça vous dit pou tout vilain zaffaire yé?

— Tout ça pou ein femme, dit Compair Lapin, faut nous seyé, mo zami, pas trouvé nouzottes dans yé procès.

— Mais comment na fait, dit Renard, yé va forcé nouzotes la dans.

— Non, dit Compair Lapin, faut to conseillé Lion, mo va conseillé Néléphant, alors comme ça nous va resté gardé et laissé ye batte tant yé oulé.

— To connin, dit Renard, Léonine tournin coté so popa et comme vouzotes té pas marié devant léglise mo croi ben Lion en train marié so fille avec ein dans so voisin ; ça pas fait toi la peine, Compair Lapin, tendé tout ça?

— Non, ça zié pas oua tcheur pas fait mal.

Dé malin yé causé bon boute, yé té si content, navé si longtemps yé té pas contré. Dans méme moment yé té paré pou parti yé oua dé chien qui tapé grongnin nez a nez et pi yé senti ye méme partout.

— Vous, Compair Renard, qui connin tout quichoge, vous capabe dit moin cofaire chien gagnin vilain nhabitude la ?

— Mo va dit vous, Compair Lapin, cofaire yé fait ça. Les otes fois, yéna longtemps, dans temps yé navé jis ein Bon Djé qui té pélé Michié Zipiter, tout chien té trouvé yé sort té malheureux, alors yé voyé ein délégation, ein bande chien pou mandé Bon Djé pou li méliorer yé condition. Quand yé té rivé au ras la maison Michié Zipiter dans ciel tout la restant chien yé té pair, yé parti, jis Brisetout, plis gros chien la bande qui resté. Li té pas pair arien, li vancé au ras Michié Zipiter, et pi li dit comme ça : — Mo nation voyé moin coté vous pou mandé vous, qui maite tout ça yéna en haut la terre, si vous croi na va gardé nous maites yé tout la journin et tout la nouite, jappé tout temps, trappé coups pied, pas mangé arien. Nous trop

"But you, why are you running so ? They are surely not going to make a soldier of you ?"

"No, you believe that. Ah, well, with all your cunning you know nothing. When the officers of the king will come to get the horses and mules for the cavalry to go to war, they will say : 'That's a fellow with long ears ; he is a mule ; let us take him.' Even if I protest, and say that I am a rabbit, they will say : 'Oh, no ! look at his ears ; you see that he is a mule,' and I should be caught, enlisted, and forced to march. It seems to me that I know you, but it is such a long time since I have seen you. May God help me, it is Master Fox, my old friend !"

"Yes, yes, it is I, my good fellow. Well ! what do you say about all that bad business ?"

"All that is for a woman," said Compair Lapin ; "we must try, my friend, to have nothing to do with that war."

"But what shall we do ?" said Master Fox. "They will force us into it."

"No, you must be King Lion's adviser, and I will be that of King Elephant, and in that way we shall merely look on and let them fight as much as they want."

"You know," said Master Fox, "Léonine has returned to her father ; and as you were not married before the church, I believe that Lion is about to marry her to one of his neighbors. Does it not grieve you, Compair Lapin, to think of that ?"

"Oh, no ; *ça zié pas oua tcheur pas fait mal* (we feel no sorrow for what we do not see)."

The two cunning fellows conversed a long time, for they were glad to meet after such a long absence. As they were about to part, they saw two dogs, that stood nose to nose, growling fiercely, and then turned around rapidly and began to smell each other everywhere.

"You, Master Fox, who know everything, can you tell me why dogs have the bad habit of smelling each other in that way ?"

"I will tell you, Compair Lapin, why they do that. In old, old times, when there was but one god, called Mr. Jupiter, all the dogs considered their lot so hard and unhappy that they sent a delegation to ask Mr. Jupiter to better their condition. When they arrived at the house of the god in heaven, all the dogs were so frightened that they ran away. Only one remained ; it was Brisetout, the largest dog of the party. He was not afraid of anything, and he came to Mr. Jupiter, and spoke thus : 'My nation sent me to see you to ask you whether you think that we are going to watch over our masters all day and all night, bark all the time, and then be kicked right and left and have nothing to eat. We are too unhappy, and we want to

malheureux et nous oulé connin si nous pas capabe temps en temps manzé moutons nous zotes maites ; nous pas capabe travaille comme ça pou arien, ça vous dit, Michié Zipiter ?

— Attende ein ti moment, mo va donnin toi ein réponse qué jamin vous zotes a envie vini bété moin encore, mo lasse tendé tout sortes plaintes, to tendé.

Alors li parlé ein langage personne té capabe comprende et ein dans so commis sorti pou couri cherché quichoge. Li dit Brisetout assite et chien la resté en haut dernier marche l'escalier. Li té cré Michié Zipiter té gagnin pou régalé li, mais premier quichoge li té connin, commis la tournin avec lote moune, yé prend Brisetout, yé marré li ben, ensuite yé prend ein pote ferblanc yé metté ladans piment avec télébentine et yé frotté chien la partout. A force ça té bourlé li, li hélé, li béglé et pi yé laché li. Alors Michié Zipiter dit li comme ça : — Va porté ça to camarades et chaque dans vous zotes qua vini plainde, ma va traité yé pareil, to tendé, hein ?

Ah non, li pas tendé, pasqué Brisetout galopé dret devant li, sans connin ou la couri. A la fin li rivé devant ein bayou, li tombé ladans et li neyé.

Quéque temps après ça Michié Zipiter té pas senti li bien, li pensé li sré quitté ciel, vini promenin ein pé en haut la terre. Dans so chimin li contré ein pommier qui té chargé avec belle dépommes, li commencé mangé et pendant temps la ein bande chien vini jappé après li. Li commandé so Baton fout yé ein bon trempe et Baton la prend tournin a droite et a gauche. Li bimin tout chiens yé et paillé yé tout, jis ein pove chien galé. Li mandé Baton la pardon, alors Baton la poussé li divant Michié Zipiter et li dit comme ça : — Chien cila té si maigre mo té pas gagnin courage bimin li. — C'est bon, dit Michié Zipiter, laissé li couri, mais si jamais chien vini jappé après moin mo va détruit yé tout. Vous zotes déja voyé ein délégation coté moin et mo traité li bien pou pas li vini encore et vous zotes déja blié ça. Pove chien maigre la dit li : — C'est vrai ça vous dit, mais nous pas jamin oua commissionaire nous té voyé coté vous, napé tende li toujou. Alors Michié Zipiter dit : — Mo va dit toi comment vous zotes sra capable reconnaite li : si vous zotes senti lein a lote, cila qui senti télébentine, c'est li vous zotes té voyé coté moin.

— Vous oua asteur, Compair Lapin, cofaire chien senti ein a lote,

know if you will allow us once in a while to eat one of the sheep of our masters. We cannot work like this for nothing. What do you say, Mr. Jupiter?'

"'Wait a moment; I shall give you such a reply that you will never wish to annoy me any more. I am tired of hearing all sorts of complaints. I am tired, do you hear?'

"Then Mr. Jupiter spoke a language that no one could under-stand, and one of his clerks went out to get something. He told the dog to sit down. Brisetout remained on the last step of the staircase. He thought that Mr. Jupiter was going to give him a good dinner; but the first thing he knew, the clerk returned with another man. They took hold of Brisetout, they tied him well, then they took a tin pan in which they put red pepper and turpentine. They rubbed the dog all over with the mixture; it burnt him so much that he howled and bellowed. When they let him go, Mr. Jupiter told him: 'You will give my reply to your comrades, and each one that will come to complain will be received in the same manner; you hear?'

"Ah, no, Brisetout did not hear; he ran straight ahead without knowing where he was going. At last he arrived at a bayou, fell into it, and was drowned.

"Some time after that, Mr. Jupiter did not feel well. He thought he would leave heaven and take a little trip to earth. On his way he saw an apple-tree which was covered with beautiful apples. He began to eat some; and while he was eating, a troop of dogs came to bark at him. Mr. Jupiter ordered his stick to give them a good drubbing. The stick began to turn to the right and to the left, and beat the dogs so terribly, that they scattered about in a minute. There remained but one poor dog, who was all mangy. He begged the stick to spare him. Then Stick pushed him before Mr. Jupiter, and said: 'Master, that dog was so thin that I did not have the courage to beat him.' 'It is very well,' said Mr. Jupiter, 'let him go; but if ever any dog comes to bark at me again, I shall destroy them all. I don't want to be bothered by you, I say. You have already sent me a delegation, and I received them so well that I don't think they will like to come back to see me. Have you already forgotten that?' The poor lean dog replied: 'What you say is true, but we never saw again the messenger we sent you; we are still waiting for him.' Mr. Jupiter then said: 'I will tell you how you can find out the messenger you had sent to me: let all dogs smell one another, and the one which will smell turpentine is the messenger.'

"You see now, Compair Lapin, why dogs smell one another. It

c'est Michié Zipiter qui fait ça. Pove vieux Michié Zipiter li perdi tout so pratique pasqué pape ordonnin tout moune quitté li et li té bligé fermé so boutique. Li parti et personne pas connin ou li couri. Vous comprende, Compair Lapin, toujou même quichoge, ein moune fini par dégouté, alors yé prend ein lote Bon Djé et ein lote religion. Cila nous gagnin asteur mo croi li bon.

— Merci, merci, Compair Renard, et pou prouvé vous nous toujou bon zamis mo va dit vous ça nous capab fait. Comme mo déja dit vous na va resté tranquille. Comme Néléphant yé oulé couri taqué Lion chez li même na va fait en pont pou passé larmée et sitot li va fini na va marché dret sans rété nille part jisqua nous rendi coté Lion. Nous oulé surprende li ; pas dit ça personne, vous tendé.

Yé serré la main et yé séparé. Renard prend so chimin et Lapin couri trouvé Roi Néléphant et pi li dit tout charpentier et forgeron dans pays faut yé couté li. Quand tout zouvrier té réini Compair Lapin commencé fait so pont qui té vite fini. Au boute pont la, coté yé, li fait ein grand parc. C'était barre di fer qui té planté dans la terre disse pieds haut et pi si pointi au boute qué ein démouche té pas capabe posé sans li resté pris ; et pi li couvri tout barre di fer avec la liane et tout quichoge qui té vert comme si c'était ein grand talle zéronce, pou yé douté c'était ein la trappe. Alorse li prend quatre lavache avec yé piti veaux et marré yé dans bo milié la. Après ça li mette piment, la cendre et la prise qué li paillé partout dans la trappe la. Li mette aussi plein baille dolo avec ein drogue qui té connin endormi tout souite. — La, Compair Lapin dit, nous paré, laissé Lion vini taqué nous zotes.

Renard té apé voyagé toujou pou couri rende compte so commission, mais li té si pair couri coté Lion sans Compair Lapin qué li pensé li té vaut mié pas couri ditout. Dans so chimin li contré ein poule, li tchué li, li prend so disang et barbouillé ein vié linge. Li marré so patte darriere et li prend boité, sauté en haut trois pattes A la fin li rencontré Bourriquet et li dit comme ça : — Mo cher zami, rende moin ein ti service, to oua comme mo malade. Tant prie, couri coté Lion et dit li mo pas capable vini. Yé cassé mo patte coté néléphant pasqué mo té couri réclamé Compair Lapin.

— Oh, non, dit Bourriquet, to té toujou conte moin avec Compair Lapin, couri to méme.

was all Mr. Jupiter's doing. Poor old fellow, he has now lost all his clients, since the pope ordered everybody to leave him, and he has had to close his shop. He left the heaven, and no one knows where he went to hide. You understand, Compair Lapin, people get tired of having always the same thing ; so they took another religion, and I think that the one we have now is good."

" Thank you, thank you, Master Fox, for your good story ; and in order to show you that I am your old friend, I will tell you what we can do. As I told you already, we must remain very quiet. As the elephants want to go to attack King Lion in his own country, they will make a bridge for the army to pass. When the bridge will be finished they will go straight ahead, without stopping anywhere, to attack King Lion, for they want to take him by surprise. Don't you tell that to anybody, you hear."

Compair Lapin and Master Fox then shook hands, and they parted. Master Fox went on his way, and Compair Lapin went to the king of elephants and asked him to give orders to all the carpenters and blacksmiths in the country to obey him. When all the workmen were assembled, Compair Lapin began to make the bridge, and soon finished it. On the side of the river which was in the country of the elephants, he made at the end of the bridge a large park. These were bars of iron planted in the earth ; they were at least ten feet high, and so sharp that a fly could not touch one without being pierced through. Compair Lapin then covered the bars of iron with branches and brambles to make it appear like a patch of briers, in order that they might not know that it was a snare. Then he took four cows with their calves, and tied them in the very middle of the pit. Then he put in it red pepper, ashes, and tobacco snuff. Then he placed in the trap a great number of tubs of water, in which there was a drug that made people go to sleep right off. After he had finished all this, Compair Lapin said : " Now let King Lion come to attack us."

Master Fox was still travelling to render an account of his errand to King Lion ; but he was so much afraid to return without Compair Lapin, that he concluded that it was better not to return at all. On his way he met a hen ; he killed it, and covered an old rag with the blood. He tied his hind paw with the rag, and he began to limp, and jump on three feet. At last he met Bourriquet, to whom he said : " My dear friend, render me a little service ; you see how sick I am. I pray you to go to King Lion, to tell him that I cannot come to see him. The elephants broke my leg because I had come to claim Compair Lapin."

" Oh, no ! " said Bourriquet ; " you were always against me with Compair Lapin. Go yourself."

— C'est bon, dit Renard, *c'est pas jis ein fois la bouche besoin man-ger*, ta va besoin moin avant longtemps, si to té connin ça mo oua et ça mo connin, to té couté moin.

— Eh ben, dis moin tout, mo va couri, dabord vous pas capabe marcher.

— C'est ben, couté alors : Néléphant conté vini taqué Lion chez li ; pou ça yé fait ein grand pont pou passer et yé va vini tout souite surprende Lion. Si Lion connin quichoge, la fait mié couri taqué néléphant avant yé vini soulever li sans li douté arien.

Alors Bourriquet parti grand galop et quand li rivé coté Lion li dit tout ça Renard té conté li. Lion té si content li dit ein so moune donnin Bourriquet ein pé lapaille pou mangé. Bourriquet té pas content, li babillé ein pé, alors cila qui donne li la paille dit li : — To connin *qué ein choal donnin to doite pas gardé la bride.*

— Mo té croi, dit Bourriquet, mo sré gagnin meillère récompense, mais ma prend ça toujou, pasqué *ein ti zozo dans la main vaut mié qué plein ti zozos quapé voltigé dans bois.*

Tout dein coup yé tendé ein grand boulvari. C'était Lion avec tout so zanimo, tigue, lours, loup et tout ça li té capabe ramassé. Renard té déjà tournin pou verti Compair Lapin yété apé vini.

Léonine té dans la bande et a tout moment so popa té apé dit li : — Mo content to vini, Compair Lapin gagnin pou payer tout so farce, faut to traité li comme li traité toi.

Lion té en tête la bande ; quand yé té proche pont la li contré Compair Renard qui té couché dans chimin avec so patte cassé.

— An, an, dit Lion, c'est comme ça yé traité toi, yé gagnin pou payé tout ça.

— Couri vite, dit Renard, pas attende yé vini taqué vous zotes, passé pont la tout souite, vous zotes va dérouté yé.

Yé continué yé chimin, yé tout té apé galpé et yé prend pou passé pont, Lion en tête avec so fille. Quand yé vini coté la trappe la et yé oua lavache layé qui té apé béglé, Lion et so la bande mangé yé tout. Ensuite yé prende batte et yé voltigé la cendre et piment et la

"That is good," said Master Fox; "*c'est pas jis ein fois la bouche besoin manger* (I shall have my chance again, you will need me again). If you knew what I have seen and what I know, you would listen to me."

"Well, tell me all," said Bourriquet; "and I will go, since you cannot walk."

"That is all right; listen well. The elephants intend to come to attack King Lion in his country. They are making a bridge to cross the river, and as soon as the bridge will be finished they will come immediately to surprise Lion. If the king understood his business, he would hasten to attack the elephants in their own country, before they come to lift him up before he knows it."

As soon as Master Fox had finished speaking, Bourriquet galloped away and went to King Lion, to whom he said what Master Fox had related to him. The king was so glad that he ordered some one to give Bourriquet a little hay to eat. Bourriquet was not very much pleased, and he began grumbling. "Don't you know, Bourriquet," said the king's servant, "*qué ein choual donnin to doite pas gardé la bride* (that you must not look at the bridle of a horse which was given to you)."

"Well," said Bourriquet, "I had expected a better reward, but I'll take that anyhow, because *ein ti zozo dans la main vaut mié qué plein ti zozos quapé voltigé dans bois* (a bird in the hand is better than two in the bush)."

All at once they heard a dreadful noise. It was King Lion, who was starting for the war with all the animals which he could find: tigers, bears, wolves, all King Lion's subjects were there. As to Master Fox, he had run back to notify Compair Lapin that the enemies were coming.

Miss Léonine was with the army, and her father used to tell her all the time: "I am glad that you came; Compair Lapin will have to pay for all his tricks; you must treat him as he treated you."

King Lion was at the head of the army, and coming near the bridge he saw Master Fox, who was lying in the road with his leg broken.

"Oh! oh!" said Lion, "this is the way they treated you! They shall have to pay for all that."

"Make haste," said Master Fox; "don't wait till they come to attack you; pass the bridge immediately; that will throw them in confusion."

The army went on. They all ran to pass over the bridge, King Lion at the head, with his daughter. As soon as they arrived at the place where was the snare, and they saw the cows and their calves, King Lion and his troops killed them and began to eat them. Then

prise et ça té aveuglé yé. Yé batte, yé massacré yé méme et pi ça yé qui té resté boi dolo la. Dé zère après ça yé tout té apé dromi.

Alors néléphant vini tchué yé et jété yé dans dolo. Yé corché Lion, yé prend so lapeau et coude Bourriquet ladans. Yé metté ein tas la paille avec godron après so la tcheu, et yé metté di fé ladans et pi yé laché li pou couri porté la nouvelle dans pays Lion.

Quand Bourriquet passé en haut pont, a force li galpé vite moune té cré c'était tonnerre qui té apé roulé plis dé cent charretées. Quand Bourriquet rivé dans pays Lion so boute la tcheu té tombé a force li té bourlé, li dit c'était dans ein bataille yé té donne li ein coup sabe. Malgré li té porté ein triste nouvelle yé ri après li pasqué li té trop drole comme ça.

Quand tout ça té fini, Compair Lapin couri trouvé Compair Renard et li ménin li coté Roi Néléphants. Compair Lapin présenté li et dit lé roi qué Renard té ein so bon zamis et li sré content si Roi té accepté li et yé dé sré rende bande services. Roi néléphants dit yé : — Mo croi vous zotes cé dé malin, dans zaffaire nous té gagnin avec Lion mo croi Compair Renard té *galpé avec chévreil et chassé avec chien.* Enfin c'est bon, li capabe resté icite. Tant qu'a pou toi, Compair Lapin, mo oulé to marié, ala ein Mamzelle Lapin Blanc qui riche, c'est to zaffaire, demain mo oulé la noce la.

Lendemin tout moune té réini et yé célébré la noce Compair Lapin avec Mamzelle Lapin Blanc et Compair Renard té so premier garçon d'honnair. Trois semaines après la noce Madame Compair Lapin gagnin dé piti, ein té blanc, lote té noir comme la souie chiminin. Compair Lapin té pas content, li couri oua Roi néléphant pou dit li ça.
 — Ah bah, dit lé Roi, to pas connin arien, to bien marié devant léglise, mo pas capabe donnin toi divorce, et pi mo va dit toi, c'est nhabitude dans famille Madame Compair Lapin gagnin piti qui noir, c'est quand madame yé pair la nouitte, ainsi consolé toi.

Ça fait Compair Lapin consenti resté avec so femme jisqua li mouri et c'est comme ça li marié avec tout so frédaine.
Comme mo té la quand tout ça rivé mo vini pou conté vous ça.

they quarrelled among themselves and began to fight. They scattered about the ashes, the red pepper, and the tobacco snuff, and were completely blinded. They fought terribly; they massacred one another; then those that were left drank the water in the tubs. Two hours later they were all sound asleep.

The elephants, which had remained prudently at a distance, hearing no more noise, came to the bridge. They killed all the animals that were left in Lion's army, and threw their bodies in the river. They flayed King Lion; they took his skin and sewed Bourriquet into it; then they tied some straw, covered with pitch, to Bourriquet's tail; they put fire to the straw, and they let him go to announce the news in Lion's country.

When Bourriquet passed on the bridge, he was galloping so fast that one might have thought that it was thunder that was rolling on the bridge, as if it were more than one hundred cart-loads. When Bourriquet arrived in his country his tail was entirely consumed by the fire, but he said that he had lost it in a battle. Although he announced very sad news, no one could help laughing at him: he was so funny without his tail, and so proud of his glorious wound.

As soon as all was over at the bridge, Compair Lapin went to get Master Fox, and took him to the king of the elephants. He presented him to his majesty, and told him that Master Fox was his good friend, and if the king wanted to accept his services, they would both be his very faithful subjects. The king of elephants said to them: "I believe that you are two cunning rascals, and that in my war with King Lion, Master Fox *té galpé avec chévreil et chassé avec chien* (had been on both sides of the fence); but all right, he may remain here, if he wants. As for you, Compair Lapin, I want you to get married. Here is Miss White Rabbit; she is rich, and will be a good match for you. To-morrow I want to dance at the wedding."

The next day all the people assembled, and celebrated with great splendor the marriage of Compair Lapin with Miss White Rabbit. Master Fox was the first groomsman. Three weeks after the wedding, Mrs. Compair Lapin gave birth to two little ones; one was white and the other as black as soot. Compair Lapin was not pleased, and he went to see the king of elephants.

"Oh! you know nothing," said the king; "you are married before the church, and I will not grant you a divorce. Besides, I must tell you that in the family of Mrs. Compair Lapin it happens very often that the little ones are black. It is when the ladies are afraid in a dark night; so console yourself, and don't be troubled."

Compair Lapin consented to remain with his wife until death should part them, and that is how he married after all his pranks.

As I was there when all that happened, I ran away to relate it to you.

PART TWO:
Märchen.

XVI.

LÉ ROI PAN.

In fois yavait in madame qui té si joli, si joli, qué li té jamin oulé marié. Tou cila qui té vini, li té trouvé quichoge pou di — Oh, toi to trop laide — Oh, toi, to trop piti. Oh, toi, to la bouche trop grand. Enfin chacunne té gaingnin quichoge qui té pas dréte. Asteur ein jou in vaillant michié vini. Li té dans in carrosse tout en or, et yavait huite choals blancs qui té apé trainin carrosse la. Li mandé madame la pou marié. Li té jamin oulé. Michié la té si en colère, li dit madame la qué dans in an li sré gaingnin in fille qui sré boucou, boucou pli joli qué li. Madame la di li couri, qué li té pas oulé mette so giés enho li encor.

Asteur, jisse in an après ça madame la té gaingnin in joli joli piti fille. Quand li oua li té si joli li frinmin li dans in lachambe au boute so la maison : et li mette so nourice, pou gardé. Ti fille la vini grand, et plis li té pé grandi, et plis li té pé vini joli. Jamin so nourice té laissé li sorti dans lachambe la. In jou, li té pé balayé, fille la gadé déyors, et li oua in gros zozo.

— Oh, moman Tété, li di, comment to pélé zozo la, li si joli?

— Ça, mo piti, c'est in pan.
— Oh, li di li, moman Tété, si mo jamin marié, molé marié lé roi Pan. — Lors so gadgienne di li : — Bon Djié tendé toi, mo piti.
Jou la méme moman la vini, li pélé gadgienne la dans in coin, li tiré en bas so romaine in gros couteau et li di li : — Molé to tchué mo fille. Lapé vini plis joli qué moin.

Gadgienne la parti crié, mandé pardon pou so pove piti, mais ça té pas la peine, caire noir la té pas tendé arien. Asteur quand lé soir vini, gadgienne la di so fille : — Mo pove piti, fo mo tchué toi, to moman oulé ça.

Pove piti, la té si bon, li di : — Ah ben, moman Tété, fé li, pisse moman oulé ça.

Mais li di fille la : — Mo pas gaingnin courage fé sorte louvrage la, mo piti. Tiens, ala trois graines, ta jetté to méme dans pi et pi ta neyé. Mais avant to tombé dans pi valé inne dans graines yé, to va pas souffri ditout comme ça.

Fille la bo so moman tété et li prend so chimin pou couri. Li marché jouqu'a li rendi coté in grand pi. Li descende ladans, et

XVI.

KING PEACOCK.

There was once a lady who was so pretty, — so pretty that she never wanted to marry. She found something to criticise in all the suitors who presented themselves, saying of them : " Oh, you are too ugly." " You are too small." " You have too large a mouth." One day a fine man came ; he was in a golden carriage, drawn by eight horses. He asked the lady to marry him, but she refused. He fell into a passion, and told her that in one year she would have a daughter that would be much, much prettier than herself. The lady sent him away with scorn.

Well, a year later she had a pretty little girl. When she saw that the child was so pretty, she shut her up in a room at the further end of the house, with her nurse to attend to her. As the girl grew up she became handsomer every day. The nurse never allowed her to leave her room, or even to look through the window. One day, however, while the old woman was sweeping the floor, she left the door open, and the young girl saw a large bird.

"Nurse," said she, "how do you call that bird which is so pretty ? "

The woman was obliged to reply, and said : " That is a peacock."

" If ever I marry, I want to marry King Peacock."

" May God hear you, my child."

That very day the mother came, called the nurse into a corner, drew from under her skirt a great knife, and said, " I want you to kill my child. She has become prettier than I."

The nurse began to cry, and begged the lady to spare the poor child, but all in vain ; that black heart could not be softened. When night came, the nurse said to the girl : " My poor child, I have to kill you, your mother wants you to die."

The girl was so good that she replied : " Well, kill me, nurse, if my mother wants it to be so."

But the nurse answered : " No, I have not the heart to do any such thing, my little one. Here, take these three seeds, throw yourself in the well and drown yourself ; but before jumping in the well, swallow one of these seeds, and you will not suffer at all."

The girl thanked the nurse, and went to drown herself. She walked until she arrived at a large well. She threw herself into it,

avant li rivé coté dolo, li jetté in graine dans so la bouche. Mais
au lieu li couri dans so labouche li tombé dans dolo. Asteur pi li
vini tout sec. Mamzelle la té si chagrin. Li sorti dans pi et li
marché, marché loin dans bois, jouqu'a li tombé enho in piti la maison. Li cognin enho la porte, et in vié femme vini ouvri. Li jetté
in cri quand li oua joli mamzelle la. — Oh bon Djié Seigneur, mo piti,
ça to vini fait icite. To pas connin qué mo mari c'est in norgue, li
mangé moune.

Alors fille la di li : — Ah ben, madame, c'est ça molé, mo moman
dit fo mo mouri.

Lors vié femme la di li : — Si c'est ça, entré, mo pove piti, mais ça
bien dommage.

Pove piti la assite apé crié et apé tende norgue la. Tout d'in coup
yé tendé in gros pas qui té apé marché. Sitot la porte la ouvri,
norgue crié : — Oh, mo femme, mo senti la vianne fraiche, et ou ça
yé ? Li gardé coté fille la, qui jisse gardé li avec so grand giés et
norgue la tchullé, et li di : — Oh, mo femme, esqué to croi qué mo
capabe mangé in joli fille comme ça ? Non, li jisse bon pou yé
gardé li.

Fille la di li li té si lasse, alors li minnin li dans in joli lachambe,
et li cou chaché in ventail avec déplime pan et li di so femme vanté
li tout temps li dromi.

Alors pove fille la di : — Vo mié mo mouri einne foi, pasqué
pété té dinmain norgue la va envie mangé moin. Li prend so piti
graine, li metté li dans so labouche et pi li parti dromi, dromi, et
femme norgue la té pé vanté li tout temps. Yavait trois jours li té
pé dromi, norgue la vini gadé li et li di so femme : — Mo croi li
mouri, et c'est dommage. Li couri laville, et li porté in cercueil
tout en or. Li metté fille la ladans et li posé li enho flève. Asteur
cercueil la parti descenne, descenne flève. Rivé loin, lé roi Pan té
pé pranne la fraiche enho la levée avec tout so prince yé. Quand li
oua ça qui té pé clairé enho flève, li di so moune yé, couri bien vite
oua qui ça. Yé tout prend skif et yé parti. Yé crié : — Cé in cercueil,
et yé minnin li coté lé roi. Quand li oua joli mamzelle la qui té jisse
sembe apé dromi, li di : — Minnin li coté mo lachambe, molé seyé pou
réveillé li. Li fermin li méme dans so lachambe, li frotté mamzelle
la avec dolo cologne, mais ça té pas fait arien. Alorse li ouvri so
labouche, et li té pé gardé comme li té gaingnin joli dents. Li oua
quichoge qui té rouge dans so dent dévant, li prend in épingle en or,
et li oté ça. Li jisse ote ça, fille la ouvri so gié et li dit : — Mo content oua vous.

Alors li roi dit li : — Moin, cé lé roi Pan, et molé marié avec vous.

but before touching the water she took one of her seeds to put it in her mouth. The seed, however, fell in the water, and immediately the well dried up. The young lady was very sorry to see that there was no water left in the well, and getting out she walked as far as a wood, in which she found a small house. She knocked at the door, and an old woman showed herself. When she saw the pretty young girl, she said : "Oh ! my child, what do you come to do here ? Don't you know that my husband is an ogre ? He will eat you up !"

Then the girl answered : "That is what I want. My mother wants me to die."

The woman replied : " If that is the case, come in, but it is a great pity."

The poor girl sat down in a corner, and cried while she was waiting for the ogre. All at once they heard big footsteps, and as soon as the door was opened, the ogre said : " My wife, I smell fresh meat in here," and he ran towards the young girl. She, however, merely looked at him with her large eyes, and he stepped back, saying to his wife : "Do you think that I can eat such a pretty girl ? She is so beautiful that I want to look at her all the time."

The girl said she was tired, so the ogre took her to a beautiful room, and ordered his wife to fan her with peacock feathers while she would be sleeping.

The young lady said to herself : " It is better for me to die now, for perhaps the ogre will change his mind to-morrow and will eat me." She put one of her seeds in her mouth, and fell in a deep sleep. She slept and slept, and the ogre's wife was fanning her all the time. When three days had passed, and she did not awake, the ogre looked at her, and said : " It is a great pity, but I believe she is dead." He went to the town, and brought a coffin all made of gold. He put the girl in it, and placed it on the river. The coffin then went floating down the river. Very far away, King Peacock was one day on the levee, with all his princes, to enjoy the cool breeze, when he saw something shining in the river. He ordered his courtiers to see what that was. They took a skiff, and exclaiming, " It is a coffin," they brought it to the king. When he saw the pretty young girl, who appeared to be sleeping, he said, " Take her to my chamber," for he wished to try to awaken her. He put her on a bed and rubbed her hands and face with cologne water, but to no avail. Then he opened her mouth to see what pretty teeth she had. He saw something red in her front teeth, and tried to take it off with a golden pin. It was a seed which fell on the floor. The young girl awoke and said, " I am so glad to see you."

The king replied : " I am King Peacock, and I want to marry

Mamzelle la dit : — C'est ça, et yé fait in gros la noce, et yé di moin couri conté ça partout, partout.

XVII.

DES OS QUI CHANTÉ.

Yavait eine fois ein n'homme et ein fame qui té gagnin vingt-cinq pitis. Yé té très pove, n'homme la té bon, fame la té mauvais. Tous les jous quand mari la té révini so louvrage fame la té servi li dinin, mais toujou laviande sans des os.

— Comment ça fait la viande la pas gagnin des os ?

— Pasqué des os ça pésé, et c'est meilleur marché sans des os. Yé donnin plis pou largent.

Mari la mangé et pas dit arien.

— Comment ça fait to pas mangé la viande ?

— To blié mo pas gagnin dents. Comment to lé mo mangé la viande sans dents ?

— C'est vrai, dit mari la, et li paix pasqué li té pair fait la peine so fame qui té aussi laide qué li té méchant.

Quand moune gagnin vingt-cinq pitis moune pas capabe pensé yé tout temps et moune pas oua si yé na ein ou dé qui manqué. Ein jou après so dinin, mari la mandé so pitis. Quand yé té coté li li compté yé et jiste trouvé quinze. Li mandé so fame ou té disse les otes yé. Li réponde yé té chez yé grandmoman et tous les jous li voyé ein lote pou yé changé l'air. Ça té vrai, tous les jous yavait eine qui manqué.

Ein jou mari la té on so pasporte divant ein gros la pierre yé té gagnin la. Li tapé pensé so pitis et li té oulé couri chercher yé chez yé grandmoman, quand li tendé des lavoix qui tapé dit :

> Nous moman tchué nous,
> Nous popa manzé nous.
> Nous pas dans la bière,
> Nous pas dans cimetière.

En prémier li té pas rende compte ça ça té, mais li lévé la pierre la et li oua ein grand quantité des os qui recommencé chanté. Li comprende alors c'était des os so pitis so fame té tchué et qué li té manzé. Alors li té si en colère li tchué so fame et terré des os so pitis dans cimetière et li couri resté sel chez li. Dipi temps la li jamais manzé la viande pasqué li té toujou cré c'était so pitis li té apé manzé.

you." The young girl said "yes," and there was such a wedding that they sent me to relate the story everywhere, everywhere.

XVII.

THE SINGING BONES.

Once upon a time there lived a man and a woman who had twenty-five children. They were very poor ; the man was good, the woman was bad. Every day when the husband returned from his work the wife served his dinner, but always meat without bones.

" How is it that this meat has no bones ? "

" Because bones are heavy, and meat is cheaper without bones. They give more for the money."

The husband ate, and said nothing.

" How is it you don't eat meat ? "

" You forget that I have no teeth. How do you expect me to eat meat without teeth ? "

" That is true," said the husband, and he said nothing more, because he was afraid to grieve his wife, who was as wicked as she was ugly.

When one has twenty-five children one cannot think of them all the time, and one does not see if one or two are missing. One day, after his dinner, the husband asked for his children. When they were by him he counted them, and found only fifteen. He asked his wife where were the ten others. She answered that they were at their grandmother's, and every day she would send one more for them to get a change of air. That was true, every day there was one that was missing.

One day the husband was at the threshold of his house, in front of a large stone which was there. He was thinking of his children, and he wanted to go and get them at their grandmother's, when he heard voices that were saying :

Our mother killed us,
Our father ate us.
We are not in a coffin,
We are not in the cemetery.

At first he did not understand what that meant, but he raised the stone, and saw a great quantity of bones, which began to sing again. He then understood that it was the bones of his children, whom his wife had killed, and whom he had eaten. Then he was so angry that he killed his wife ; buried his children's bones in the cemetery, and stayed alone at his house. From that time he never ate meat, because he believed it would always be his children that he would eat.

XVIII.

JEAN SOTTE.

Yavait eine fois ein bougue a force li té béte tout moune té pélé li Jean Sotte. Li té si simple qué tout moune té foute dé li. Li té coutume limin la lampe lé jou et teigné li lé soi. Jamin li té pas prend so parasol dans jou, jis la nouitte, quand li té fait ben noir. Dans l'été li té mette so gros capot et l'hiver li té couri tout ni et prend ein grand vantail ; li té fait tout quichoge a la rebours bon sens. Ça fait lé roi Bangon qui té laimin fait farce tendé parlé tout faits et geste Jean Sotte, alors li voyé chercher li pou amuser tout so camarade. Quand Jean Sotte rivé coté lé roi yé prend ri a force Jean té paraite gauche. Lé roi mandé li comme ça si li té connin compter. Jean réponde li té connin compter dézefs, qué hier li trouvé quatre et pi dé. — Combien ça fait en tout ? dit lé roi. Jean compté en haut so la main et pi li dit ça fait quatre et pi dé.

— C'est ça méme, dit Bangon ; yé dit moin c'est Compair Lapin qui to popa ? "

— Oui, dit Jean Sotte, c'est li méme.

— Non, non, dit ein lote moune qui té la, mo croi plitot c'est Compair Bouki.

— Oui, oui, dit Jean, li aussite.

— Non, dit ein vié fame qui té apé passé, c'est Renard qui to popa.

— Oui, oui, dit Jean Sotte, tout ça yé, c'est tout mo popa, chaquéne dans yé quand yé passé dit moin : — Bonjou, mo piti, alors mo croi yé tout c'est mo popa.

Moune yé ri boucou après Jean Sotte, alors lé roi dit li : — Mo oulé to porté moin demain matin ein bouteille di lait taureau, c'est pou fait réméde pou mo fille qui malade, li gagnin ein point coté dans dos.

— C'est bon, dit Jean Sotte, demain matin bonne haire ma porté li.

Et pi roi Bangon dit li comme ça :

— Premier avril prochain dans ein mois, ta vini, na gagnin pou dévinin ein quichoge. Cila qua trouvé gagnin pou marié avec mo fille, mais cila qui seyé troi fois, si li pas trouvé, mo bourreau gagnin pou coupé so cou.

— C'est bon, ma seyé, dit Jean Sotte, et pi li parti, soi disant pou chercher di lait taureau.

Quand li rivé coté li, li raconté tout ça so moman, et vié femme prend

XVIII.

JEAN SOTTE.

There was once a fellow who was so foolish that everybody called him Jean Sotte. He was so simple that every one made fun of him. He would light the lamp in daytime, and put it out at night; he would take an umbrella with him only when it was very dark. In summer he would put on a great coat, and in winter he would go nearly naked. In short, he did everything contrary to common sense. King Bangon, who loved to play tricks, heard of the sayings and deeds of Jean Sotte, and sent for him to amuse his friends. When Jean came to the king all began to laugh, as he looked so awkward. The king asked him if he knew how to count. Jean replied that he knew how to count eggs; that yesterday he had found four and two. "How much does that make?" said the king. Jean went to count the eggs, and on returning said there were four and two.

"Exactly," said the king, "but tell me, Jean Sotte, they say that Compair Lapin is your father?"

"Yes, he is."

"No, no," said some one else; "I think it is Compair Bouki."

"Yes, yes," said Jean Sotte; "it is he also."

"No, no," said an old woman who was passing; "it is Renard who is your father."

"Yes," said Jean Sotte, "all of them; they are all my fathers. Every time one of them passes by me he says, 'Good-morning, my child.' I must believe, then, that they are all my fathers."

Everybody laughed at Jean Sotte; then the king said: "Jean Sotte, I want you to bring me to-morrow morning a bottle of bull's milk. It is to make a drug for my daughter, who is sick, and has a sideache in her back."

"All right," said Jean Sotte, "to-morrow morning early I shall bring it."

King Bangon then said: —

"On the first of April, in one month, you will come. I want you to guess something. If you guess, I will give you my daughter in marriage, but if you try three times, and do not succeed, my executioner will have to cut your neck."

"All right," said Jean Sotte, "I will try." And then he went away, pretending to go and get the bull's milk.

When he reached home, he related to his mother all that had hap-

crié, crié, pasqué tout sotte so garçon té yé moman la té laimin li
quand méme, pasqué c'était jisse ein piti li té gagnin.   Li défende
Jean Sotte couri, ménacé li marré li ou ben fait sheriff jété li dans
prison.   Jean Sotte té fout ben tout ça ; li parti anvant jou, li prend
so la hache et anvant li té fait clair li té dévant la maison lé roi.   Li
grimpé dans la tête ein chéne qui té dévant la maison et pi li commencé :— Caou, caou, biché, biché.   Comme ça té fait train et révéillé
tout moune ein domestique lé roi sorti et vini oua.   Quand li jété so
zié en haut Jean Sotte, li dit comme ça : — Mais qué commerce tapé
méné, bougue d'animal, réveillé tout moune comme ça ?

Ça pas gardé toi, to tendé, dit Jean Sotte, toi c'est chien pou jappé
dans la cour.   Quand to maite, lé roi Bangon, a vini, mo va dit li
ça mapé fait ici.

Alors lé roi vini oua, li gardé li longtemps et pi li mandé li ça li té
apé fait dans la tête nabe la.   Jean Sotte réponde li té apé biché
l'écorche chéne pou fait la tisane pou so popa qui té malade, li té
accouché la veille, so popa té fait dé jumeaux.

— Aïe, dit lé roi, mais pou qui to prend moin, Jean Sotte, ou ça
to déja tendé ein n'homme accouché?   Mo pensé to oulé foute toi
dé moin.

— Comment ça fait vous mandé moin hier ein bouteille dit lait
taureau, réponde Jean Sotte, si vous té gagnin raison, moin aussite.

Alors lé roi dit li comme ça :— Mo pas croi to aussi sotte qué to
oulé sayé fait nous zotes croi.   Couri la quisine, ya donne toi to dé-
jéner et pi couri coté to la maison et pas blié vini premier avril pou
oua cila dans nous zotes qua mangé posson d'avril la.

Quand Jean Sotte tournin coté so moman li raconté tout ça.   Vié
femme la prend crié et pi li défende Jean couri coté roi encore, li té
pair yé sré coupé cou so pove piti.   Quand jou la vini Jean monté en
haut so choal et li parti sans so moman té connin.   Compair Bouki
qui té traite et malfaisant, dit comme ça : — Moin mo va péché Jean
Sotte couri dévinin, pasqué mo connin li si sotte yé va coupé so cou
et pi gardé so choal, vaut mié moin mo profité et prend choal la, pas
dit arien, ta oua ça ma fait.

Li prend ein grand panier gateaux qui té poisonnin et pi li metté
yé en haut ein pont ou Jean Sotte té gagnin pou passé. — La, quand
li va mangé gateaux la yé la mouri et ma vini prend so choal.

Bouki té connin Jean Sotte té gourmand et li té mangé pou sire
dans gateaux yé, mais Compair Lapin te laimin Jean Sotte, pasqué
ein fois li té trouvé li méme dans grand nembarras, li té trouvé dans
prison dans ein la trappe et Jean Sotte té laché li.   Pou ça Compair

pened, and the old woman began to cry, and could not be consoled, because, however foolish her boy was, she loved him, as he was her only child. She forbade him to go to the king, and threatened to tie him in her cabin, or to have the sheriff throw him in prison. Jean Sotte paid no attention to his mother, and started before day-break, with his axe on his shoulder. He soon arrived at the house of the king, and he climbed into a big oak-tree which was before the door. He began, "caou, caou, caou," to cut down the branches with his axe, and he woke up everybody in the house. One of the servants of the king came out to see what was the matter; and when he saw Jean Sotte on the top of the tree, he said: "But what is your business there? Fool that you are, you are disturbing everybody."

"It is not your business, — do you hear?" said Jean Sotte. "Are you the watch-dog to be barking thus in the yard? When your master, King Bangon, comes, I will tell him what I am doing here."

The king came out, and asked Jean Sotte what he was doing there. He replied that he was cutting the bark to make some tea for his father, who had been delivered the day before of two twins.

"What!" said the king, "for whom do you take me, Jean Sotte. Where did you ever hear of a man in childbirth? I think you mean to make fun of me."

"How is it that yesterday you asked a bottle of bull's milk? If you were right, I am also."

The king replied: "I believe that you are not so foolish as you want to make people believe. Go to the kitchen, and they will give you your breakfast. Don't forget to come on the first of April, that we may see which of us will be the April fool."

On the first of April Jean Sotte mounted his horse and went out without his mother seeing him. Compair Bouki, who is deceitful and evil-minded, said: "I shall prevent Jean Sotte from going, because I know he is so foolish that they will cut his neck and keep his horse. It is better that I should profit by it, and take his horse. Don't you say anything; you will see what I shall do."

He took a large basket full of poisoned cakes, and put it on a bridge where Jean Sotte was to pass. "If he eats those cakes, he will die, and I shall take the horse."

Bouki knew that Jean Sotte was greedy and that he would surely eat the cakes. Compair Lapin liked Jean Sotte, because one day, when he was caught in a snare, Jean Sotte had freed him. He did not forget that, and said: "I want to protect the poor fellow," and

Lapin dit li méme : — Mo va protégé pove ninnocent la. Li tende
Jean Sotte longtemps dans chimin anvant jou et quand li rivé li dit :
— Jean Sotte, mo vini pou rende toi service, couté moin ben, pas
mangé ni bois arien dans chimin pendant to voyage, quand méme tapé
mouri faim et soif. Couté moin, to tendé, ye gagnin pou poisonné
toi si to boi ou mangé. Quand lé roi a mandé toi pou dévinin ta
reponde li jisse ça mo va dit toi dans to zoreille ; vancé, mo pas oulé
personne tendé.

Alors Compair Lapin dit li tout doucement ça pou réponde.
— An, an, oui, oui, dit Jean Sotte, mo comprende, et pi li rit. Oui,
oui, c'est ça méme.

— Asteur, dit Compair Lapin, pas blié moin quand ta marié avec
fille lé roi, voyé chercher moin et na fait bon zaffaire.

— Oui, dit Jean Sotte, mo va pas blié vous.

— Eh ben, bon voyage, fait ben tention tout ça to oua, gardé partout, couté ben et ça va profité toi.

Alors Jean Sotte metté li en route et ein piti moment après li rivé
coté pont en haut la rivière. Prémier quichoge li oua, c'était panier
bel gateaux Compair Bouki. Yé té senti bon, ça té donnin envie
mangé. Jean Sotte gardé yé, li taté yé, li té proche envie mordé
ladans, mais li rappelé ça Compair Lapin dit li, ça fait li rété ein ti
moment. Laissé moin oua si ya fait mo choal mal. Li prend ein
demi douzaine gateaux et donne so choal. Pove béte la mouri ein ti
moment après, li tombé raide en haut pont la, c'était fini dans ein ti
moment. — Gardé si mo té pas prend précaution. Ah, Compair
Lapin té raison ; ein pé plis mo té fouti.

Anvant li parti li culbité so choal dans la rivière et quand pove
béte té apé dérivé dans courant trois carencros vini posé en haut li
et commencé mangé so pove choal. Jean Sotte gardé li longtemps
jisqua li disparaite derrière la pointe. — Compair Lapin dit moin
gardé, couté et pas dit arien, c'est bon, moin aussite mo va gagnin
pou mandé lé roi dévinin quichoge.

Quand Jean Sotte rivé coté lé roi yé navait déjà plein moune qui
té sayé dévinin ça lé roi té proposé yé, et après yé té sayé trois fois
so bourreau té coupé yé cou. Yavait cinquante qui té déjà mouri.
Alors tout moune dit : — Ala Jean Sotte, li va sayé dévinin aussite,
li si sotte vous zotes a oua comme ya coupé so cou, laissé li fait,
dabord li si béte.

Lé roi prend ri quand li oua Jean Sotte et li dit li comme ça. — Qui
ça qui bon matin marché en haut quatre pattes, a midi en haut dé
pattes, et lé soir en haut trois pattes ?

before daybreak he waited on the road for Jean Sotte. When he saw him, he said : " Jean Sotte, I am coming to render you a service, listen to me : don't eat or drink anything on your way, even if you are dying of hunger and of thirst ; and when the king will ask you to guess, you will reply what I am going to tell you. Come near ; I don't want anybody to hear."

Compair Lapin then told him what to say. " Yes, yes, I understand," said Jean Sotte, and he began to laugh.

" Now," said Compair Lapin, " don't forget me when you marry the king's daughter ; we can have good business together."

" Yes," said Jean Sotte, " I shall not forget you."

" Well, good luck, pay attention to all you see, look on all sides, and listen well."

Then Jean Sotte started, and a little while afterwards he arrived at a bridge on the river. The first thing he saw was the basket full of cakes which Compair Bouki had placed there. They smelled good and they were very tempting. Jean Sotte touched them and felt like biting one, but he remembered what Compair Lapin had told him. He stopped a moment and said : " Let me see if they will do harm to my horse." He took half a dozen cakes and gave them to his horse. The poor beast died almost immediately and fell on the bridge. " See, if I had not been prudent, it is I who would be dead instead of my horse. Ah ! Compair Lapin was right ; a little more and I should have been lost. Now I shall have to go on foot."

Before he started he threw his horse into the river ; and as the poor beast was being carried away by the current, three buzzards alighted on the horse and began to eat him. Jean Sotte looked at him a long time, until he disappeared behind the point in the river. " Compair Lapin told me : 'listen, look, and don't say anything ;' all right, I shall have something to ask the king to guess."

" When Jean Sotte came to the king nobody was trying to guess, for all those who had tried three times had been put to death by the king's executioner. Fifty men already had been killed, and every one said, on seeing Jean Sotte : " There is Jean Sotte who is going to try, they will surely cut off his head, for he is so foolish. But so much the worse for him if he is such a fool."

When he saw Jean Sotte the king began to laugh and told him to come nearer. " What is it," said he, " that early in the morning walks on four legs, at noon on two, and in the evening on three legs ? "

— Si mo dévinin, vous va donnin moin vous fille ?

— Oui, dit lé roi.

— Oh, ç'est pas arien pou dévinin.

— Eh ben, hourrah, fait vite si to pas oulé mo coupé to cou.

— C'est ein piti moune qui marché en haut quatre pattes. Quand li vini grand li marché en haut dé, et quand li vini vié li bligé prend ein baton pou apiyer li, ça fait trois pattes.

Tout moune resté la bouche ouvri a force yé té étonné.

— To dévinin jiste, dit lé roi, mo fille pou toi. Asteur nimporte qui dans vous zotes mandé moin ein quichoge et si mo pas trouvé, pasqué mo connin tout ça yé na dans moune, alors mo va donnin li mo place avec mo fortine.

Alors Jean Sotte dit lé roi : — Mo oua ein mort qui té apé porté trois vivants et apé nourri yé. Mort la té pas touché la terre ni li té pas dans ciel, dis moin qui c'est ou ben mo va prend vous place avec vous fortine.

Roi Bangon sayé dévinin, li dit c'est ça et tout plein quichoge, li pas fouti dévinin et li té bligé bandonné la partie. Alors Jean Sotte dit li comme ça : — Mo choal mouri en haut ein pont, mo jété li dans la rivière et quand li té apé dérivé carencros posé en haut li et mangé li dans dolo. Li té pas touché la terre ni li té pas dans ciel.

Alors tout moune oua qué Jean Sotte té boucou plis malin qué yé tous ensembe. Li marié avec fille lé roi, li prend so place et c'est li qui té gouverné pays la après. Li prend Compair Lapin pou so premier colombe, et pi après ça yé pende Compair Bouki pou so coquinerie. Après ça yé changé nom Jean Sotte et pélé li Jean l'Esprit.

XIX.

MARIAZE DJABE.

Ein jou yé té gagnin ein joli jeine fille mais li té fière. A chaque fois des michiés té vini fé li lamour, li té toujougagnin prétexes. Ein té tro piti, lote té tro grand, ci la, so chivé té trop rouge. Enfin li té jamin oulé marié yé. In jou, so moman dit li : — Mo fille, to oua gros nabe, haut, haut, milié fléve, malé metté giromon ça to oua on nabe la au boutte branche plis fèbe la, et cila qua capable trappé giromon la, ta marié avec li.

Ça fait fille la dit oui. Yé metté ça en haut tous la gazette. La

"If I guess, you will give me your daughter ? "

"Yes," said the king.

"Oh ! that is nothing to guess."

" Well, hurrah ! hurry on if you don't want me to cut your neck."

Jean Sotte told him, it was a child who walked on four legs; when he grew up he walked on two, and when he grew old he had to take a stick, and that made three legs.

All remained with their mouths wide open, they were so astonished.

"You have guessed right; my daughter is for you. Now, let anybody ask me something, as I know everything in the world ; if I do not guess right I will give him my kingdom and my fortune."

Jean Sotte said to the king : "I saw a dead being that was carrying three living beings and was nourishing them. The dead did not touch the land and was not in the sky ; tell me what it is, or I shall take your kingdom and your fortune."

King Bangon tried to guess ; he said this and that and a thousand things, but he had to give it up. Jean Sotte said then : " My horse died on a bridge, I threw him into the river, and three buzzards alighted on him and were eating him up in the river. They did not touch the land and they were not in the sky."

Everybody saw that Jean Sotte was smarter than all of them together. He married the king's daughter, took his place, and governed the kingdom. He took Compair Lapin as his first overseer, and hanged Compair Bouki for his rascality. After that they changed Jean Sotte's name and called him Jean l'Esprit.

XIX.

THE DEVIL'S MARRIAGE.

One day there was a pretty young girl, but she was very proud, and every time the young men came to court her, she found a pretext to send them away. One was too small, another was too tall, another had red hair ; in short, she refused all her suitors. One day her mother said to her : " My daughter, you see that tall, tall tree in the middle of the river? I am going to put this pumpkin on the smallest branch at the top of the tree, and that young man who will be able to climb up and catch the pumpkin will be your husband."

The daughter said she had no objection, so they put a notice in

sémaine après yé té gagnin in tas jeine nommes la. Yé té gagnin ein qui té si bien habillé, si joli, ça té djabe et personne té pas connin ça. Li té allé bien avec mamzelle la. Mamzelle la dit so moman : — Mo sré voudré li té capabe trappé giromon la.

Tout moune seyé, et yé tout dit yé té pas capabe. Ça fait tour djabe la vini. Dans ein minite li té on nabe la avec giromon la on so la main. Li descende et li dit mamzelle la : — Vini asteur, vini dans mo la maison.

Fille la habillé li méme bien, et parti avec djabe. Enho chimin cin moune oua djab et dit li : — Donne moin mo cravate, et mo col, ça mo té prété toi.

Djabe oté so cravate et so col, et dit : — Tchiens, tchiens, to vié cravate et to vié col. Ein pé plis loin ein lote nhomme oua djabe et dit : — Donne moin mo chimise, ça mo té prété toi. Djabe oté so chimise et dit : — Tchiens, tchiens, to vié chimise. Ein pé plis loin li oua ein lote nhomme qui dit li : — Donne moin mo capot, ça mo té prété toi. Djabe oté so capot et dit li : — Tchiens, tchiens, to vié capot. Ein pé plis loin li oua ein lote nhomme qui dit li : — Donne moin mo tchilottes, et mo caneçons ça mo prété toi. Djabe oté so tchilotte et so caneçons et dit li : — Tchiens, tchiens, to vié tchilottes et to vié caneçons. Plis loin encore, ein lote mandé li pou so chapeau. Li ouété so chapeau et donné li. Li descende so la voitire, et yé pas oua li pendant ein piti moment. Li révini bien faraud comme anvant.

Fille la commencé pair. Plis loin encore ein lote dit li : — Donne moin mo choal yé mo té prété toi. Djabe descende et donne li so quatre choal yé. Lors li dit fille la : — Descende et trainin moin ; fille la descende et so caire té apé batte fort. Li trainin djabe jisqua coté so la maison.

Li couri dans so jardin, et dit fille la : — Resté avec mo moman. Quand djabe té bien parti, moman djabe dit fille la : — Ah, mo fille, to tombé mal marié. To marié djabe.

Fille la té si chagrin li té pas connin ça pou fait. Li dit vié fame la : — Tan prie, mo bon vié madame, vous pas capabe donne moin monien pou chappé. Fame la dit : — Oui, attende jouqua dinmain matin, et vini oua quichoge. Li minnin fille la dans ein ti la chambe. Li ouvert ti la chambe la. Li dit : — Vini oua quichoge, mo fille. Fille la gardé dans ti la chambe la. Ça li oua ? Ein tas fames pende en haut ein déclou. Li té si pair li té pas connin ça pou dit. Li mandé fame la, si li té pas capabe caché li méme en quéque part,

the newspapers. The next week a crowd of young men presented themselves, and among them one who was beautifully dressed and exceedingly handsome. He was the Devil, but nobody knew him. The young girl told her mother : " I wish he would catch the pumpkin."

All the young men climbed on the tree, but no one could succeed in reaching the pumpkin. When the turn of the Devil came, in one minute he was up the tree, and had the pumpkin in his hand. As soon as he was down he said to the young girl : " Come now, come with me to my house."

The girl put on her best dress and went away with the Devil. On the road they met a man, who said to the Devil : " Give me my cravat and my collar which I had lent to you."

The Devil took off his cravat and his collar, and said : " Here, take your old cravat and your old collar." A little further on, another man saw the Devil and told him : " Give me my shirt which I had lent you." The Devil took off his shirt and said : " Here, here, take your old shirt." A little further, he saw another man, who said to him : " Give me my cloak which I had lent to you." The Devil took off his cloak, and said : " Here, here, take your old cloak." A little further, another man asked for his trousers, then another one for his hat. The Devil took off the trousers and the hat, and said : " Here, here, take your old trousers and your old hat." He came down from his carriage and disappeared for a few minutes, then he returned as well dressed as before.

The young lady was beginning to be very much frightened when they met another man, who said : " Give me my horses which I had lent to you." The Devil gave him his four horses, and said to his wife : " Get down from the carriage and hitch yourself to it." She drew the carriage as far as the Devil's house, and was so frightened that her heart was almost in her mouth.

The Devil entered his garden, and said to his wife : " Remain here with my mother." As soon as he was gone the mother said to the young lady : " Ah ! my daughter, you have taken a bad husband ; you have married the Devil."

The poor girl was so sorry that she did not know what to do, and she said to the old woman : " Can you not tell me how I can run away ? " The old woman replied : " Yes, wait until to-morrow morning ; but come, let me show you something." She opened the door of a little room, and said : " Look, my daughter." The girl looked in the room, and what did she see ? A number of women hanging from a nail. She was so frightened that she asked the old woman if she could not hide her somewhere until the next morning. The

jouqua dinmain matin. Fame la dit oui, mais, quitté mo dit toi in monien pou chapper. Quand djabe la dit toi a soir faut donne so coq qui réveillé li tous les matins ein sac maïs, au lieu donne li ein donne li trois, pou tchombo li apé mangé plis qué tous les matins, pou pas li hélé trop vite. Fame la dit aussite : — Couri dans poulailler, prend six dézefs sales. Pas prend dézefs propres, mo piti ça va porté toi malhére.

Lendemin matin fille la donne coq la trois sacs maïs. Li prend so dézefs et li parti. Quand coq la fini so trois sacs maïs li chanté. Djabe réveillé vite : — Quéquenne dans la maison parti, li dit. Djabe lévé vite et parti. Fille la gardé derrière li. Ça té la fumin et di fé. Ça té djabe minme. Li prend ein dézef, li cassé dézef la. In gros barrière en dibois poussé. Djabe la té gagnin pou tournin chez li, cherché so ti la hache pou cassé barrière la. Li cassé barrière la, li tournin chez li, porter so la hache.

Fille la tendé di bri, li gardé derrière li, li oua la fumin et di fé. Ça té djabe méme. Li cassé ein lote dézef ein la barrière en fer poussé. Djabe tournin chez li pou chercher so ti la hache en or. Li cassé la barrière la et tournin porté so la hache.

Fille la gardé derrière, li oua la fumin et di fé, li cassé ein lote dézef, ein gros di fé limin. Djabe te gagnin pou tournin chercher ein la jarre dolo pou taingnin di fé. Li té gagnin pou couri rapporté so la jarre.

Fille la gardé encore, li oua la fumin et difé. Ça té djabe. Li cassé ein lote dézef, ein la barrière en briques poussé. Djabe té gagnin pou couri chercher so la hache en or, et li tournin rapporté li.

Fille la gardé encore, li oua la fumin et di fé, ça té djabe. Li cassé ein lote dézef, ein ti fléve poussé. Yé té gagnin ein ti pirogue, li traversé et djabe la nagé.

Fille la gardé derrière li encore. Li oua la fumin et di fé. Ça té djabe. Li cassé ein lote dézef, ein gros fléve poussé. Yé té gagnin ein gros caïman on bord apé chauffé dans soleil ; fille la chanté : — Ten prie, grandmoman, traversez moin, sauvez mo la vie, belle, belle, tonié belle. Cocodrille dit : — Monté on mo dos, ma sauvé to la vie.

Djabe oua magnière fille la té gagnin pou traverser, li dit ; cocodrille la :— Traversé moin, cocodrille, traversé moin. Cocodrille dit : — Monté on mo dos, ma traversé toi. Rendi dans milié fléve li calé, li calé en bas dolo et li neyé djabe.

woman said: "Yes, but let me tell you how you can escape from here. When the Devil tells you to give one sack of corn to his rooster which wakes him up in the morning, you will give him three sacks that he may eat more and not crow so early. Then you will go to the chicken house and take six dirty eggs. Take care not to take clean eggs; that will bring you bad luck."

The next morning the young lady gave the rooster three sacks of corn, she took her eggs, and ran away. When the rooster had finished eating his three sacks, he crowed: "Mr. Devil, awake quickly; some one has run away from the house!" The Devil got up quickly and started running after his wife. The poor girl looked behind her, and saw smoke and fire — indeed, the Devil himself. She took an egg and broke it: a high wooden fence arose in the middle of the road. The Devil had to return home to get his golden axe to cut down the fence. After he had broken down the fence he took his axe to his house.

The girl looked behind her; she saw smoke and fire — the Devil himself. She broke another egg: there grew up an iron fence. The Devil went home to get his golden axe, and had to take it back after breaking the fence.

The girl looked again; there was fire and smoke. She broke another egg: a great fire rose up in the road. The Devil went to get his jar of water to put out the fire, and then had to take the jar back.

The girl heard again a noise; it was fire and smoke. She broke another egg: a brick wall grew up. The Devil went to get his golden axe, and carried it back after breaking the wall.

The girl looked again: she saw fire and smoke. She broke another egg: a small river appeared, in which was a small canoe. She entered the canoe and crossed the river. The Devil was obliged to swim across.

The girl looked again; she saw fire and smoke. She broke another egg: a large river appeared. There was a big crocodile on the other side of the river warming himself in the sun. The girl sang: "Grandmother, I pray you, cross me over; grandmother, I pray you, save my life." The crocodile said: "Climb on my back, my little one, I shall save your life."

The Devil saw in what way the girl had crossed the river, so he said to the crocodile: "Cross me over, crocodile; cross me over." The crocodile replied: "Climb on my back; I shall cross you over." When he reached the middle of the river, he dived under the water, and the Devil was drowned.

Anvant fille la té parti chez so moman, so moman té dit li : — Eh ben, mo fille, ça tolé mo fait avec corps to vié choal blanc ? Fille la dit so moman : — Mo pas inquiété li, laché li dans la savane, et laissé li mouri si li oulé. Fille la oua so vié choal dans la savane, et li dit li : — Ten prie, vié corps, sauvé mo la vié, ten prie, vié corps, sauvé mo la vie. So vié choal blanc réponne li : — Oui, c'est comme ça to traité moin ; to dit to moman quitté moin mouri, si molé, asteur tolé mo sauvé to la vie. Monté on mo dos, ma minnin toi chez to moman."

Fille la descende, li bo so choal et so moman, et resté avec so moman. Li té plis oulé marié encore, pasqué li té marié djabe.

XX.

TI DOIGT.

Anvant nous vini icite, nouzotte pove djabe, nous té libe ; nous té pas bligé travaille pou ein maite. C'est blancs yé qui vini dans nous pays, l'Afrique, pou chercher nous ; ye volé quéquenne dans nous, yé acheté lézotte nous popa pou ein tignon rouge, in bouteille tafia ou in vié fisi. Quand nous couri la guere cila yé yé trapé yé vende blanc yé qui vini fait zaffaire on bord lamer. Yé té minnin nous taché dé par dé, et quand nous rivé coté lamer comme bande zanimo, nommes, fames et piti mounes, yé té changé nous pas pou largent mais pou tout sorte marchandise, et blanc yé metté nous dans bateau et minnin nous icite. C'est comme ça nouzottes vini nesclaves dans Namérique.

Quand Manga, mo grandmoman, rivé coté lamer, li oua ein joli piti laville, avec piti lamaisons. Yé té gagnin plein bateaux, et yé té gagnin l'air apé dansé on la mer ; quéquesennes té lévé et lézotte té baissé. Cété divent, vous connin, qui tapé soufflé et rémié lamer. Mo pove grandmoman, qui té zéne alors, té pair quand li oua yé tapé metté tous négue yé a bord navire. Li té cré yé té oulé neyé yé dans lamer. In nomme blanc vini coté li et acheté li avec so maite. Li minnin li chez li et li dit li dans so langage : — Mo acheté toi pou gardé mo piti garçon. Li té gagnin ein joli la maison avec ein magasin ladans, et ein joli jardin. Derrière la maison yé té gagnin plein zoranger, et nabe yé té si grand qué yé té fait bon nombe. Pou montré coman pays mo grandmoman té bon mo va dit vous qué

When the girl had left her mother's house with her husband, her mother had said to her: "Well, my child, what do you wish me to do with your old white horse?" The girl said to her mother: "I don't care what you do; put him out in the pasture and let him die if he wants to." However, when she crossed the river on the crocodile's back, she saw her old horse in the pasture, and she said to him: "I pray you, old body, save my life!" The horse replied: "Ah, you want me now to save your life; did you not tell your mother to let me die, if I wanted? Well, climb on my back, I shall carry you to your mother."

The girl soon reached her mother's house. She got down from the horse and kissed him, then she kissed her mother. She remained at home after that, and did not wish to marry again, after having had the Devil for her husband.

XX.

THE LITTLE FINGER.

Before we came here, poor devils, we were all free, we were not obliged to work for any master. It is the whites who came into our country, Africa, to get us. They stole some of us; they bought some of us from our fathers for a red handkerchief, for a bottle of tafia, or an old gun. When we went to war those who were caught were sold to the whites who came to trade on the seacoast. We were led away, tied together, tied two by two; and when we reached the seacoast like a herd of cattle, men, women, and children, we were exchanged, not for money, but for any kind of merchandise, and the whites put us into ships and brought us here. This is how we became slaves in America.

When Manga, my grandmother, arrived at the seacoast, she saw a pretty little town with small houses. There were many ships, and they seemed to be dancing on the sea; some were going up, others down. It was the wind, you know, that was blowing and shaking up the sea. My poor grandmother, who was young then, was afraid when she saw they were putting all the negroes on board the ships. She thought they were going to drown them in the sea. A white man came to her and bought her from her master. He took her to his house and told her in her own language: "I bought you to take care of my little boy." He had a pretty house with a store in it, and a pretty garden. Behind the house was an orange grove, and the trees were so large that there was a fine shade under-

zoranger té en flére tout l'année ; yavé flére et piti zorange, et zorange mire tout temps.   La maison la té coté lamer et tous les matin
Manga te minnin ti Florimond baignin.   Ti garçon la té si joli et so
popa et so moman té si bon qué Manga sré pas laissé yé pou arien
dans moune.   Li té lainmin ti Florimond si tant ; so chivé té bouclé, so zié blé, so la peau blanc et rose.   Tout moune té adoré pove
ti garçon la, li té si, si joli et *smart*.   Li té connin chanté si bien et
imité tout zozo si bien qué souvent yé té cré c'était Nita qui tapé
chanté dans nabe.   Nita c'est ein ti zozo Nafrique qui chanté la
nuite quand la lune apé clairé.   Li perché en haut plis grand nabe,
et si yé gagnin divent li chanté mié, pasqué quand branche la balancé ça idé piti zozo la chanté, comme hamac idé ein nomme chanté.
Florimond té imité Nita si bien qué tout moune té trompé, et ça té
amisé ti garçon la boucou.

Papa Florimond té fait zaffaire avec négue qui vive loin dans bois,
et ein jou li parti pou chercher la poude d'or et dent néléphant.
Quand li parti li dit Manga : — Prend bien soin mo fame et mo piti
garçon ; to connin mo dija donne toi ein paire soulier, mo sra donne
toi quand ma revini ein joli robe et ein collier. — Premier fois Manga
metté so soulier yé té fait li si tant mal li té pas capable a peine marcher.   Li oté yé, quand li rivé la maison et li assite on n'escalier apé
gardé so zorteilles. — Soucouyé, soucouyé, pove quichoge, li dit.
— Vous té en prison tout a l'hére, vous libe asteur, vous content,
hein ? Oh, mo sra jamais fermin vous encore, mo pas comprende
comment blanc yé capabe metté yé zorteille dans quichoge comme
ça.   Dépi temps la Manga jamin metté soulier.

Eh bien, maite la couri dans grand bois et trois jou après ça
madame la dit Manga prend Florimond et minnin li baignin dans
lamer.   Pendant ti garçon la té apé joué avec coquille et di sabe yé
oua ein nesquif avec plein nomme rivé.   Ein blanc descende et passé
coté Mange et li senti quéque choge drole comme si malhére allé
rivé.   Zié nomme la té brillé comme quenne chatte dans la nouitte.
Quand li passé li dit : — Bonjou, Florimond, mais piti garçon la pas
réponde arien.   Quand yé couri la maison madame la voyé yé joué
dans la cou, et chaque fois maite la té pas la nétranger la té vini la
maison.   Florimond té pas oulé oua li et ein jou li dit li sré dit so
popa on nétranger la.   Cila la dit Manga : — Piti djabe noir, si jamin
to ouvri to la bouche pou dit ça to oua icite ma coupé to la langue
avec mo gros couteau, et ma porté toi dans mo bateau, coude toi
dans sac et jetté toi dans lamer pou posson mangé toi.   Manga té si
pair qué li sré pas dit ein mot méme si yé té taillé li tout la journin.

neath. To show you how my grandmother's country was a good one, I will tell you that the orange-trees were in bloom the whole year; there were flowers and little oranges and ripe oranges all the time. The house was near the sea, and every morning Manga took little Florimond to take a bath. The little boy was so pretty, and his father and mother were so good, that Manga would not have left them for anything in the world. She loved little Florimond so much; his hair was curly, his eyes were blue, his skin was white and rosy. Everybody adored the poor little boy, he was so pretty and smart. He could sing so well and imitate all birds so admirably that often they thought it was the Nita that was singing in the trees. Nita is a little bird in Africa which sings at night when the moon is shining. It perches on the top of the tallest tree; and if there is a light breeze it sings better, for the swinging of the branch helps the little bird to sing, as the rocking of the hammock helps a man's lullaby. Florimond imitated the Nita so well that everybody was mistaken, and it amused the boy very much.

Florimond's father used to trade with the negroes that lived far in the woods, so one day he started to get gold dust and elephants' teeth. On leaving he said to Manga: "Take good care of my wife and my little boy. You know I gave you already a pair of shoes; I will give you, on my return, a fine dress and a necklace." The first time Manga put on her shoes they hurt her so much that she could hardly walk. She took them off on arriving at the house, and sat on the steps looking at her toes: "Wiggle, wiggle, poor things," she said, "you were in prison just now: you are free now, you are glad, is it not? Oh! I shall never shut you up again. I don't understand how white folks can put their toes in such things!" From that time Manga never put shoes on.

Well, the master went into the big woods, and three days afterwards the lady said to Manga to take Florimond to the sea and give him a bath. While the little boy was playing with the shells and the white sand, they saw a skiff with several persons come ashore. A white man disembarked, and passed by Manga, and she felt a peculiar sensation, as if some misfortune was to happen. The eyes of the man shone like those of a cat in the dark. As he passed, he said: "Good morning, Florimond," but the little boy did not reply anything. When they arrived home the lady sent them to play in the yard, and every time the master was away the strange man would come to the house. Florimond did not want to see him, and he said one day he would tell his father about the stranger. The latter said to Manga: "You little black imp, if ever you open your mouth about what you see here, I will cut your tongue with my big knife; then I will carry you to my ship, sew you up in a sack, and throw

Soir la Florimond crié si tant qué Manga té gagnin boucou tracas fait li dromi.   So litte té a coté quenne piti garçon la.   Pendant la nouitte li oua pirate la entré dans lachambe la avec ein gros baton. Li frappé piti garçon la on so latéte et li dit : — Li mouri, ma metté li dans trou la mo fouillé dans jardin, asteur ma fait zaffaire ti né-gresse la.

Mais Manga té déjà parti couri dans la cou, et nomme la couri on chimin pou trapé li.   Moman Florimond vini dans lachambe, li prend ti garçon la et li terré li dans ein trou coté la Manga té yé.   Li té pas fini so vilain nouvrage, quand li tendé dibri et li galpé couri. Li rencontré nomme la qui dit : — Mo croi fille la couri dans bois, pas bésoin pensé li encore, lion et tigue va mangé li bien vite.   As-teur faut mo couri a bord mo bateau et quand ma révini ma prend vous avec moin.

Madame la rétournin la maison et Manga sorti.   Li té si faibe li té pas capabe resté diboute, mais anvant li parti li bo la terre ou so pove ti maite té terré.   Li dit : — Adié, ti nange, et li couri dans bois.   Li té laimin mié resté avec zanimo sauvage qué avec mauvais moman la.

Li marché quéque temps si vite li capabe et li rété coté ein bayou dans bois ; li boi dolo et assite pou posé.   Li commencé dromi, mais li tendé moune apé parlé fort et li réveillé.   Li oua nomme autour li et so maite qui té gagnin l'air très colère : — Qui ça tapé fait icite si loin mo la maison, mo laissé toi pou gardé mo ti garçon, mo pensé to fait quichoge mal et to chappé.   Manga pas réponde arien, pasqué li rappelé ça pirate la té dit.   Maite la ordonnin yé minnin li la maison et li rétournin chez li aussi vite li capabe.   Li trouvé so fame apé crié et li dit li : — Oh qué malhor ! Manga quitté Florimond tombé on so latéte et nous pove ti garçon mouri.   Mo té oulé tchué négresse la, mais li parti couri et mo pas connin ou li yé.   Si jamin mo trappé li ma tranglé li.

Quand pove nomme la tendé so cher ti garcon té mouri, li tombé par terre.   Yé metté li dans so litte et li resté quinze jou dans délire. Pendant temps la madame la dit Manga li sré tchué li si li ouvri so la bouche.   Li fermin fille la dans ein cabane et donnin li jisse dipain et dolo.

Popa Florimond lévé mais li té vé pas consolé et li crié tout la

you into the sea for the fish to eat you." Manga was so frightened that she would not have said a word even if they had whipped her for a whole day. In the evening Florimond cried so much that it was with great difficulty that Manga succeeded in putting him to sleep. Her cot was near the bed of the little boy, and during the night she saw the pirate enter the room with a big stick. He struck the little boy on the head and said: "He is dead. I will put him in the hole which I dug in the yard. Now I must attend to the black girl."

Manga, however, had already run away into the yard; but the man, thinking that she was in the road, ran out to catch her. Florimond's mother came into the room, took the little boy's body in her arms, and buried him in a hole near the place where Manga was. She was not quite through with her ugly work when she heard a noise and ran away. She met the man, who said: "I believe the girl has gone to the woods; we need not trouble about her any more; the lions and tigers will soon eat her up. Now I must go on board my ship, and when I come back I will take you with me."

The lady went into the house, and Manga came out of her hiding-place. She felt so weak that she could hardly stand, but before she left she kissed the ground where her dear little master was buried. She said: "Farewell, little angel," and ran into the woods. She preferred to stay with the wild animals than with the cruel mother.

After walking for some time as fast as she could, she stopped by a bayou in the wood, drank some water, and sat down to rest. She fell asleep, but soon she was awakened by loud talking. She saw some men standing around her, and among them was her master, who seemed to be very angry: "What are you doing here so far from my house? I left you to take care of my little boy. I suppose you did something wrong and ran away." Manga did not reply anything, because she remembered the threats of the pirate. The master ordered his men to bring her back to his house, and he hastened to go home. He found his wife, who was weeping bitterly, and she said to him: "Oh! what a dreadful misfortune! Manga let Florimond fall on his head, and our poor little boy is dead. I wanted to kill the negress, but she ran away, and I don't know where she is. If ever I catch her I will strangle her with my own hands."

When the poor man heard that his dear boy was dead, he fell in a swoon. They put him in bed, and he remained fifteen days delirious. During that time the lady said to Manga that she would kill her if she opened her mouth. She shut the girl in a cabin, and gave her nothing but bread and water.

At last Florimond's father got out of bed, but he would not be

journin pou so piti garçon. Comme Manga té dans prison so maite té pas oua li. Ein jou li tapé marché dans la cou, li gardé temps en temps la tombe so piti garçon et délarme coulé dans so zié. Nita tapé chanté on ein nabe a coté li et so chanson té si triste qué pove nommé la senti plis triste que jamin. Ça té sembe li c'était Florimond qui tapé chanté, et li vancé coté la tombe la et gardé li longtemps. Tout d'ein coup pove popa la té croi li tapé révé, li oua quichoge si drolle qué plein moune va pas cré ça, mais si tant moune dit moin méme nistoire la qué mo cré li sire comme soleil apé clairé. Quand madame la té terré ti garçon la li té pas gagnin temps couvri tout so corps et ein piti lamain té déhors, et c'était joli ti doigt la qui tapé rémué comme si li tapé fait signe pou pélé quéquenne. Ti doigt la rémué ein coté et lote coté et jamin fini pélé, nous capabe dit. Pove popa la enlevé la terre avec so lamain et découvri corps la. Li trouvé li fraiche comme si yé té sorti terré li, et li prend li dans so bras et porté li la maison. Li metté garçon la on litte et li frotté li si tant, qué piti la réveillé. Popa la voyé cherché ein médecin qui commencé soignin li et qui dit li sré bientot vive encore. Yé té pas gagnin danger pou so la vie, pasqué so latéte té pas cassé ; piti la té sélement dans targie et bientot li sré bien encore. Quéque jou après Florimond té apé galpé comme si pas arien té rivé, mais li jamin dit arien on so moman et nétranger la, et madame la laissé Manga sorti so prison. Moman Florimond té gagnin remor, li maigri tous les jou, et ein soi, malgre yé soignin li bien, li mouri. So dernier mots té : — Oh ! Bon Djié, pardonnin moin. Yé terré li dans tombe so ti garçon ; Pirate la jamin révini. Yé dit yé pende li.

Après lamort so fame popa Florimond parti Nafrique et li vende pove Manga. Yé metté li a bord ein navire, et c'est comme ça li vini nesclave dans la Louisiane et li raconté moin nistoire ti doigt.

consoled, and he wept all day for his little boy. As Manga was still in her prison, her master did not see her, and did not think of her. One day as he was walking about in the yard, he looked from time to time at his dear boy's grave, and tears flowed from his eyes. In the mean time the Nita was singing on a tree near by, and its song was so sad that the poor man felt more sad than ever. It seemed to him it was his Florimond who was singing, and he came to the grave and looked at it a long time. All at once the poor father thought he was dreaming. He saw something that was so strange that many people will not believe it ; but so many people told me the same story, that I believe it is as sure as the sun is shining. When the lady had buried the little boy, she had not had time to cover the body completely, and one little hand was out of the grave, and it was the pretty little finger which was moving as if it was making a sign to call some one. The little finger moved on one side and then on the other, and never stopped beckoning, so to say. The poor father dug up the earth with his hand and uncovered the body. He found it as fresh as if it had just been buried, and he took it in his arms and carried it to the house. He put the boy on a bed and rubbed him so long that the child came back to consciousness. The father sent for a surgeon, who began to attend to the boy, and said that he would revive. There was no danger for his life, as the skull was not broken ; the child was only in a state of lethargy, and would soon be well again. Indeed, in a few days Florimond was running about as if nothing had happened, but he never said anything about his mother and the stranger, and the lady at last allowed Manga to leave her prison. Remorse had taken hold of Florimond's mother ; she grew thinner every day, and one evening, in spite of the most tender care, she died. Her last words were, " Oh ! my God, forgive me ! " She was buried in the grave where her little boy had been ; and as to the pirate, he never came back. They say that he was hanged.

After his wife's death Florimond's father left Africa, and sold poor Manga. She was put upon a ship, and this is how she became a slave in Louisiana, and related to me the story of the little finger.

XXI.

STATIE ST. ANTOUÈNE.

Ein cordonnier dans ein piti la ville té gagnin ein belle fille. Ein jou li oua ein jéne nomme entré dans la maison coté so quenne et li vini amouré li. Li mandé so vié quisiniére ça li capabe fait pou fait jéne nomme lainmin li. Vié fame la conseillé li prié St. Antouène. Li fait li, mais pou arien.

— Pététe li sourd, dit quisiniére la, anon fait ein trou dans so zoreille.

Quand yé tapé seyé percé ein trou dans zoreille statie dibois la domestique nomme la jéne fille la té lainmin vini dans boutique. Li mandé dé fame yé ça yé tapé fait. Yé dit yé té oulé St. Antouène tendé ein prière. Domestique la fait trou dans zoreille statie la et li tende déhors pou tendé prière jéne fille té si tant oulé mandé. Quand li tendé jéne fille té apé mandé St. Antouène fait so voisin lainmin li, li couri raconté so maite nistoire la. Jéne nomme la té si flatté belle fille la té lainmin li qué li vini amouré aussite et li marié fille la.

XXII.

PITI GARÇONS ET GÉANTS.

En fois yavé dé ti garçons qui té vive dans ein lamaison avec fléve dréte derrière. Yé parent té défende yé couri au ras fléve, mais ein jou yé chappé et yé prend ein nesquif qui té dans fléve et yé commencé ramain, ramain, mó cré yé doite ramain des millions milles. Quand lé soi rivé yé té bien pair et yé té pas connin ou pou couri. Yé oua ein lumière loin, loin, et en minme temps géants vini pou trappé yé. Yé monté on nabe, mais géants jisse soucouyé nabe la et pove garçon yé tombé. Géants yé porté yé dans yé la maison ou yé trouvé boucou lotte piti garçon. Yé te donnin yé mangé di-laite et digri pou yé vini gras, et tous les jou yé té tchui quéque ti garçon pou géants mangé.

Pas loin la maison géant yé yé té gagnin in vié fame qui té sor-cière. Ein jou popa dé ti garçon yé qui té chappé vini coté la maison vié fame la avec so zamis et li mandé li si li pas oua so garçon.

XXI.

THE STATUE OF ST. ANTHONY.

A shoemaker in a small town had a beautiful daughter. One day she saw a young man enter the house next to hers, and she soon fell in love with him. She asked her old cook what she could do to be loved by the young man. The old woman advised her to pray to St. Anthony. She did so, but without effect.

"Perhaps he is deaf," said the cook; "let us make a hole in his ears."

When they were trying to bore a hole in the ears of the wooden statue, the servant of the young man whom the girl loved came into the shop. He asked the two women what they were doing. They said they wanted St. Anthony to hear a prayer. The servant made the holes in the ears of the statue and waited at the door outside to hear what was the request the young girl was so anxious to ask. As soon as he heard that the young girl was asking St. Anthony to obtain for her the love of her neighbor, he ran to his master and related the story to him. The latter felt so much flattered by the love of the beautiful girl that he fell in love with her, in his turn, and married her.

XXII.

THE LITTLE BOYS AND THE GIANTS.

Once upon a time there were two little boys who lived in a house not far from a river. Their parents had forbidden them to go near the river; but one day they ran away, and, taking a skiff which was in the river, they rowed and rowed. I believe they rowed millions of miles. When night came they were very much afraid, and did not know where to go. While they were looking at a light far away the giants came to catch them. They climbed upon a tree, but the giants merely shook the tree and the poor boys fell down. They were carried to the house of the giants, where they found many other little boys. They were all fed on milk and hominy, that they might grow fat, and every day a few of the little boys were cooked and eaten by the giants.

Not far from the house of the giants lived an old woman who was a witch. One day the father of the two little boys who had run away came to the old woman's house with his friends, and asked her

Li répondé yé té dans la maison a coté divant qui yé té gagnin ein caillou pas plis grand qué ein piti canique. Nomme yé couri coté la maison la mais yé trouvé qué caillou la té tournin ein lapierre grand comme ein lamontagne. Yé té gagnin boucou tracas pou oté lapierre la et ouvri la porte, mais yé entré dans la maison la, ye tchué géants yé et yé raminnin piti garçon yé.

XXIII.

NOMME QUI TOURNIN ZOZO.

Ein fois yavé ein madame qui té gagnin douze piti, onze garçon, et ein fille. Pove madame la mouri et so mari marié avec ein lotte madame qui té ein sorcière et qui té bien méchant. Dans la journin li té fait onze piti garçon yé tournin zozo et révini nomme lésoi. Fille la li fait li tournin négresse pou tout temps. So popa té pas capabe réconnaite li et li metté li déhors. Sorcière la té fait tout ça piti so mari, pasqué li té oulé li donnin so quenne piti so fortine.

Quand yé metté pove fille la déhors li couri joinde so frère yé et li dit ça yé té fait li. Yé dit lendemin matin yé sré minnin li dans lote pays. Yé fait ein litte avec feille, et lendemin, quand yé té zozo encore chaquenne prend ein boutte litte avec yé bec et yé voltigé avec yé sére loin dans lotte pays. Yé ménin li dans ein bois et bati li ein joli ti cabane. Alors ein jou ein vié sorcière passé coté cabane la et quand li oua jéne fille la li mandé li ça li tapé fait tout séle la. Jéne fille conté ça so belle-mère té fait li, et alors vié fame la dit li comme ça li connin ein moyen pou fait so frère resté nomme tout temps. Li sré gagnin pou fait ein chimise pou chaquenne so frère yé, mais faut pas li coude chimise yé, jisse tissé yé, et faut pas li parlé anvant tous chimise yé sré préte. Ça prend li longtemps pou fait louvrage la, et quand li té gagnin jisse ein lamanche pou fini on dernier chimise la, so belle-mère vini connin ou li té et li fait rété li pasqué li dit li té sorcière. Yé tapé minnin li dans prison dans ein vié charrette, alors so onze frère yé vini voltigé autour charrette la. Li jetté tout suite chimise layé on yé et yé tournin nomme encore et fait descende yé sére. Par exemple quand li jété chimise la qui té gagnin jisse ein lamanche fini, frère la, qui té trouvé gagnin chimise la, resté tout so lavie avec ein zéle zozo pou so bras.

if she had seen his boys. She replied that they were in the house near by, before the door of which was a pebble not larger than a small marble. The men went to the house, but found that the pebble had become a rock as big as a mountain. They had much trouble in putting aside the rock and opening the door, but at last they entered the house, killed the giants, and brought back their little boys.

XXIII.

THE MEN WHO BECAME BIRDS.

Once upon a time there was a lady who had twelve children,— eleven boys and one girl. The poor lady died, and her husband married again. His second wife was a witch, who was very bad. In the daytime she changed the eleven boys into birds, and allowed them to take their human form only at night. As to the girl, she changed her into a negress. Her father did not know her any more, and put her out of his house. The witch treated her husband's children in that way because she wanted him to leave his money to her own children.

When the poor girl was put out of her father's house, she went to see her brothers and told them what had happened to her. They said that the next morning they would take her to another country. They made a bed with leaves; and the next day, when they were birds again, each one took hold of the bed in his beak, and they carried their sister far away into another country. They placed her in a forest, and built a pretty little hut for her. One day an old witch passed by the hut, and when she saw the young girl she asked her what she was doing there. The poor girl related her story, and the witch told her she would tell her how to make her brothers remain men all the time. She must make a shirt for each one of her brothers, and not sew the shirts but weave them, and stay without speaking until the shirts were ready. It took her a long time to do the work; and when she was nearly through, — only one sleeve was missing to one shirt, — her stepmother found out where she was and had her arrested as a witch. They were taking her in a cart to prison when her eleven brothers came flying around the cart. She immediately threw the shirts over them, and they became men again and rescued their sister. As one of the shirts had only one sleeve, the brother who had received that shirt had all his life, instead of an arm, a bird's wing.

XXIV.

EIN BON TI DOMESTIQUE.

Ein fois yavé ein michié qui té bien riche et bien bon. So fame té tout temps dit li té malade et li té bésoin tout sorte drole réméde qué so mari té gagnin pou couri chercher pou li. Fame la té fait ça pou so mari sorti so chimin et pou li capabe gaspiller so largent. Ein jou li dit faut li gagnin dolo lamer ou la mouri. Michié la té gagnin ein ti domestique yé té pélé Ti Margot et qui toujou couri voyagé avec li. Michié la parti cherché dolo lamer, mais li pas minnin Ti Margot fois cila, et ti domestique la oua ça so maitresse tapé fait avec largent so mari. Li té oulé donnin ein grand bal et ein grand souper. Ti Margot couri dit so maite ça li té oua et li mandé li laissé li trappé li. Yé révini sans personne connin, et Ti Margot dit domestique yé suive li et fait ça la dit yé. Li metté so maite dans grand panier et li caché dans panier la boucou fouette. Pendant bal la Ti Margot vini dans la salle la avec dé nommes qui tapé porté panier la, et lotte domestique yé. Maitresse la et so ninvité té cré c'était quéque joli cadeau et yé vançé coté panier la pou oua. Alorse tout suite Ti Margot dit : — Ala mo maite révini, et li prend fouette yé dans panier la et li donnin yé so maite et domestique yé, et yé batte raide ninvité yé et madame la. Michié la metté so fame dihors et li dit li : — To pas bésoin dolo lamer pou guéri toi.

XXV.

CORBEILLE FLÈRE.

Ein fois yavé ein ti fille yé té pélé Marie ; li té pas gagnin parents ditout, li té resté avec so vié grand-père. Li couri prend ein place pou travaille chez moune qui té bien méchant, et moune la yé té gagnin ein pie voleuse. Ein jou pie voleuse la volé ein bague qui té on la fénétre ; alorse quand yé manqué bague la yé acquisé Marie, et yé prend li et mette li dans prison. Pendant li té dans prison yé fait li plein boucou lamisère et yé batte li pou fait li dit c'était li qui té vole bague la.

So pove grand-père té crié tout la journin et li té couri la prison

XXIV.

THE GOOD LITTLE SERVANT.

There was once a gentleman who was very rich and very good. His wife always pretended to be sick and needed all kinds of extraordinary remedies, which her husband had to go and get for her. The woman did that to get her husband out of the way and to be able to squander his money. One day she said she must have some sea water or she would die. The gentleman had a little servant called Little Margot, who always went with him on his journeys. When the gentleman went to get the sea water, Little Margot was left behind and saw what the mistress was doing with her husband's money. She was preparing to give a great ball and a great supper. Little Margot went to tell his master what he had seen, and asked him to let him act. They came back secretly to the house, and Little Margot told all the servants to follow him and do whatever he would order them. He put his master in a large basket and hid in the basket a number of whips. During the ball Little Margot came in the dancing-hall with two men carrying the basket, and followed by the other servants. The mistress and her guests thought it was some fine present and crowded around the basket. All at once Little Margot said: " Here is my master come back ; " and taking the whips from the basket, he gave them to the servants and to his master, who whipped the guests and the lady unmercifully. The gentleman put his wife out of his house, and said to her: " You do not need any sea water now to cure you."

XXV.

THE BASKET OF FLOWERS.

There was once a little girl called Marie ; she had no parents, but lived with her old grandfather. She went to work for some people who were very wicked, and those people had a magpie. One day the magpie stole a ring which was on the window ; and now when the ring was missed Marie was accused of the theft, and she was taken and sent to prison. While she was in prison she was treated very badly, and they beat her to make her say it was she who had stolen the ring.

Her poor grandfather used to cry all day long, and he went to the

oua li. Dernier jou la qué yé té gagnin pou jiger Marie yé dit yé sré voyé li la pénitentiaire. Li sitant prié la Sainte Vierge qué jou la yé té donnin li so sentence, yé scié ein nabe dans la cou madame et dans cré nabe la yé trouvé bague la.

Quand madame la trouvé so bague li couri dans prison la et li dit li trouvé li. Mo blié dit vouzote qué quand Marie té sitant prié la Sainte Vierge li té promette li, si yé té laché li li sré couri dans bois chercher pli belle flère layé li sré capabe trouvé. Alorse, quand madame la tendé connin promesse la Marie té fait la Sainte Vierge, li fait ein corbeille avec plis belle flère layé li té capabe trouvé dans so jardin, et li donnin li ein ti la maison pou li et so grand-popa resté.

XXVI.

JEAN DES POIS VERTS.

Ein vié négue yé té pélé Jean des Pois Verts té vive dans ein cabane coté palais lé roi. Comme yé tapé volé tout ti poulet lé roi li té oulé sauvé so dézoi et li mandé Jean ou pou metté yé. Jean té bien content, et dézoi diparaite méme manière qué ti poulet yé. Lé roi mandé Jean ou pou caché so largent et Jean dit li pou metté so lor ou li té metté so dézoi. Lor disparaite aussite. Voisin yé alorse persiadé lé roi qué c'était Jean qui té volé li, et lé roi couri avec so soldat pou rété vié nomme la. Jean té connin ça yé té allé fait et li mette on so latabe ein dézoi avec pièce lor en bas so lézaille. Quand lé roi vini Jean montré li dézoi la et li dit li, si li jamin bésoin largent dézoi la sré donnin li, si li joué violon. Roi acheté dézoi la, mais quand li oua coman Jean té trompé li, li fait mette li dans ein sac pou yé jetté li dans flève. Nomme yé qui tapé porté sac la soulé yé méme et pi quitté Jean in moment on chimin. Li tendé ein berger apé vini avec so troupeau et li commencé crié li pas oulé marié fille lé roi. Berger la prend place Jean dans sac la pou marié fille lé roi, et vié négue parti couri avec mouton yé. Lé roi contré Jean, et Jean dit li li té trouvé mouton yé et lor la au fond larivière.

Lé roi jété li méme dans flève et li neyé li méme. Pove roi qui té béte, li té quitté ein palais pou sauté dans fléve.

prison to see her. On the last day before she was to be tried, they said she would be sent to the penitentiary. She prayed so much to the Holy Virgin that on the very day when judgment was passed upon her, they sawed a tree in the yard of the lady, and in the hollow of the tree they found the ring.

When the lady found the ring she went to the prison and said that she had found it. I forgot to tell you that when Marie prayed so much to the Holy Virgin she made a vow that if she would be freed, she would go to the woods and get the most beautiful flowers she could find. Now, when the lady heard of Marie's vow, she filled a basket with the finest flowers she could find in her garden, and she gave her a little house for herself and her grandfather.

XXVI.

JOHN GREEN PEAS.

An old negro, called John Green Peas, lived in a cabin by the king's palace. As all the chickens of the king were being stolen he wanted to save his geese, and he asked John to tell him where to put them. John was delighted, and the geese disappeared in the same way as the chickens. The king asked John to tell him where to put his money, and John told him to put his gold where he had put the geese. The gold disappeared also. The neighbors then convinced the king that John was the robber, and the king went with his guards to arrest the old man. John knew what was going on, and he placed on his table a goose with gold coin under its wings. When the king arrived John showed him the goose, and told him that whenever he needed money the goose would give him some, if he played on the fiddle. The king bought the goose; but when he saw how John had deceived him, he had him put into a bag to be thrown into the river. The men who were carrying the bag got drunk and left John for some time in the road. He heard a shepherd coming with his flock, and he began crying that he would not marry the king's daughter. The shepherd took John's place in the bag, in order to marry the king's daughter, and the old man went away with the sheep. The king met John, and the latter told him that he had found the sheep and the gold at the bottom of the river.

The king threw himself into the river and was drowned. Poor simple king, to leave a palace to jump into the river.

XXVII.

EIN POVE TI GARÇON.

Yé té gagnin ein fois ein fame qui té coutime dit li té pove et li té pas gagnin arien pou manger. Tous les jou so mari té couri travaille et souvent so lestomac té vide. Ein jou ein ti garçon vini frappé on laporte madame la et li mandé li si li té capabe entré pou chauffé liméme, et si li oulé donnin li mangé et couché. Fame la refusé et li dit li pas gagnin difé, pas arien pou manger et pou coucher.

Ti garçon la té bien faché, mais li couché par terre divant cabane la et li oua dans lafente laporte tout ça yé fait dans cabane la. Li oua fame la limin ein grand difé, fait biscuit, tchui cochon, et li oua ein nomme qui té cache dans lachambe sorti et vini chauffer coté difé.

— Ah! Ah! dit ti garçon la, ala pouquoi li pas laissé moin entré dans la maison la. Quand so mari pas la li fait bal. Lapé laissé moin mouri faim et frette dihors, mais la payé moin ça.

Ein ti moment après ça fame la tendé marcher, et comme li pensé c'était so mari, li caché cochon la dans garde manger, biscuit yé en bas ein tamis et nomme la en bas litte. Quand mari la rivé li oua ti garçon la couché par terre qui tapé gélé, et li dit li : — Qui ça tapé fait la, pouquoi to pas chez toi ? To pas mandé mo fame entrer. Nous pove, mais nous sré toujou trouvé ein ti coin pou toi.

— Mo pas chez moin pasqué mo pas gagnin popa ni lamaison, mo pas chez vous, pasqué vous fame dit moin ya pas place pou moin.

— Vini avec moin ; mo fame va changé nidée.

Li prend ti garçon la et li fait li entrer. So fame té étonnin oua so mari avec ti garçon la, et li té pair li té oua ça yé té fait dans cabane et li té couri conter ça so mari. Mais mari la té gagnin l'air tranquille et li dit li li té content oua li trouvé quéque morceau dibois pou fait difé, pasqué yé fait bien frette et li mandé si li gagnin souper pou li. Li dit non, alorse mari la tiré ein dipain dans so sac et li dit li pas travaille boucou et c'était tout ça li té capabe porter. Li partagé dipain la en trois morceaux, pou li, so fame et ti garçon la.

Chaquenne mangé so dipain, et quand yé té fini mari la dit : — Anon conter conte pou passer temps anvant nous couri coucher.

XXVII.

A POOR LITTLE BOY.

There was once a woman who used to say that she was poor and had nothing to eat. Every day her husband went to work, and often with an empty stomach. One day a little boy knocked at the woman's door and asked her if he could come in to warm himself, and if she would give him something to eat and a place to sleep. But the woman refused, and she said she had no fire, nothing to eat, and no place for him to sleep.

The little boy was very sorry, but he lay down on the ground in front of the cabin, and he saw through a crevice in the door all that was being done in the cabin. He saw the woman light a big fire, make biscuits, cook a pig, and he saw a man, who was hidden in the room, come out and warm himself by the fire.

"Ah! ah!" said the little boy; "that is why she did not let me come into the house. When her husband is not there she has a high time. She is letting me die of hunger and cold outside, but she will pay for that."

A little while later the woman heard some one walking; and as she thought it was her husband, she hid the pig in the cupboard, the biscuits under a sieve, and the man under the bed. When the husband arrived he saw the little boy lying on the ground freezing, and he said to him: "What are you doing there? Why are you not at home? Did you not ask my wife to let you come in? We are poor, but we would always find a little corner for you."

"I am not at home, because I have no father and no home. I am not at your house, because your wife told me there was no room for me."

"Come with me; my wife will change her mind."

He took the little boy, and made him come in; his wife was astonished to see her husband with the little boy, and she was afraid that he had seen what had happened in the house and had told her husband. But the husband appeared very quiet, and he told her that he was glad to see that she had found some pieces of wood to make a fire, because it was very cold, and he asked her if she had any supper for him. She said no; then her husband drew out a loaf of bread from his sack and said he had not had much work, and that was all he was able to bring. He divided the bread into three shares, — for him, his wife, and the little boy.

Each one ate his bread, and when they were through, the husband said: "Let us relate stories as a pastime before we go to bed."

— Bon, dit fame la, pasqué li té connin conte té fait so mari dromi et li sré capabe fait nomme la chappé qui en bas so litte.

— Eh bien, dit mari la, commencé prémier, ti garçon, pasqué c'est toi qui plis jéne.
— Mo pas connin conte, dit ti garçon la. Mo popa té toujou dit moin dit la vérité, mo pas connin conte, mais mo connin des vérités.

— Dis-nous vérités, alorse, dit mari la.
— Eh bien dit ti garçon la, mo connin yé na biscuit en bas tamis la, laviande cochon dans garde manger et ein nomme en bas litte.
— Ça c'est pas vrai, dit fame la, qui tapé tremblé pair. Na pas arien ditout.
— Anon gardé toujou, dit mari la, et li trouvé biscuit yé, cochon la et nomme la.
Mari la té si colère oua so fame té trompé li qué li mette li déhors avec nomme la, qui té pas oulé li, pasqué si li trompé ein nomme, li capabe trompé ein lotte. Li mouri frette dans bois. Mari la prend ti garçon la pou resté avec li et li té cré li té ein zombi, pasqué li té pas dit li coman li té connin ça li té dit.

"All right," said the woman, because she knew that stories made her husband go to sleep, and she would be able to make the man escape who was hidden under the bed.

"Well," said the husband, "commence first, little boy, because you are the youngest."

"I do not know any stories," said the little boy. "My father always told me to tell the truth. I do not know any stories, but I know some true things."

"Tell us true things, then," said the husband.

"Well," said the little boy, "I know there are biscuits under the sieve, pig's meat in the cupboard, and a man under the bed."

"That is not true," said the woman, who was trembling with fright. "There is nothing at all."

"Let us look, nevertheless," said the husband; and he found the biscuits, the pig, and the man.

The husband was so angry to see that his wife had deceived him that he put her out with the man, who did not want her, because, if she deceived one man, she might deceive another. She died of cold in the wood. The husband took the little boy to stay with him; and he thought he was a sorcerer, because the boy did not tell him how he found out what he had said.

PART THREE:
Bits of Louisiana Folk-Lore.

Bits of Louisiana Folk-Lore.

Introduction.

Folk-lore may appear to many persons as being of little importance, but the great interest which philologists take in it, is the best proof of its usefulness. I shall, therefore, give what I know of folk-lore in Louisiana, presenting the text, in the patois, of some popular tales, songs and proverbs, and making a few critical remarks about that most interesting dialect spoken by the Negroes in Lower Louisiana.

Tales.

It is quite difficult to make a complete collection of the negro tales, as the young generation knows nothing about them, and most of the old people pretend to have forgotten them. It is a strange fact that the old negroes do not like to relate those tales with which they enchanted their little masters before the war. It was with the greatest trouble that I succeeded in getting the following stories.

While reading these tales, one must bear in mind that most of them were related to children by childlike people; this accounts for their *naïveté*. As to their origin, I shall not attempt to explain it. I shall be satisfied to give the text and to comment upon it with regard to the morphology and idiomatic expressions. Some of the tales, such as ' Ti Bonhomme Godron ' and the stories about *Bouki* and *Lapin* are probably to be found in all Creole speaking countries, but modified by variants in the different localities. I have heard negro women relate a story one way, and the next day, change it considerably. The Louisiana Creole tales are probably amplifications of some well known theme. The ' Arabian Nights,' or La Fontaine's fables, or popular tales from Europe, have doubtless been the origin of many of our local stories. It is nevertheless, interesting to note what changes have been made in the foreign tales by a race rude and ignorant, but not devoid of imagination and of poetical feeling.

I give below ten tales, viz: 'Piti Bonhomme Godron,' 'Compair Bouki é Compair Lapin' Nos. 1, 2, 3, 4, 5, and 6, 'Ein Vié Zombi Malin,' 'Choal Djé,' ' Ein Fame Ki tournin Macaque.'

XXVIII.—*Piti Bonhomme Godron.*[1]

[2]*Bonnefoi, Bonnefoi; Lapin, Lapin!* [3]Mo va raconté [4] vouzote [5]ein kichoge ki [6]ben drolle, com vouzote va oua, é [7]ki té rivé yen a lontan, lontan.

Can zanimo té gagnin la terre pou yé minme é yé navé pa boucou [8]moune encor, Bon Dgié té ordonnin yé [9]com ça pou pa manzé yé entre yé minme, pa détruit yé minme, mé ké yé té capab manzé zerbe avé tou qualité fri ké yè navé dan moune. Ça té vo mié, pasqué yé tou so criatire é ké ça té fé li la peine can yé té [10]tchué leine à lote ; mé ké aussi vite ké yé sré manjé zerbe avé fri, Li Bon Dgié, li sré pran plaisir pou té fé yé poussé encor aussi vite pou yé plaisir.

Mé yé pa couté le Maître! Michié Lion comancé [11]manzé mouton, chien manzé lapin, serpent manzé ti zozo, chatte manzé déra, hibou manzé poule. Yé metté yé à manzé entre yé minme, yé sré fini par détruit yé minme, si Bon Dgié té pa vini rété tou ça. Li voyé ein gran [12]la sécheresse pou pini yé dé yé criauté. Cété ein kichoge ki ti ben drole tou dé minme, com vouzote a oua.

[13]Lair té boucanin, com can yé api bourlé baton coton, té semblé com si yé navé ein ti brouillard. Après soleil couche, ciel té résté rouge comme di fé! Temps en temps kéke nétoile té tombé en ho la terre. Lamer, fleve, lac, bayou, tou té pran baissé, baissé, tou té baissé a la foi, jika yé navé pa ein goutte dolo ki té resté. Ni la rosée té pas tombé [14]bo matin pou mouillé zerbe.

Ah! mo di vouzote, mo zami tou zanimo té trouvé yé dan ein grand nembara. Yé té apé [15]navigué partou, yé lalangue té apé panne ; yé té vini még, még.

Yé nave parmi yé ein doctair ki té pélé [16]Michié Macaque, li té batar sorcier, batar voudou. Yé di li té connin boucou kichoge, mé cété ein [17]grand parlair, piti faisair. Li di les ote zanimo ké cété aforce ké yé té fé péché, que Bon Dgié té voyé tou malhair layé pou pini yé, ké si yé navé parmi yé ki té oulé payé, li sré prié pou la pli té tombé. Li té dija réissi plein foi, can li té mandé kichoge; Bon Dgié dan ciel té toujou couté [18]so priére à li.

Yé navé aussi ein famé volair la, cété [19]Michié Rénard, ki té manzé tou poule ké yé navé dan so voisinage. Li di les ote zanimo: " pas bésoin couté Doctair Macaque, cé ein coquin, la pran vou lagent sans donnin vouzote arien pou ça. Mo connin li, cé ein canaille, vouzote pa apé gagnin la pli ditou. Vo mié nou fouillé ein pi nouzote minme. Cé pa la peine conté en ho lote kichoge. Anon! Hourrah! tou souite, si vouzote com moin, pasqué mo ben soif."

Astér Michié Macaque di li. " Mo pensé ben ké to soif, pirate ké to yé, astér to fini manzé tou poule ké yé navé ici. [20]Tapé vini fé to vantor ici."

Maite Rénard di: " Pou ça, to ben menti, to connin ben ké hibou, fouine avé blette apé manzé tou poule, é to vini di cé moin. To connin si yé na ein volair, cé toi, marchand priére."

Tou lote zanimo, tig, lion, loup, néléphan, [21]cocodri, serpent té apé navigué pou cherché dolo; yé to trouvé yé tou rassemblé pou tendé dispite Doctair Macaque avé Michié Rénard.

[22]I fo mo di vouzote ké si ein cochon connin grognin, chien jappé, loup hirlé, lavache béglé, chaque qualité zanimo gagnin yé tchenne langage. Ein tig, ou ben lion, ou néléphant pa capab parlé la langue ein lote bétail, chakenne parlé so tchenne langage, mé can yé tou ensemb chakenne compranne lein a lote: cochon a grognin, chien a jappé, yé va compranne yé ben. Cé pa com vouzote moune, si ein l'allemand vini parlé avé ein Français ou ein Méricain, li pa lé compranne, pas plis ké si l'Anglais té parlé avé ein Pagnol ké pa compranne nanglais. Nouzote moune, nou bligé apprenne la langue les ote nachion, si nou oulé causé ave yé. Zanimo, cé pa ça ditou; yé compranne yé minme com si yé té tou parlé minme langage.

Astér, fo mo fini di vou Michié Rénard té prétende ké si li té fé ein si grand sécheresse, dipi ein an la pli té pas tombé en ho la terre, ké tou zerbe té grillé, é ké nabe té apé perde yé feille é ke yé navé pas ni flér ni fri, cé pasqué yé navé pas niage dan ciel pou donnin nouzote dolo, é ké yé navé pas ein prière ka fé la pli tombé. "Tou dolo la rentré dan laterre, i fo vou fouillé ein gran pi pou vou tou capab boi. Couté moin mo zami é vou va gagnin dolo."

²³Lion ki té le roi ouvri so la djole. Li rigi, la terre tremblé aforce li parlé fort; li batte so flan avé so la tchié, ça té résonnin com ²⁴ein gros papa tambour yé gagnin dan cirque. Tou lote zanimo couché por terre. Li di com ça : Cré mille tonnair! prémier là ki va vini parlé moin pou la priére; mo va fout li ein kichoge ki li va connin moin. Comme si mo pa bon boug! Où ça mo déja manjé ein lote bétail? Cé ben menti é moin mo di ké ti navoca Rénard, ²⁵cé ein vaillant ti boug; li raison, i fo vou fouillé ein pi pou vou gagnin dolo tou souite! Vini ici, toi compair Bourriquet, cé toi ki gagnin pli bel la voie ici; can to parlé ya di ein trompette soldat. Ta couri partout verti tou zanimo ké moin lé Roi mo di com ca i fo yé vini fouillé et gratté la terre pou vou gagnin dolo. Ca yé qua pa oulé vini travail, ta rapporté yé, ²⁶ta vini drét pou mo forcé yé fé yé part louvrage ou ben payé lote zanimo dan yé place."

A force Bourriquet té contan cété li ki té gagnin pou servi gazette, li commencé braire ké ça té assourdi tou moune.

Alorse ²⁷Bourriquet la maté é pi corcobié, li té cré li tapé fé joli kichoge; ça té rende li tou fier lé roi té metté so confiance dan li, é pi ça té metté li en position vini commandé les ote vinj au nom lé roi lé Lion. Can li parti, li baissé so la tête, pi li voyé vous ein démi douzaine paire cou pié; en minme tan li donnin vou ein pétarade, ça té pareil comme si yé té déchiré la cotonnade! Ça cé so maniére salié la compagnie can li contan.

Alors, tou zanimo Bourriquet rencontré li di yé ké yé té pa vini tou souite pou gratté é fouillé la terre pou fé ein pi pou yé gagnin do lo, pou sir, lé roi lé Lion té manzé yé tou cri. Yé té tou si tellement pair ké yé tou vini, jis compair Lapin ki tapé grignotté ein vié ti boute zerbe sec.—Pas vini couté ça mo di toi, resté toujou la, é pa vini tou souite, ta oua ça lé roi a fé avé toi.—²⁸Mo fout pas mal toi avé lé roi tou ensemb, vini tou les dé ta oua comme ma rangé vouzote. To capab couri au diab; esqué mo boi moin? Où ça mo té jamin bésoin dolo? Pou sir, cé kichoge ki nonveau pon moin. To dija bîte, sotte animal bossale, Bourriquet ké to yé; mo jamin boi. Lapin pa boi, mo popa ni mo grand-popa té pa connin boi é com moin cé ein vrai lapin, mo pa servi dolo. ²⁹Lapin pa jamin fé piti sans zoreille, to tendé. Si yé navé kéke monne ki té tendé toi yé

sré capab cré ké mo tein batar! Couri, passé to chimin, gran
zoreille, pasqué si mo pran toi a coup de fouette ici, ma montré
toi to chimin, ma fé toi trotté pli vite ké to jamin galpé dan tou
to la vie, si to té connin moin com moin mo connin mo minme,
to sré pa rété ici, [30]pou sire."

Bourriquet là oua cété pa la peine, lì pran so chimin, mé
mé li té pa si bête fé so fion avé so geste comme li té coutime.
Li parti drét et can li rivé coté lé Lion, li di: " Mo maite, mo
fé tou vou commission, tou zanimo ké yé na dan moune, tou jis
compair Lapin ké pas oulé tendé raison. Li di li pa bésoin
dolo é li fout ben tou dolo yé na dan moune. Ça yé ki bésoin
dolo, yé capab couri cherché li. Dé plis ké si vou pa contan,
la pran vou, a coup de pié é fé vou trotté raide. Vou pa gagnin droit commandé li, li libre, libre com lair, [31]li pu gagnin
maite, jis [32]Bon Djié."

Can lé roi tandé ça li di ein tig ki té la avé ein l'ousse couri
cherché compair Lapin, rété li, minnin li ici tou souite. " Pran
garde, vouzote manzé li en route, pasqué vou va trapé ein
tourné comme vouzote jamin trapé encor, mo garanti vouzote
ké [33]ma montré vouzote coman cabri porté la tchié ; vouzote
tendé, hein? Eh ben! couri astér."

Yé parti, yé voyagé bon boute avan yé rivé. Tou tan la, les
ote zanimo té apé fouillé dir, chakenne té gagnin so part louvr-
rage, minme yé té quitté ein bon morceau, pou la tâche compair
Lapin, avé ça yé ki té couri pou rété li. Yé cherché partout,
dan la plaine, dan boi, en ho montague ; à la fin [34]yé vini bitté
en ho compair Lapin ki tapé manzé ein racine [35]zerbe coquin ki
té gagnin plein dolo ladan.

Va connin ké lapin connin fouillé é crézé la terre, cé en ba
la yé pran yé dolo dan racine.

Dan minme moment yé rivé coté li, compair Lapin té apé
chanté [36]ein ti chanson li té fé en ho lé roi. Li té di ladan ké lé roi
té ein fouti sotte, ké li pa capab gouverné, é so fame gagnin plein
mari. (Compair Lapin té apé ri li tou seul) é ké pététe après yé
sré fini fouillé pi la, li lé roi té fé tou zanimo payé taxe pou boi
dan pi la ké yé té crézé avé yé la siér ! Mo pa si sotte moin, mo
pa apé couri travail. Rangé les ote si yé bête, moin
mo fout ben lé roi com chien fout ben dimanche. Trala la
la etc." . . . . . .

Tig la proché tou doucement é pi li di li com ça: "Bonjoo,
compair Lapin, mo mandé vou ben pardon si mo dérangé vou,

mé mo pa fé par exprés. Lé roi lé Lion ordonnin moin vini pou
rété vou, mo bligé couté li, vou connin : [37]Ravet pa gagnin raison
divan poule ; cé pou ça mo conseillé von pa fé résistance,
pasqué compair l'ousse et pi moin na va bligé manzé vou. Pran
mo conseil, vini tou tranquillement, pététe va sorti clair ; [38]vou
gagnin la bonche doux, va capab gagé Michié Rénard pou
défende vou, cé ein bon ti navoca, li pas pran cher ; anon, vini !"

Cau compair Lapin oua li té pa capab fé autrement, li laissé
nofficié lé roi rété li. Yé mette la corde dan so cou é pi yé
parti.

Cau yé rivé proche la où lé roi té coutime resté, yé rencontré
Doctair Macaque en route. Li di compair Lapin : Mo pense to
tein élève Maite Rénard, to gagnin pou payé ça cher, va ! To
fouti, mo vié ; coman to yé àstér ? To pa senti kichoge kapé
frédi dan toi. Ça va montré toi lire gazette é oquipé toi la
politique tou lé dimanche, au lié to couri tranquillement la
messe.

Compair Lapin réponde li bréf : " Mo fout ben ça to capab di,
vié Macaque ! E pi ta connin : [39]Béf dan poto pa pér, couto.
Pai to la djole, fouti canaille, tapé sayé fé moin di tor, mé pét-éte
ben la farce a resté pou toi, [40]mo pencor rendi au boute quarante
narpen to tendé ; [41]pét-éte to minme avan lontan ta batte les
taons. [42]Chaque chien gagnin so jou, cé tou ça mo gagnin pou
di toi."

Alorse, com yé té rivé coté [43]ein gros di boi ké di vent té getté
par terre, Lion la té assite au ra la, Tig avé l'ousse, so dé
nofficier ki tapé méré compair Lapin di li : Roi, com ça [44]ala
gaillard la, nou méné li."

Maite Rénard té proché tout doucement derrière compair
Lapin, li di li dan so zoreille : " Can li va mandé toi [45]cofair to
parlé mal en ho li, di li com ça cé pa vrai, cé Bourriquet la ki
menti en ho toi pou fé toi di tor. E pi flatté li plein, [46]fé li
bande compliment avé kèke piti cado, ta sorti clair. Si to fé
com mo di toi, ta trouví toi ben, autrément, si to assé bête pou
di tou ça ki dan to tchor, pran gar pou toi, ta sorti sale. Mo
garanti toi lé roi va fé ein salmi avé toi."

" Vou pa bésoin pair, Maite Rénard, mo connin ça mo doi fé ;
merci pou vou bon conseil, mo tein navoca mo minme."

Compair Lapin [47]té gagnin doutance ké ye sré vini rété li
pou tou ça li té di, li té parlé si mal en ho lé roi é gouverné-
ment ; cé pou ça li té metté so pli bel nabi avé gros la chaîne

en or dan so cou. Li té di ein so voisin yé ké yé pélé Michié
Bouki, avé ki li té gran camarade, (li té lamouré so fame avé so
fïe é li té dan la mison compair Bouki com si li té ché li) oui, li
di compair Bouki : " Vou mandé moin où mapé couri faro comme ça; eh ben ! mo va pa tardé couri coté lé roi et, com ⁴⁸cé
la plime ki fé zozo, cé pou ça mo billé moin faro com vou oua ;
ça toujou fé bon effet avé moune ki fier é ki béte.

Can lé roi té paré pou comancé procès compair Lapin, li di
so garde méné prisonnier la pou li jigé li.

Alorse compair Lapin vancé, li di com ça : " O Lion, mo cher
Maite, to fé di vini, ala moin, ça to oulé ?

Lion la di li com ça : " Mo gagnin pou condané toi, pasqué
⁴⁹to tro connin batte to la djole en ho moin, é pi to té pa oulé
travail pou fouillé pi napé fé pou boi. Tou moune apé travail,
jis toi, é can mo voyé Bourriquet cherché toi, to di li ké mo té
ein bon arien é ké to sré méné moin a coup fouette. Ta connin
ké si yé dja mette fouette en ho to do, moin mo té jamin taillé,
minme mo défin moman té pa fouti touché moin. Ça to gagnin
pou di, zoreille lorgue kapé pande ; mo pense cé a force chien
tayo coursé toi ké to zoreille si longue, parlé tou souite, ou ben
⁵⁰ma crasé toi com ein plaquemine ki ben mir."

Compair Lapin té pa perdi so sangfroid, li té connin tou ça
⁵¹cété ein gros di vent ki pa méné la pli ni tonnair. Li froté so
né avé so dé patte, pi li grouillé so zoreille, li terné é pi li assite
é li di : " Lé roi, cé la jistice en ho la terre, com Bon Djié jiste
dan so saint Paradis ! Gran roi, ⁵²vou ki brave passé nouzote
tou ensemb, va tendé la verité : Can vou voyé Bourriquet coté
moin, li ki plis Bourriquet ké tou Bourriquet yen a den moune ;
li vini la mison can mo té malade. Mo di li com ça : ' ta di lé
roi ké mo ben chagrin mo pa capab couri astér, mé ala ein bel
la chaîne en or ; ta porté ça lé roi en cado é ta di ⁵³ma gagé
quarante donze lote zanimo pou travail dan mo place pasqué ta
di li cé kichoge tro vécessaie gagnin ein pi, cé la vie ou la mort
é nou pa capab fé sans ça. Yé na jis ein gran roi com li ki té
capab gagnin ein pareil lidé é assé la tête pou sauvé nou tou.
Ça vou cré li di moin ? Li réponde moin ki li té fout ben la
chaîne l'or, li pas manzé ça li ; ⁵⁴si mo té donnin li ein la manne
maï ou ben di foin, oui li sré manzé, mé la chaine ! pét-éte lé
roi té attelé dan chari ave minuve la chaine la li tí ben faché
porté li.' E pi li parti é li di moin : ' va toujou, popa, mo va
rivé anvan toi ; ta connin ké ⁵⁵Béf ki divan toujou boi dolo clair.

Mo pense li té oulé di ké li sré parlé avan yé té gagnin la chance tendé moin. Com [56]mo lé lé roi cré mo pa apé fout li dé blague, mo gagnin ein témoin ki té la, ki tendé tou mo conversachion. Si lé roi oulé gagnin la bonté couté li, [57]la tendé pareil com ça mo sorti di li.'" Alorse compair Lapin salié lé roi é li vini metté la chaîne lór dan so cou é pi li assite on coté é li souri, tan li té sir ké so cado té fé ein bon neffet pou idé li sorti clair dan so tracas.

Alorse Lion la di maite Rénard parlé vite : "Mo connin tou zaffair la, si to vini ici pou menti, ma cassé to cou, to pa bésoin balancé to la tchié é fé la grimace, com si tapé manzé fourmi. Anon, hourra! parlé, mo pa gagnin tan."

"Mo cher Maite, di Rénard, mo va di vou tou com ça té ; compair Lapin ké vou oua ici, cé meilleir zami ké vou gagnin· La préve cé ké li porté ein gros la chaîne l'or pou fé vou cado ; jamin va oua ein Bourriquet fé ca, cé pa pet-éte. Mo di vou ké li cé pli gran paillasse dan moune ; [58]Dan Rice pran virgt et un ans pou dressé ein Bourriquet. Li di can minme yé donnin li $100,000—[59]li papé récommencé jamin encor, jamin la entrepran ein pareil job ; li lainnim mié dressé cirquante mille lion [60]pasqué ya manzé li tou souite, ou ben la fé kichoge dé bon avé yé. Alorse, pou di vou, Michié Lion, vou ki roi tou zanimo, minme Bourriquet la, ké vou té voyé pou répresenté vou r.intérét, [61]vini menti en ho vou, é compair Lapin, li blan com la neige. Malgré Doctair Macaque dan vou confiance, cé li kapé gouvernin en cachette é conseillé tou moune é metté yé en révolte contre lé vou pou fé ein ote gouvernement, où minme Doctair Macaque avé Bourriquet gognin pou gouvernin dan von place can ya réissi fou vou dihor. Cé ça yapé sayé dipi lantan, é cé ça moin avé compair Lapin té oulé di vou."

Can lé roi tendé ça, li di : "Cé bon, mo contan vouzote di moin ça. To capab couri toi avé compair Lapin, mo tchombo li quitte."

Mé pendau yé tapi fé procés la, Doctair Macaque avé Bourriquet té pensé ça té pa sain pou yé tou lé dé. [62]Ouchon! yé té dija loin, yé chappé can yé oua ça té apé chauffé manvais coté, [63]yé fout yé can raide, personne pa oua coté yé passé, aforce yé té ben caché.

Apris ça, compair Lapin é Maite Rénard tou lé dé resté dan minme paroisse où lé roi lé fé so résidence. Maite Rénard sé to dépité ou so prémié comis, é lote té [64]maite d'équipage ; cé li ki commandé tou monne é fé tou lesotes travail pou fini fouillé pi la avé yé patte.

A la fin, pi la té fini net! Tou zanimo pran boi é yé tou té vini gaillard encor. Ça fé Lionne vini gaillard aussi, é kèke tan apré ça, li fé douze piti ki té jaune com l'or, yé té tou pli joli l'ein ké lote. A force lé roi té contan, li pardonnin tou ça ki té condanné dan pénitentiaire, ça yé ki té exilé aussi li permette yé vini encor. Cau li donnin yé la grace, li di yé couri boi dolo dan pi la.

Alorse, vou pèt-y-cré ké Doctaire Macaque avè so complice Bourriquet tou lé dé sorti dan yé trou é yé vini encor parmi les ote ; mé yé pran espionnin é djetté tou ça ki té apé passé ou tou ça yé di. Ein jou yé sencontré Maite Rénard ki té apè parlé zaffair gouvernement pou augmenté taxe. Li avé compair Lapin, yé té trouvé navé pa assé l'argent dan trésor piblic pou yé té vini riche vite.

Can Doctair Macaque oua yé tou lé dé ensemb, li pran souri. Li vancé coté yé, li salié, é pi li di : "Anon! blié tou ça ki té passé. [65]Cé pa la peine nou couri cherché tou vié papier layé, annon fé camarade é vive tranquille com bon voisin." Vou té cré yé trop bon camarade can yé séparé.

Doctair Macaque di so padna Bourriquet : " To oua, dé boug layé, compair Lapin avé Maite Rénard, cé dé canaille, mo gagnin pou oua yé boute, ou ben ya bimin moin ; cé tou ça mo connin.

Com compair Lapin té di li té pa jamin boi dolo, can Lion té jigé li, lé roi té di li : " Pran gar to pa jamin sayé boi dan pi la, molé oua si cé vrai ké to jamin boi, é mo ordonnin tou moune dyetté toi."

Vouzote [66]palé cré moin si mo di vouzote ké cé la vérité Lapin pa jamin boi dolo, yen a toujou assé pou yé dan zerbe yé manzé. Mé jis pasqué yé té défend li boi dan pi la, compair Lapin té envi. Tou les ote zanimo té tan vanté dolo la com li té clair, com, li té bon, ça té donne li soif soif ; tou moment, li té altéré com si li té manzé [67]la vianne salé ki té ben pimenté.

Alorse li di com ça : " Mo fout pas mal, ma couri boi a soir minme, mo oulé oua ça ka péché moin, mo assé malin pou yé pa trapé moin. E pi si yé trapé moin ma toujou trouvé [68]protection fie lé roi ; cé mo Dombo, la toujou trouvé kèke moyen pou pa yé tracassé moin, pasqué li capab fé boucou avé so popa lé Lion."

Li fé com li di, tou lé soir, li té couri boi plain. Mé à la fin li té oulé boi dan jou aussi.

Cété ein drole pi, so dolo té pa semb lote dolo, mé li té connin soulé pareille com ouiski. Sélement, au lié rende ein moune malade, apré chaque bitire vou té trouvé vou boucou pli gaillard. [69]Tou ça yé ki té vié té apé vini jéne encor; minme léguime ké yé té rosé dan jardin avé dolo la, aussi vite vou coupé yé, lendimin yé tou poussé encor pli bel ké jamin.

Can compair Lapin commencé oua bon neffet dolo la, li di com ça: "I fo mo gagnin pou dan jou aussi, ça fé boucou di bien, é com mo boucou pli vié ké fïe lé roi, fo mo vini aussi jeine ké li. Laissé moin fé, mo va rangé ça. Di pa arien."

Ça fé can li ti fé noir, li pran [70]so piti calebasse ki té tchombo à pé prés dé bouteil, é li couri coté pi la, é li rempli so calebasse. Mé li té pran si ben so précaution ké la gard yé té metté tou lé soir au ras pi té jamin oua arien.

Doctair Macaque avé Bourriquet té fé la gard tou tan pasqué yé té pa capab blié coman compair Lapin té trompé yé si ben dan so procés. Aussite yé té fé serment ke yé sré trapé li. Mé tou ça yé té fé yé perdi yé la peine é vé tan. Enfin ein bon jou Doctair Macaque vini trouvé Bourriquet so camarade é li di li:

"Vini la mison coté moin, ma montré toi ein kichoge." Li fé li oua ein ti Bonhomme Godron. "Cé avé ça mo lé trapé gaillard la. Foi cila, com mo va capab prouvé ké li coupab, mo va gagnin tou so l'agent, ké lé roi sra confisqué pou donnin nouzote, si nous dénoncin li."

Yé pran Ti Bonhomme la, yé metté li dan ti chimin ou compair Lapin té bligé passé au ra, au ra do lo, é pi yé parti. Yé connin yé té pa bésoin djetté; Ti Bonhomme Godron té fé so zaffair san moune té bésoin idé li. Mo pa connin si compair Lapin té douté kichoge, li vini ben tar soir là.

Jamin li té rivé minme lhére, mé li té toujou gagnin dolo, é yé té pa capab trapé li. Can li rivé soir la yé té posé Ti Bonhomme Godron, li oua ein kichoge ki noir. Li gardé li lontan, li té jamin oua arien com ça anvant. Li tournin tou drét é li couri couché.

Lendimin soir li vini oua encor; li proché pli proche, li gardé lontan, [71]li soucouyé [72]so la téte. Dan minme moment ein [73]grounouille sotté dan dolo: [74] *Tchoappe.* Compair Lapin crasé a force li té pair: dan dé sot li té rendi coté li. Li resté trois jou sans vini, é Doctair Macaque é Bourriquet té comancé

desespéré, yé té comancé cré ké cété vrai compair Lapin té pa
boi dolo di tou.   Mé siffit li té privé ça té donnin li encor pli
envi boi.

"Oh tiens! li di, mo fout ben! ma risqué, mo gagnin ein pé
l'agent ici, mé [75]la restan mo fortine caché dan [76]gran zéronce.
Si yé trapé moin ma payé la police é yé va laché moin, é pi mo
gagnin la protection fille lé roi—tou lé soir, li vini dan mo la
chambre—mo connin [77]li lainmin moin com cochon lainmin la
boue. Si li pa fé kichoge pou moin, ça té ben drole. E pi mo
toujou dressé la police pou li laché ein nomme can nomme la
gagnin l'agent, é mo pensé yé va pa fé nexception pou moin,
pasqué ye sré perdi l'agent, mo sré donnin yé.

Alorse ça té rassiré li, li parti lé soir, li té fé ein bel clair la
line ; moune té promenin tar jou la, pasqué cété la fin printemps.
[78]Chévrefeille té bomé l'air, moquair té apé chanté dan pacanier ;
yé navé ein ti divent ki té fé feille nabe dansé, ça té péché personne tendé li marché.

Can li parti, tou moune té couché, jis [79]chien ki tapé japé
après gros niage ki té apé galpé divan di vent. "Cé mo tour
astér, moin compair Lapin, mo gagnin pou boi, mé ein boi
complète.

Can li rivé coté Ti Bonhomme Godron, vié Ti Bonhomme té
toujou là. Li té fé chand dan la journin é godron la té mou.
Compair Lapin gardé li é li di: Hum! Hum, ya assé lontan to
dan mo chimin, mo pa vini pou boi, cé ein kichoge mo jamin fé,
mé mo lé baingnin a soir; sorti dan [80]mo chimin. To vé pa
réponde, hein?   Mo di toi mo oulé baingnin, noiraud.

Bonhomme Godron pa réponde, ça té fé compair Lapin en
colère ; li fout li ein tape, so la main resté collé.

"Laché moin, ou ben mo va fout toi avé lote la main."
Bonhomme Godron pa réponde, li fout li *cam* avé lote lamain,
li resté collé aussite.

"Ma fout toi coup pié, si to pa laché moin, fouti coquin!"
Li fout li, mé pié la resté collé aussite é pi lote pié aussite.

Alorse, li di : "Tapé tchombo moin pou yé fé mauvais kichoge avé moin ; vouzote apé sayé volé moin ; mé arréte, ta oua,
ça ma fé avé toi. Laché moin ou ben mo va fout toi avé mo
latéte é ma crasé to la djole."

Com li di ça, li fout li, é ein milet té pa fouti cognin fort com
ça, aforce li té faché. Mé so latéte, mo cher zami té resté collé
aussite. Li pri, li ben pri.

Au jou, ein pé avan soleil lévé, Doctair Macaque avé Bourriquet rivé. Can yé oua compair Lapin la, yé ri, yé jouré li. Yé pran ein charrete pou minnin li en prison. Tou di lon chimin, yé raconté tou moune coman yé té metté ein la trape pou trapé pli famé coquin yé navé dans l'inivers ; cété cé famé compair Lapin ki té gaté nom fïe lé roi, [81]li té sali so répitation hors service ké yénavé pas ein prince ki té oulé mamzelle Léonine, aforce compair Lapin té couri paillé partout ké mamzelle Léonine té so Dombo.

Maite Rénard, ki tapé passé, tendé tou manvais parole Doctair Macaque avé Bourriquet en ho compair Lapin ; ça fé, li di : "Oui, cé ben vrai, na pas com ein volair peu trapé ein lote volair."

Can charrette la té apé minnin compair Lapin en prison, tou ça yé ki tapé passé dan chimin voyé la brique avé caillou, on compair Lapin, yé fé ein vrai paillasse avé li.

Can lï té divant lé roi, li di com ça : "Mo oulé connin ça to gagnin pou di astér pou to capab sorti clair ici."

Lapin réponde : "Ça mo capab di ; [82]can di boi tombé cabri monté ! Mo connin mo gagnin pou mouri jis ein foi, mo fout ben. Si cé mo l'agent yé oulé, tou ça yé ki vini fé ein bande conte en ho moin, mo garanti vou, yé trompé. Tan mo té lib, jamin Bourriquet ni Doctair Macaque sayé gagnin train avé moin, [83]cochon marron connin où yé frotté. Mo garanti vou cé dé famé scéléra."

"To pa doit parlé com ça divant lé roi, can mo la. Mé lé roi va gagnin pou jigé toi dan ein piti moment."

"[84]Ça mo di, li ben di, mo paré pou tendé mo sentence." Après lé roi avé tou so zami té consilté ensemb, yé trouvé compair Lapin *coupable,* é yé condanné lï à mort ! Yé ordonin li sré couri en prison en attendan yé té capab trouvé ein bourreau bonne volonté pou exéquité li.

Lé roi té pensé li té débarrassé ein bougre ki trop malin pou li, é pi cété pou vengé lï dé cé compair Lapin té compromette Mamzelle Léonine, so fïe ; cété ein vrai scandale. [85]Ein fïe ki té mince, com ein di cane é dan cinq mois aprè compair Lapin té sorti clair dan so procès, fïe la té tournin gros com ein bari farine ; vou oua ben yé navé kichoge ladan ki té pas ben !

Pendan compair Lapin té en prison, lï tapé zonglé coman li sré trouvé jou pou sorti é chapé pou toujou. Li pensé so zaffair té ben sale é cété pli mauvais position li té jamin trouvé lï. Lï di com ça li minme : "Diab, tou ça [86]cé pa baptême

catin, mo crében mo fouti! Enfin, com mo lasse boucou, si
mo [87]dromi, ça va fé moin di bien. Li couché pa terre, é ein
piti momeut après li té apé ronflé. Li pran révé bel Léonine,
fïe lé roi tapé fé li signe pou di li pa bésoin pair, li va rangé tou
ça; alorse li réveillé contan.

[88]A la barre jou, jolié la vini ouvri la porte so la prison, é pi li
di li: "Yé trouvé ein bourreau bon volonté pou exéquité toi, mé
avan, yé gagnin pou coupé to zoreille, cé Bourriquet ki offri so
service pou voyé toi dan lote moune. Pran courage, mo vié;
ça fé moin la peine pou toi; to tein bon gaçon, mé si to té pa
risqué si souvan, to té pa la ou to yé. To connin: 'pran gar
vo mié passé pardon,' astér li trop tar. Bon voyage, mo camarade!"

Dan minme moment la, shérif la vini avé so dépité pou
ménin li ou yé té doi fé li mouri. Yé rivé au bor ein ti la
riviére; l'écore té àpic é yé té gagnin gran nabe, zerbe é pi
zéronce partou. Yé choisi ein ti place clair.

Can yé rivé, navé plein mouue: Madame, Michié, plein nen-
fant. Tou té vini pou oua coman yé sré tchué compair Lapin.
Roi té la avé so famille. Mamzelle Léonine, fïe lé roi, té la
aussite. [89]Oh! mé li té bel, avé so chivé tou bouclé ki té clairé
com l'or dan soleil! Li té gagnin ein robe la mousseline blanc
com la neige, avé ein cintire riban blé, é pi ein couronne dé rose
en ho so la téte. Zié tou moune té braqué en ho li. A force li
té bel. yé blié compair [92]Lapin net, [91]ki té apé tremblé com ein
feille liard. [90]Oui, oua, li té chagrin fini quitté in si gran
fortine é ein si joli fame com fïe lé roi.

Ça ki té fé pli la peine, cé can li pran pensé pét-éte Doctair
Macaque ou ben Bourriquet té maié avé Mamzelle Léonine sito
li sré mouri, pasque tou lé dé té vanté yé ké compair Lapin té
dan yé chimin; sans li, yé té di pét-ete té na lontan zaffair té fé.

Alorse lé roi di: "Anon fini avé tou ça; vancé Bourriquet
coté compair Lapin lire li so sentence."

Lé roi té [93]donnin lï so choix pou choisi so la mort com li té
oulé: néyé dan rivière la ou ben bourlé vivan, ou ben penne
dan nabe, ou ben coupé so cou avé ein sabe.

"Oui, oui, di compair Lapin, [94]tou ça ensemb, ou ben l'aine
apé l'ote; si ça fé vouzote tan plaisir mo mouri, mo ben, ben contan. Sélement, mo té pair vouzote té jetté moin dan gran
zéronce; ça té déchiré mo la peau, mo té soufri trop lontan, é
pi serpen avé dgièpe té piqué moin. Oh! non, non, pa ça

ditou! Di lé roi fé tou, tou, cepté jetté moin dangran zéronce, pou l'amou Bon Djié dan ciel ki gagnin pou jigé vouzote com vouzote jigé moin.

"Han, Han, to pair zéronce, Coquin, cé souffri nou oulé oua toi, souffri, to tendé."

Yé fé si bande di train: "[95]Ça ça yé, di lé roi ki té proché au ra avé Mamzelle Léonine, so fïe, ki té vini pou oua si compair Lapin té mouri com ein brave, di moins, cé ça tou moune té cré, mé cété pou donnin li courage é rassiré li. Can li té dan prison Mamzelle Léonine té fé di li, can minme la corde té dan so cou, li sré rivé en tan pou oté li é sauvé li, pasqué li té linmin compair Lapin plis ké tou kichoge dan moune.

Yé raconté lé roi avé Mamzelle Léonine ça compair Lapin té di é com li té pair yé jetté li dan zéronce, li té pair tro souffri. [96]Mamzelle Léonine vancé, li di: "Popa, mo gagnin ein grace pou mandé vou, mo connin vou haï compair Lapin, é moin aussite, pasqué li gaté mo nom: eh ben! mo lé fé vouzote tou oua tou ça yé di té menti. Mo lé oua li souffri pou tou so conte, é mo mandé vou ké yé jetté li dan zéronce é quitté li pourri la, cé ein assé bon place pou ein canaille com ça."

Alorse, tou moune batte yé la main, aforce yé té contan. "Fout li, fout li, cé la minme fo yé fout li," di lé roi, "fo li souffri, anon, vite, hourrah vouzote."

Astér yé pran compair Lapin a cate, yé balancé li ein foi: pove djabe la té apé crié: "Non, non, pa dan zéronce, dan di fé, coupé mo cou, pas dan zéronce."

Yé di: "dé foi."—"Jésus, Marie, Joseph, pa dan zéronce!"

Troi foi, Vap! yé voyé li dan ein gran talle zéronce.

Com compair Lapin tombé dan so payis, li assite, li gratté so nin, soucouyé so zoreille, é pi li di: "Merci, tou moune, mo té pa cré vouzote té si béte, mé [97]cé la minme mo moman té fé moin, mo ché moin ici, adieu, tou vouzote, mo connin ou mapé couri."

Mamzlle Léonine aussite té contan, li té connin ou li sré contré compair Lapin.

Ca prouvé vouzote ein kichoge, ké compair Lapin té ein niprocrite é li plaidé faux pou gagnin vrai, Ça prouvé vouzote aussi ké can ein fame lainmin ein nomme, la fé tou ça nomme la oulé, é fé tou ça li capab pou sauvé nomme la, é nimporte où nomme a couri fame a couri joinde li—Cé pou ça yé di ké [98]nimporte kichoge ein fame oulé, Bon Djié aussite.

[99]Com moin mo té la can tou ça rivé, yé voyé moin ici pou raconté vouzote ça.

[100]Mo fini.

XXIX.—*Compair Bouki é Compair Lapin.*—No. 1.

Ein jou ¹compair Bouki rencontré compair Lapin. Coman, li di, compair Lapin, cé vou ki là? vou pa connin jordi cé jou ké tou moune apé vende yé moman pou mangé.

" Ah! oui, di compair Lapin, moin aussite ma couri cherché mo moman é ²ma vende li pou ein chaudièr di gri é ein chaudière gombo."

Astér yé tou lé dé parti. Compair Bouki couri marré so moman avé ein lacorde, é pendan tan la ³compair Lapin marré so kenne avé ein fil zaraigné et avan li monté dan charrette li di com ça: "asteur, moman, sitôt va rivé côte zéronce, va sotté, é va chapé la mison."

Compair Bouki veude so moman é rétournin daus so charrette avé so chaudière di gri et so chaudière gombo. Pendan lapé revini, li oua ein lapin couché dans chimin, é ein pé pli loin ein ote lapin ; li couri encor ein pé, et li oua ein ote lapin.

Quand li rivé côté troisième lapin, li di : " Cé pa possib, lapin layé apé mouri faim aulié vende yé moman, laissé moi descende trapé yé.

Li tépa capab trapé arien, pasqué cété compair Lapin ki té
fé semblan mouri pou fé compair Bouki laissé so charrette, tan
la, compair Lapin galopé côté charrette compair Bouki, volé
so dé chaudière, ⁴coupé la tché so choal, planté li dan la terre.
mainin so charrette pli loin é couri caché.

Compair Bouki révini cherché so charrette, mé li oua jis la
tché so choal planté dans la terre.

Li commencé fouillé la terre com li té cré so choal é so charrette té tombé dans ein trou é li pélé moune pou idé li. Tig
sorti dans bois é idé compair Bouki fouillé.

Compair Bouki trouvé Tig si gras ké li mordé li on so dos é
li chapé. Tig mandé compair Lapin ki ça li capab fé pou
vengé li même en haut compair Bouki. Compair Lapin dit:
fo donnin grand bal, viní a soi chezmoin."

Tig é compair Lapin pren bon misicien é yé invité plein
moune. Alors compair Lapin mouté on so la garli é li commencé chanté :

⁵Vini dan gran bal
Ça qui perdi yé fame
Bel négresse Sénégal.

Compair Bouki ki tendé ça galopé côté compair Lapin et li
crié : cé mo kenne fame, pas besoin invité plice moune.

Mé compair Lapin fé comme si li pa tendé é li batte tambour
é chanté :

⁶Simion, carillon painpain,
do.   do.   do.

Compair Bouki entré dan cabane compair Lapin é li pren
Tig pou ein fame, pasqué li té caché so labarbe é té billé com
ein mamzelle. Quand bal fini compair Bouki resté sél avé Tig
ki donnin li ein bon volé é chapé avé compair Lapin. Astair cé
pa tout. Tig é compair Lapin té pa connin côté compair Bouki
té passé. Quand compair Lapin vini côté so cabane, li crié ;
bon soi, mo cabane, bon soi, é li di : cé drole mo cabane ki
toujour réponne, pa di arien jordi.

Compair Bouki ki té pa malin ditou, réponne : bonsoi, mo
maître bonsoi : Ah ! nous tchombo li, di compair Lapin, couri
cherché di fé, nouzote va boucanin compair Bouki dan cabane la.

Yé brilé povre compair Bouki, é compair Lapin té si content
ké li sotté com cabri et chanté

⁷Aïe, aie, aïe, compair Lapin
Cè ein piti béte ki connin sotté.

XXX.—*Compair Bouki é Compair Lapin.*—No. 2.[1]

Ein jou, compair Bouki couri oua compair Lapin. Quand li entré dan cabane là, li oua ein gros chaudière qui té apé tchui dévan di fé é ça té senti si bon compair Bouki té pa capab resté tranquille.

Quand mangé la té tchui, compair Bouki té gagnin aussi so par; li trouvé ça te bon ké li commencé embêté compair Lapin pou connin où li pren la vianne ki si bon.

" Tan pri, compair Lapin, di moin où vou pren la vianne là."

" Non, compair Bouki, vous tro gourman."

" Campair Lapin, mo pove piti apé mouri faim, di moin où vou trouvé la vianne là," Non, compair Bouki, vou tro coquin.

Enfin, li embêté compair Lapin si tan, si tan: ké compair Lapin di " Couté, compair Bouki, mo va di vou mais fo pa vou di personne é i fo vou fé com mo dí vous. Vou connin béf lé roi ki dans la plaine é ki si gras, eh ben! vou va pren ein sac et ein coutau, vou va guetté quaud li ouvri so la bouche pou mangé, [2]vou va soté dans so la gorge, é quand vou rendi dans so vente, vou va commencé coupé la vianne é metté dan vou sac, astér fé ben attention, pa coupé côté so tcher, pasqué vous va tchué li; quand li va ouvri so labouche pou mangé encor vou va soté déhor é galopé ché vou, fo pas vou laissé personne oua vou.

Lendimin matin compair Bouki pren so sac é so couteau, li galopé dan la plaine é quand Bef lé roi ouvri so la bouche pou mangé, li soté dan so vente et la li commencé coupé la vianne et metté dans so sac, coupé la vianne, metté dans so sac, ; pli li té apé coupé, pli li té apé vancé côté tchér béf le roi, li oua la vianne la té si bel, si gras, li dí, " ki ça fé si mo coupé ein piti morceau, ça va pas tchué li; li pren so conteau, li coupé ein morceau, tien, béf lé roi tombé mouri et voila compair Bouki ki pli capab sorti dans so vente.

Tou moune vini oua ki ça ki té rivé, coman béf lé roi ki té si vaillan, té mouri comme ça.

Yé di, faut nous ouvri so vente pou oua ki ça li té gagnin.

Quand yé fé ça, ki ça yé oua?

Compair Bouki! Ah! compair Bouki, cé vou ki tchué bèf lé roi, vou té oulé volé la vianne, attend, nouva rangé vou.

Yé prend compair Bouki, yé ouvri so vente, yé oté so létripe et [3]yé bourré li avé di sable, et yé mette ein bouchon pou fermin trou là.

Quand compair Bouki tournin ché li, li té benhonte; so piti galopé vini oua bon la vianne li té porté, "Popa, donnin nou la vianne"—Ya pas, mo piti—"Oui, popa, kichoge senti bon en haut vous."

Et piti apé vancé, vancé, compair Bouki apé tchoulé, tchoulé.

Piti commencé senti bouchon la, yé trouvé li senti bon pasqué ⁴yavé di miel en haut la; piti commencé sicé bouchon, sicé bouchou, tien! voila bouchon ki parti, tou di sable sorti é compair Bouki ki mouri dret là, li té plate par terre.

XXXI.—*Compair Bouki é Compair Lapin.*—No. 3.[¹]

Ein jou, piti compair Bouki rencontré piti compair Lapin ki té gagnin bel robe dimanche é soulier néf.

Can yé rétournin ché yé; yé mandé yé popa cofer li pa donnin yé bel zabi comme kenne piti compair Lapin.

Compair Bouki couri oua compair Lapin é li mandé li, ou li pran tou bel kichoge li donnin so piti.

Compair Lapin té pa oulé réponne mais compair Bouki embété li sitan ké li di: "couri biché dan boi é can to va lasse, gadé dans milié boi, to va oua ein gro nabe. Dromi en ba li et can to va réveillé di: " ²nabe, comme to doux." Nab va di: si mo té ouvri, ça, to sré di?" Toi, to va réponne: si to té ouvri, mo sré ben conten. "Can nabe la ouvri, entré didan, la va réfermé, é to sra oua plein joli kichoge, Pren ça to lé, é di nabe: 'ouvri,' pou to capab sorti."

Compair Bouki fé ça compair Lapin té, di, mais can li oua tout ça yé té gagnin dans nabe la li té oulé pran sitan kichoge ké li blié di "nabe ouvri." Nabe la té pou dé volér ki té serré yé kichoge la dan, yé révini dans bois é yé trouvé compair Bouki apé volé yé bitin. Mo pas bésoin di vou ké yé donnin pove compair Bouki ein si bon volé ké li té pa capab grouillé.

XXXII.—*Compair Bouki é Compair Lapin.*—No. 4.[¹]

Compair Bouki é compair Lapin té couri ensemble oua Mamzelle. Pendan yé tapé causé, compair Lapin di comme ca mamzelle layé: vou oua compair Bouki, li pa moune, li cé ein choal mo popa laissé moin en néritage. Mamzelle yé di: oh! non, compair, nou pa capab cré ça. Astér, compair Lapin rétournin chez li, é can jou vini pou li couri oua mamzelle, li fé ein bel toilette, et li couvri avé lapeau cochon.

Can compair Bouki rentré, li di: "Eh ben, compair, vou prête?" Compair Lapin réponne: " mé non, vou pa oua coman mo couvri, mo frêt et mo gagnin sitant mal au pied ké mo pas connin coman ma fé pou marché."

Compair Bouki ki té toujou si bête, di: "monté en ho mo dos, et can nou va proche pou rivé vou va descende."

Compair Lapin di: mo pa connin si mo va capab monté on vou dos, mé ma seyé."

Sans compair Bouki oua, compair Lapin metté so zéperon, é li monté on dos compair Bouki.

Pendant li on dos compair Bouki, compair Lapin té ²nec apé grouillé. Compair Bouki mandé li ça li gagnin. "Ma pé souffri sitant, ké mo pa connin coman assite." Compair Lapin di ça, mais li tapé grouillé pou oté so lapeau cochon.

Can yé rivé coté la mison mamzelle layé, compair Lapin piqué compair Bouki avé so zéperon é compair Bouki parti galopé. Compair Lapin sotté par terre é li entré dans la mison mamzelle.

"Vou oua ben, ké mo té raison, quand mo di compair Bouki cé ein choal mo popa té laissé moin."

XXXIII.—*Compair Bouki é Compair Lapin.*—No. 5.[1]
CONTE NÈGRE.

Ein jou bon matin, Compair Lapin lévé et li senti la faim apé gagné li. Li charché tou côté dan cabanne, li pa trivé aién pou manzé.

Li parti couri côté Compair Bouki. Tau li rivé, li ouâ Compair Bouki apé guignoté ein dizo.

—Eh! Compair Bouki, mo té vini dijiné avé toi; mo oua to pa gagné famé kichoge pou don mouen.

—Tan dire, Compair Lapin; ²na pi rention dans cabanne, jiche dizo cila qui rêté.

Compair Lapin zonglé tan.

—Eh ben! Compair Bouki, si to olé, ma va couri la chache dézef torti.

—Topé! allon, ³na couri tou souite.

Compair Bouki pran so pagné avé so la pioce et yé parti couri côté bayou dan di boi.

—Compair Lapin, mo pa souvan couri la chache dézef torti; mo pa boucou koné trive yé ben.

—Pa kété, Compair Bouki; mo tou tan trivé place koté torti pondi dézef. Toi, ta fouyé yé.

Kan yé rivé au ra bayou, Compair Lapin marcé douceman, apé gardé ben, côté ci, côté là.

Ben tô li rêté drète.

—Compeir Bouki, torti cré li malin. Li graté la té avé so gro pate et li pondi so dézef dan trou ; pi li mété ti brin sabe on yé et li parpillé feille on so ni. To ouâ bîte cila ? Oté feille la yé et graté avé to la pioce, sire ta trivé dézef.

Compair Bouki fé ça compair Lapin di li, et yé ouâ ein ta dézef apé cléré dan trou là.

—Compair Lapin, to malin passé mouen ; mo ben contan gagné toi pou mo zami.

Compair Lapin patagé dézef yé, li doné la moké à Compair Bouki.

—Compair Bouki, mo boncou faim, ma pé manzé mo kenne dézef ti suite.

—Fé com to olé Compair Lapin mouen ma pé porté mo kenne côté mo fame pou fé yé tchi.

Yé couri plin enco et ye trivé plin dézef. Compair Lepin touzou manzé so kenne ; Compair Bouai pa léimé dézef cri ; li mété yé tou dan so pagné.

—Compair Bouki, mo commencé lasse ; mo cré tan mo tonrné.

—Mo gagné acé dézef pou zordi, Compeir Lapin, allon no tour né.

Tan yé té apé couri divan, Compair Lapin zouglé li meme :

Compair Bouki pa coné trivé dézef torté ; cé mouen ki trivé yé, yé té doi tou pou mouen. Fo mo fé méké pou gagué yé.

Tau yé proche rivé divan, Compair Lapin di :

—Compair Bouki, mo blié porté dézef pou mo vié moman. To té doi ben prêté mouen ein douzène. Ma ranne toi yé ein lotte foi. Compair Bouki donne li ein douzène, et yé couri chakenne so chimin.

Compair Lapin couri mété so douzène dézef dan so cabanne, pi li parti couri côté Compair Bouki. Tan li procé cabanne compair Bouki, li comancé plène apé tchombo so vante. Compair Bouki sorti dihor.

—Ça to gagué, Compair Lapin ? Samblé com to pa gaya.

—Oh nou ! Compair Bouki dézef torté yé poisonné mouen. Can pri, vite couri charché metcin.

—Ma couri tan vite mo capa, Compair. Si vite Compair Bouki parti, Compair Lapin couri dan kisine et tombé manzé dézef torti.

—Méci bon djié, ma manzé mo vante plin zordi.   Metcin la rêté loian, mo gagné tan manzé tou avan yé vini.

Tau Compair Lapin proce fini manzé dézef, li tendé Compair Bouki apé parté dihor.

—Doctair Macaque, mo ben contan mo contré vou on chimin ; mo zami boucou malade.

Compair Lapin pa perdi tem.   Li ouvré la finétre et soté dihor.   Compair Bouki rentré dan cabanne, li pas oua Compair Lapin.   Li couri dan kisine, coquil dézef parpillé tou partou— Compair Lapin dija rendi dan clô.

Compair Bouki raché so chivé, tan li colair.

Li parté galopé apé Compair Lapin.

Compair Lapin si tan manzé dezéf, li pa capa galopé vite.

Tau lé ouâ Compair Bouki sofé lé tro proce, lé fourré dan trou di boi——

Compair Bouki pélé Compair Torti ki té apé passé dan chimin,—Compair Torti, tan pré, vini guété Compair Lapin qui volé tou to dezéf.   Ma couri charché mo la hache pou bate dé boi là.

—Couri vite, Compair Bouni, ma guété cokin là ben.

Tau Compair Bouki parti, Compair Lapin di :

Compair Torté gardé dan trou là, ta ouâ si mo gagné to dézef.

‹ Compair Torti lévé so la tête.

Compair Lapin voyé boi pouri dan so jiés.

Compair Torti couri lavé so jiés dan bayou : Compair Lapin sapé té souite.

Compair Bouki vini bate di boi, li ouâ Compair Lapin dija sapé.

Li té si tan colair, li couri trivé Compair Torti au ra bayou, et li coupé so la tchie avé so la hache.

Cé cofair la tchié torti coute com ça jika zordi.

XXXVI.—*Compair Bouki et Compair Lapin.*—No. 6.[1]

CONTE.

Ain jour compair bouki, qui ta pé crévé faim, courri 'oir so vié zami, compair' lapin.

[2]Li trouvé li apé zouglé arien et en train nettayer poëssons. Bouki mandé li oulé li té prend tou ça.   So vié zami conté li so l'histoire.   Li di li : "To ôir compair mo courri guetté charrette poëssons [3]su chimin.   Quand mo oir li proché, mo couché dan

chimin comme si mo té mourri. Gouvernair charrett 'la descende tout' suite pou 'ramassé moin. Li secouillé moin ain 'ti
brain, et pi après ça li jetté moin dan so charrett 'dan' ain tas
poëssons. Mo pas remuillé mo pattes com mait' renard. Mo
veillé ben vié gouvernair-là jisqué à mo 'oir li té' blié moin,
mo commencé vite jetté poëssons dan' chimin la jisqué 'à nous
té presse fait ain mille pli' loin, pi 'quan' mo jigé que mo té
gagnin assez, mo sauté par terre et mo ramassé tou 'poësson
la yé que mo té fou dan' chimin.

Yé té gagnin cent ou mille,—mopá compté mo té tro pressé.
Mo metté yé tout seul su mo do, pli vite qué mo té capab,' et
mo vini tout droet 'ici pou' mangé yé."

Compair bouki zonglé ain bon boute li té gagnin ain pé pair
qué si li té sayé fait la même chose li sré met li encore dan
tracas.

Compair lapin, qui ta pé guetté li avec so bon gié, 'oir qué so
zami ta pé tro zonglé. Li di li: 'Vié zami ta pé crévé faim,
fai com' moin, courri guetté charret, su chemin, et volé tou ça
to capab: et nous zaut va fai gran 'gala.'

Vié bouki qui té groumand té pi capab 'tchombo, li parti,
courri couché dan' chimin com si li té mouri pou même, li
levé so pattes yé en l'air pou mié trompé moune. Quand gouvernair charret' la proché tout près, li oir vié bouki qui ta fé so
macaqueries, pou' trompé li, li descende en bas avec 4ein gro
couarte l'habitation, et donné li 5ein fouet qui té gagnin piment,
di poivre et di sel, aforce ça té broulé. Compair 'bouki resté
ain moi' couché dan' so lit après ça. Yé voyé médecin pou
coudre so vié des zos. Li té pli gagnin ain seul la plume qui
té resté et li té gagnin colique jusqu á 'dan' so bec. Yé donné
li plein tafia pou donné li la force; yé mette li dan gro bain fé
avec gombo, et yé fé li boir di thé lorier tou temps après ça.

Quan comperè bouki guéri, li jiré, mais ain pé tar, qué compair lapin sré' pli fou-li en dedans ain aut' fois.

> Tou bouki layé qui pas coquins
> Douait gagnin peur dé vié lapins.

6MAN HENRIETTE.

XXXV.—*Ein Vié Zombi Malin.*[1]

Yé té gaignin ein foi ein prince qui té trés riche. Ein jou,
princesse so fille perdi ein gros diamant. Pendant li tapé crié,
ein vié nomme vini dan la cou et di li cé zombi. Prince la promette li ça li oulé si li dit où diamant la yé. Zombi jiste mandé

trois repas é dit li sra trouvé bijou là. Yé donnin li ein faıné déjénin é et quand li té mangé tout, li dit: voila ein qui pris. Domestiques prince commencé tremblé, pasqué cé té yé qui té volé diamant là. Apris so dinain, zombi di: voila dé ki pris. Domestiques tremblé pli fort. Aprés sonuper, zombi di: voila trois qui pris. Quand yé tendé ça, trois voleurs yé tombé à ginou divant zombi é di yé sré rende diamant la si li pa di yé maite arien.

Aster zombi pran diamant la metté li, dans ein boule la mie di pain et jété li divant ein dinde dans la cou. Dinde la valé dipin avec diamant. Aster zombi couri cherché prince et so fille et li dit yé qué bijou princesse la dans la fale gros dínde dans la cou, et ké si yé tchié dinde la yé va trouvé diamant là. Prince fé ça nomme la di ét yé trouvé diamant princesse dans la fale gros dinde. Prince té trop content é li di qué vié nomme la cé pli grand zombi dans moune.

A la cour prince la tout moune ta pé admiré zombi la, mais kéke jéné gen té pas bien sir si li té ein vrai zombi, et yé té oulé sayé trapé li. Yé prend ein criquette dans zerbe, yé metté li dans ein boite ét yé mandé zombi ça yé té gagnin la dan. Vié nomme la té pas connin, et li di li—même: Hé Criquette, to pris. So nom té criquitte, mais nomme layé té pas connin ça et yé cré ké zombi té divinin ké yé gagnin ein criquette dans boite la. Aussite vié nomme la passé pou grand zombi et yé donné li plain bon kichoge, et cépendant li té jiste malin et té gagnin la chance.

XXXVI.—*Choal Djé.*

[1]Choal Djé té gagnin ein vivié et li té laissé tou compair boi dan so vivié, cepté Compair Lapin. Ein jou, li trapé Compair Lapin coté so vivié. "Si mo trapé toi apé boi dan mo vivié, ma fé toi payé ein lamende. Compair Lapin réponne li: Charité bien ordonnée commence par soi même, é com vou maite, mo va pa boi dan vou vivié."

Eïn jou, yé tchué ein chivreuil, après yé té corché li, yé jetté la po là; Compair Lapin ramassé li é rentré so latête dans kenne chivreuil là, é couri boi dan vivié Choal Djé.

Can Choal Djé oua ça, li vancé é mandé Compair Chivreuil ki ça li té gagnin ké li tou marqué com ça. Compair Chivreuil réponne: [2]"cé Compair Lapin ki fé signe la croix on moin é ki metté moin dan létat cila é si vou pas quitté li boi dan vou vivié la fé minme kichoge avé vou."

—"Eh ben! vou capab di Compair Lapin, ké li capab vini boi dan mo vivié avé tou so camarade yé; mo vé pa li fé minme kichoge avé moin."

Compair Lapin couri ché li é oté lapo la é révini avé so camarade boi dan vivié.

Can Choal Djé oua li vini, li di li: boi autant ta oulé, avé to camarade."

Compair Lapin té toujou plice malin ké tou moune.

XXXVII.—*Ein Fame ki tournin Macaque.*[1]

Yavé ein foi ein michié, ki té gagnin ein champ pichetache. Tou lé jou li té oua ké kékeune apé mangé ein rang pichetache. Li mandé so fame ki ça ki mangé so pichetache. So fame di cé so frère qui mangé yé tou lé jou. Li trapé piti gaçon la et li donnin li ein bon volè. Lendimain, li oua ein ote rang pichetache mangé. Li trapé piti gaçon la é donnin li ein lote volé. Piti gaçon la di: "cé trop fort, li toujou apé batte moin, fo mo fait mo frère oua ké cé so fame ki mangé so pichetache."

Lendimin, li pa porté dinin so frère dan champ, mé li di li vini dan la mison é li sra montré li ki moune ki volé so pichetache.

Can yé rentré, fame la vini servi yé dinin, astér, piti gaçon la commencé chanté:

Tout man—, tout mangé tout, tout man—tout mangé tout.

Fame la di: cofer tapé chanté ça, mo pa oulé to chanté ça, chanté laute kichoge.—Non, cé ça molé chanté.

Li continuin chanté, é yé oua fame la commencé sotté, commencé gratté, é enfin li tournin macaque. Li galopé dan champ pichetache é li mangé ein rang.

"To oua ben, di piti la, ké cé pa moin ki mangé to pichetache; cé to fame ki tou lé jou tournin macaque.

Michié la vancé avé ein baton coté macaque la, mé li galopé dan bois é monté enho eine nabe.

XXXVIII.— DÉZEF KI PARLÉ.[1]

Yavé eune foi eune madame ki té gagnin dé fille yé té pélé Rose et Blanche. Rose té méchant, é Blanche té bon. Moman la té limmin mié Rose quand minme li té méchant, pasqué li té tou craché so moman.[2] Li té fé Blanche fé tou l'ouvrage, pendan ké Rose té assite apé bercé.[3] Eune jour li voyé Blanche coté pi cherché dolo dans eune baquet. Quand Blanche rivé là, li oua eune vié fame ki di li: "Tan pri, mo piti, donne moin enne pé dolo, mo ben soif."

"Oui, tante," dit Blanche, "ala dolo," é Blanche rincé so baquet é donnin li bon dolo fraiche pou li boi.

"Merci, mo piti, to eune bon fille, bon Djé va béni toi."

Kèke jou après ça, moman la ti si mauvais pou Blanche ké li chappé dans bois. Li té apé crié, pas connin où pou couri pasqué li té pér tournin chez li, quand li oua minme vié femme ki té apé marché devant li.

"Ah! mo piti, cofer ta pé crié, ki ça ki fé toi mal?"

"Ah! mo tante, moman batte moin et mo pér couri dans cabane."

"Eh bien, mo piti, vini avé moin, ma donne toi soupé et couché. Mais faut to prometté moin to va fai tout ça mo va di toi et to va pas ri arien to va oua."

Li prend la main Blanche. Yé commencé marché dans bois; a misire yé vancé, zéronce té apé tchoulé devant yé et fermin apé derrière yé dos. Eune pé pli loin, Blanche oua dé la hache ki tapé batte ensemb. Li trouvé ça ben drole, mais li pas di arien.

Yé marché pli loin, tiens cété dé bras qu' apé batte ensemb; eune pé pli loin, dé zambes: enfin li oua dé la tête qui apé batte ensemb, ki di Blanche, "Bon jou, mo piti, bon Djé va idé toi."

Enfin yé rivé dans cabane vié fame la, qui di Blanche, "Fé di fé mo piti, pou tchoui soupé;" et li assite coté la chimnin et li oté so la tête, li metté li en haut so ginou et li commencé cherché dépou.[1]

Blanche trouvé ca ben drole, li té pér, mais li pas di arien. Vié fame remette so la tête en place é donne Blanche eune gros dézo pou mette en haut di fé pou yé soupé, Blanche metté dézo dans chaudière, tiens, dans eune piti moment, chaudière té plein bon la vianne.

Li donnin Blanche eune graine di riz pou pilé dan pilon, voila pilon ki vini plein di riz.

Après yé té soupé, vié fame dit: "Blanche, tan pri, mo piti, gratté mo dos." Blanche gratté so dos, mais so la main té tout coupé, vié fame la té gagnin verre bouteille en ho so dos.[2] Quand li voir la main Blanche apé saignin, li jiste soufflé en ho là, la main guéri. Quand Blanche lévé, lendimin matin vié fame la dit: "As ter faut to couri chez toi, mais comme toi cé eune bon fille, mo oulé fé toi cadeau dézef ki parlé. Couri dans poulailler, tout dézef qui va di to prend moin, il faut to prend yé, tout dézef qui va di pas prend moin, faut pas prend yé. Quand to va dans chimin to va jété dézef yé derrière to la tête pou cassé yé."

A misure Blanche marché li cassé dézef : voila tout plein joli kichoge ki sorti dan dézef layé : diamant, l'or, bel voiture, belle la robe. Quand li rivé chez so moman, li té gagnin tant belle kichoge, ça té rempli la maison ; aussite so moman té ben content oua li.

Lendimin li dit Rose, faut to couri dans bois cherché pou minme vié fame là, i faut to gagnin plein belle robe comme Blanche. Rose couri dans bois, li rencontré vié fame la qui di li vini dans so cabane, mais quand li oua la hache ki apé batte, la zambe ki apé batte, la tête ki apé batte, vié fame ki oté so la tête pou gratté so dépou, li commencé ri et moqué tout ça li té oua, aussite vié fame la dit li : "Ah ! mo piti, to pas bon fille, bon Djé va pini toi."

Mais lendimin matin, li dit li, "mo vé pas renvoyé toi sans arien, couri dans poulailler, et prend dézef ki va dit prend moi, faut pas to prend cilayé ki dit va pas prend moin."

Rose couri dans poulailler, tous dézef commencé crié : "Prend moin, pas prend moin." Rose té si méchant li dit : "Ah oui, vouz ote dit, pas prend moin, mais c'est jiste ca moin mo oulé. Li prend tou dézef qui dit 'pas prend moin' et li parti avé yé. A misure li marché li cassé dézef, voila eune tas serpent, crapaud, gournouille, ki commencé gallopé derrier li yé ti gagnin minme plein fouet qui té ape taillé li raide comme tout. Rose galopé, apé poussé décri. Li rivé chez so moman, li té si lasse li pas capab parlé. Quand so moman oua tout bête et tout fouet qui té apé suive li, li té si colère, li renvoyé li, comme chien, et dit li couri resté dans bois.

XXXIX.— LA GRAISSE.

YAVÉ eune madame ki té gagnin cate filles. Yé té si joli, ké tout moune té oulé marié avec yé. Yé té pélé yé: La Graisse, Dépomme, Banane, et Pacane. La Graisse té pli joli, mais li té jamin sorti dans soleil pasqué yé té pér li va fonne. La Graisse té sorti tou les jou dans eune bel carosse en or. Fi léroi té oua li tou les jou, mais La Graisse té si joli et carosse li té si apé brillé [1] ké so zié té fait li mal ; li té gagnin pou frotté yé pou oua clair. Fi léroi té limmin La Graisse : li couri chez moman la pou mandé li pou marié avec La Graisse, mais moman la ki té connin La Graisse té pli joli li té oulé marié les otes avant.

Li pélé Dépomme : "Dépomme oh ! orimomo, orimomo !" Dépomme vini, mais michié la gardé li ben, li dit c'est pas cila là mo oulé, li sré gaté trop vite.

Moman pélé : "Banane oh ! orimomo, orimomo !" Banane vini, Michié té pas oulé, li dit la connin pourri trop vite.

Moman pélé : "Pacane oh ! orimomo, orimomo !" Pacane vini. Michié dit pacane va vini rance.

Enfin moman pélé La Graisse : "La Graisse oh ! orimomo, orimomo." La Graisse vini. Sito li oua La Graisse, li prend li et ménin li dans so bel la maison, et li marié li.

Fi léroi té couri la chasse tou les jou : pendant li té pas la, domestiques té fait la Graisse tout plein la misère. Li té pér dit so mari, et li té fait tout ça yé oulé.

Eune jou kisinière la dit, li vé pas fait dinin. I faut La Graisse fait li. Pauvre La Graisse li crié, li crié, mais yé forcé li pour resté coté di fé : mais li tapé fonne fonne. A la fin yavé pli qué La Graisse partout, la kisine la té tout plein. Piti zozo La Graisse oua ça, li trempé so zaile dans La Graisse.[1] Li volé dans bois coté michié la, si batte so zaile dans so figure.

Michié la oua La Graisse ki té on so zaile, li pensé so chère La Graisse, li galopé chez li, li trouvé so femme tout fonne par terre. Li té si chagrin, li ramassé tout La Graisse, et metté li dans vié baignoire, et quand La Graisse la vini frêt, li té eune femme encor. Mais li té jamin si jolie com avant, pasqué la terre té mélé avé li,[2] et li té tout jaune et sale. So mari té pli limmin li et renvoyé li coté so moman.

XL.— POSSON DORÉ.[1]

YAVÉ inne fois inne jene fille qui té gagnin inne l'amoureux, cété inne bel jene nomme, inne prince, mé papa li té pas oulé jene nomme té fé li l'amour. Li couri trouvé inne vié zombi ki té resté dans bois. Li dit : tan pri, zombi, fé jene nomme là laissé mo fille, mo vé pas yé marié.

Inne jou, jene fille la et jene nomme la té assite coté flève, zombi vini, li fé jene nomme la tournain posson é galopé dans dolo.

Papa li té cré ké jene fille là sré blié jene nomme là, astére li té posson. Li té pli gardé après yé, mais tou les jou jene fille la té couri assite coté flève, et li té chanté ; "Caliwa, wa, caliwa, co ; waco, maman dit oui ; waco papa dit non, caliwa, wa, caliwa, co ; sitôt li té chanté ça dolo té ouvri et inne bel posson rouge avec inne couronne en or en haut so la tête, té vini coté jene fille là ; li té porté li gato, zorange, dépomme, pou li mangé.

Papa la oua ké so fille couri assite coté flève tou lé jou ; inne jour li guetté li et li oua ça li tapé fé. Lendémin li porté so fisi é quand jene fille chanté é bel posson la vini, li tchoué li é li porté li ché li pou tchui li. . . . Yé di jene fille la qué li té gagnin pou tchui posson là.

Quand li prend li pou coupé li, posson commencé chanté : " Coupé moin donc, wa, wa, coupé moin donc, wa, wa. Gratté moin donc wa, wa, gratté moin donc, wa, wa. Brassé moin donc, wa, wa. Mettez di sel wa, wa. . . .

Après, quand posson là té tchui, yé metté li on la table. Jéne fille li té pa oulé mangé ; li tapé crié pou so posson, mais papa li té si gourmand li mangé si boucou qué so vente crévé et plein petit posson sorti la dans é chapé dans flève.

Après dinin jene fille li couri assite la où yé té jété lécail so posson ; li crié si boucou ké la terre ouvri et li parti dans trou là pou couri coté so posson. Quand so maman vini cherché li li oua jisse boute so chivé qui tapé sorti dans la terre la.[2]

XLI.— "GIVE ME." [1]

Ein foi, yé té gagnin ein jene madame ki té resté dan ein bel la mison. Li té maïé dipi lontan, mé li té pa gagnin piti. Ein jou, li té appiyé on balistrade so la garli, li oua ein vié fame ki tapé pacé avé ein pagnin dépomme on so latête. Can madame la oua bel dépomme yé, li té envi manzé ein ; li pélé vié fame la et li di li ké li oulé acheté ein dépomme. Vié marchan la té pa oulé vende, mé li donnin madame la ein, et li di li :

"Mo conin ké vou envi gagnin ein piti ; manzé dépomme la et dimain matin vou sra moman ein bel gaçon."

Jene fame la pren dépomme la, li ri et li pliché li. Li jété lapo yé dan la cou é manzé dépomme. Vié fame la té pa menti ; dans la nouite, jene madame la gagnin ein bel gaçon, et ça qui plice drole, cé ké ein jiment ki té laché dan la cou, manzé lapo dépomme, et li aussite gagnin ein piti dan la nouite.

Jéne madame la té ben conten gagnin ein piti, et li di ké com piti choal la té né minme la nouite ké so piti gaçon, li sré fé li cado li.

Yé tou lé dé grandi ensemb et yé té linmin yé minme boucou. Com ti choal la té né par ein mirac, li té capab sellé, bridé san personne touché li. Can piti gaçon la té oulé monté li, li crié : "Sellé, bridé, mo piti choal," et li vini tou souite prète pou yé monté li.

Can gaçon la vini ein nomme li fatigué resté ché so moman et li parti chercé zaventire. Li pa di personne ou lapé couri, li monté so choal et voyagé boucou, jiska li rivé dan pays ein grand roi.

Ein soi li rivé coté ein bel la mison ; yé di li cété démère roi et ké li té gagnin ein ben joli fïe.

Jene nomme la té envi oua la princesse ; aussite li descende so choal et fé li disparaite, pasqué mo té doite di·vou, ké choal la té capab disparaite can so maite té oulé et li minme té capab chanzé so zabi can li oulé et pren kékéfoi linge ein mendian, et kékéfoi linge ein prince. Jou cila, li pren linge ein mendian, et couri coté la kisine.

Li fé com si li té pa capab parlé ben, et tou ça yé té di li, li té réponne ein frase : "*Give me.*" Yé mandé li "To soif" — "*Give me*" — "To faim" — "*Give me.*" Yé pélé li "*Give me*" et yé permette li couché dans la kisin et dans la cende la chiminin. Li idé domestique lé roi ki té cré li té idio.

Tou la simaine, *Give me* resté dan la kisine, mé can dimanche rivé et tou moune parti pou la messe, li metté so pli bel zabi, li ordonnin so choal paraite sellé, bridé, et li commencé galopé dans tou jardin lé roi. Li cassé pot fléres, piti nabe, arien té capab rété li.

Même jou la, fie lé roi té malade et li pa couri la messe. Li resté la mison et li gardé dan jardin dan la finéte. Li oua *Give me* et trouvé li ben joli.

Give me rété galopé dan jardin can li cré la messe té presqué fini. Li fé so choal disparaite et li couri dan la kisine encor, où li répranne so zabis mendian.

Tan lé roi révini la messe, li té firié oua tou déga yé té fé dan so jardin. Li mandé so domestique layé, mé yé di ké *Give me* té sel moune ki té resté la mison. Lé roi questionnin li, mé li toujou réponne " *Give me.*"

Dimanche apé ça minme kichoge rivé, et fie lé roi resté encor la mison pou oua *Give me*. Lé roi té si colère ké li di li gagnin pou trapé canaille laki apé bimin so jardin. Troisième dimanche, li pa couri la messe, mé li caché dan la mison, et li trapé *Give me* billé com ein prince, apé galopé dan jardin on so choal.

Lé roi té ben étonnin é li mendé bel jene nomme la raconter so listoire.

Give me di li comment li té né, et li fé paraite et disparaite so choal comme li oulé, et li changé so zabis comme li oulé. Li di lé roi ké li amouré so fie et mandé so la main. Lé roi di oui, et *Give me* maïé princesse la, et voyé cherché so moman.

Yé vive lontan et yé té benhéré pasqué cété ein bon vié zombi ki té donnin moman *Give me* dépomme pou manzé.

ENGLISH TRANSLATIONS OF PART THREE

The Tar Baby (Piti Bonhomme Godron).

BONNEFOI, BONNEFOI; LAPIN, LAPIN!

I am going to relate to you something which is very funny, as you are going to see, and which happened a long time ago!

When the animals had the earth for themselves and there were yet but few people, God ordered them not to eat each other, not to destroy each other, but said that they might eat the grass with all kinds of fruits that there were on the earth. That was better, because they were all His creatures and it pained Him when they killed each other; but as quickly as they would eat the grass and fruits, He, God, would take pleasure to make them grow again to please them. But they did not obey the Master! Mr. Lion began by eating sheep, the dogs ate rabbits, the serpents ate the little birds, the cats ate rats, the owls ate chickens. They began to eat each other, they would have destroyed each other, if God had not put a stop to all that! He sent a great drought to punish their cruelty. It was a thing which was funny, nevertheless, as you are going to see.

There was smoke in the air, as when they burn cotton stalks; it looked as if there was a light mist. After sunset, the heaven remained red like fire. The sea, the rivers, the lakes, all began to fall, to fall; all fell at the same time, until there was not a drop of water remaining. Neither did the dew fall early in the morning to moisten the grass. Ah! I tell you, my friends, all animals found themselves in a great trouble. They were roaming about everywhere; their tongues were hanging out; they became thin, thin. — There was among them a doctor who was called Mr. Monkey; he was half wizard, half voudou. They said he knew a great deal, but he was a big talker, and did very little. He said to the other animals that it was because they had made so many sins that God sent them all these misfortunes to punish them; that if there were any among them who wanted to pay, he would pray to make the rain fall. He had already succeeded very often when he asked for something ; God in heaven always listened to *his* prayer. There was also a famous thief there; it was Mr. Fox, who ate all the chickens there were in the neighborhood. He said to the other animals : "Don't you listen to Dr. Monkey ; he is a d—— rascal ; he will take your money without giving you anything for it. I know him, he is a rascal ; you will have no rain at all ! It is better that we should dig a well ourselves. We need not count upon anything else. Let us go ! hurrah ! right off, if you are all like me, for I am very thirsty." Then Dr. Monkey told him : "I think indeed that you are hungry, you d—— pirate ; now that you have finished eating all the chickens there were here, you are coming to play the braggart here." Mr. Fox told him : "You are a liar ; you know very well that the owls, the polecats, and the weasels are eating all the chickens, and you come and say it is I. You know that if there is a thief here, it is you, you d—— prayer merchant." — All the other animals, tigers, lions, wolves, elephants, crocodiles, serpents, were running about to look for water. They had all assembled to hear the dispute of Dr. Monkey and Mr. Fox.

I must tell you that if a hog grunts, a dog barks, a wolf howls, a cow bellows, each kind of animal has its own language. A tiger or an elephant or a lion cannot speak the language of another animal, each one speaks his own language ; but when they are together, they all understand each other — the hog which grunts understands the dog which barks. It is not like us men; if a German comes to speak with a Frenchman or an American, he will not understand, any more than if an Englishman were to speak with a Spaniard who does not understand English. We men are obliged to learn the language of other nations, if we want to converse with them. Animals are not at all like that ; they understand each other as if they spoke the same language. Well, I must tell you that Mr. Fox pretended that if there was such a drought, the rain not having fallen for a year, so that all the grass was parched up, and the trees had lost their leaves, and there were neither flowers nor fruits, it was because there were no clouds in the heaven to give water, and not a prayer could make the rain fall. "All the water has gone into the ground ; we must dig a large well in order to have water to drink. Listen to me, my friends, and we shall find water."

Lion, who was the king, opened his mouth. He roared, the earth shook, he spoke so loud ! He beat his sides with his tail, and it made a noise like a big drum in a circus. All the other animals lay flat on the ground. He said : "By the very thunder, the first fellow who will speak to me about prayers, I shall give him something which will make him know me. I am a good fellow ; when did I ever eat another animal ? It is a lie, and I say that the little lawyer Fox is a fine little fellow. He is right, we must dig a well to have water immediately. Come here, Compair Bourriquet (Donkey), it is you who have the finest voice here; when you speak, it is like a soldier's trumpet. You will go everywhere to notify all animals that I, the king, I say that they must come to dig up and scratch the earth, that we may have water. And those that don't want to work, you will report them. You will come right off that I may compel them to do their share of the work or pay some other animal to do it."

Bourriquet was so glad he was to act as a newspaper, that he began to bray so loud that it was enough to render anybody deaf. — " Depart, depart," said the king, " or I shall strike you." Then Bourriquet reared, and thought he was doing something nice, he was so proud that the king had confidence in him, and then that gave him the opportunity to order the other animals to come, in the name of Lion, the king. On starting, he put down his head, then he kicked half a dozen times with both feet, and made a noise which was as if you were tearing up a piece of *cotonnade*. That is his way of saluting the company, when he is glad.

Now, all the animals which he met, he told them, that if they did not come immediately to dig up and scratch the ground to make a well, surely King Lion would eat them up. They were all so much afraid, that they all came, except Compair Lapin, who was gnawing a little piece of dry grass. — " Don't listen to what I tell you, remain there, and don't come right off, you will see what the king will do with you." — " I don't care a d—— for you and the king together; come both of you, you will see how I'll fix you. You may go to the devil. Do I drink? Where did I ever use water? Surely, that is something new to me. You are a fool, donkey that you are, I never drink, a rabbit never drinks. My father and my grandfather did not know how to drink, and as I am a real rabbit, I don't use water. Never did a rabbit have little ones without ears, you hear. If any one heard you he might believe that I am a bastard. Go away, you big ears; for if I take my whip, I shall show you your road, and make you trot faster than you ever galloped in your life. If you knew me as I know you, you would not have stopped here, surely."

Bourriquet saw that he could do nothing, so he went away; but he was not as proud as when he started to tell all animals that the king ordered them to come to work. As soon as he arrived near the king, he said : " Master, I went on all your errands, I saw all the animals in the world, only Compair Lapin does not want to listen to reason. He says he does not need water, let those who need it look for it. Besides, if you are not satisfied, he will make you trot. You have no right to command him, he is free, free as air; he has no master, none but God." — When the king heard that, he told Tiger, who was there, to go with the Bear to arrest Compair Lapin and bring him here. "Take care you don't eat him on the way, for if you do, I'll give you such a beating as you never had before. You hear? Well, go." — They started, and travelled a good while before they arrived. During this time, all the animals were working hard, each one had his share of the work, and they had even left a big piece as Compair Lapin's task and that of the two who had gone to arrest him. They looked everywhere: in the prairie, on the mountain; at last they fell on Compair Lapin, who was eating the root of a cocklebur which was full of water. You know that rabbits know how to dig up the earth and find water below, in the roots of plants.

At the same moment when they arrived near him, Compair Lapin was singing a little song which he had made about the king. He said in it that the king was a fool, and did not know how to govern, for his wife had many husbands, and he was laughing to himself, and that perhaps, after they finished to dig that well, the king would make all the animals pay taxes to drink the water from the well they had dug with their sweat. I am not so foolish, I am not going to work for that fellow! Let the others do it, if they are fools, I don't care any more for the king than a dog for Sunday. Tra la la, etc., . . . The tiger approached without making any noise, and then he said: "Good morning, Compair Lapin, I ask your pardon, if I disturb you, but I don't do it on purpose; the king has ordered me to arrest you, I must obey him. You know that the weak must submit to the strong; this is why I advise you not to resist, because the Bear and I will be obliged to eat you. Take my advice, come quietly, perhaps you will come out all right! Your mouth is honeyed, you will get Mr. Fox to defend you; he is a good little lawyer and does not charge dear! Come, let us go."

When Compair Lapin saw that he could not do otherwise, he let the officers of the king arrest him. They put a rope around his neck, and they started. When they were near the dwelling of the king, they met Dr. Monkey on the way. He said: "Compair Lapin, I think you are a pupil of Mr. Fox, you will have to pay for it; you are gone up, my old fellow. How are you now? Don't you feel something getting cold within you? That will teach you to read the newspaper and meddle in politics on Sundays, instead of going quietly to mass!"

Compair Lapin answered briefly: "I don't care a d—— for anything you say, old Monkey! And then, you know, he who must die, must submit to his fate. Just hush up, you rascal! You are trying to injure me, but perhaps you will be the loser ; I have not given up all hope ; perhaps, before long, you will be in trouble. Each one his chance, that is all I have to tell you." — At last they arrived at a big tree which had been thrown down by the wind, and where the king was seated. The Tiger and the Bear, the two officers who were leading Compair Lapin, said to the king : " Here is the fellow ! " — " Haw ! haw ! " said the king, " we shall judge him immediately." Mr. Fox came slyly behind Compair Lapin, and told him in his ears : " When they will ask you why you spoke badly of the king, say that it is not true, that it is Bourriquet who lied to do you harm. And then flatter the king very much, praise him and make him some presents, you will come out all right. If you do what I tell you, you will find it well for you. Otherwise, if you are foolish enough to say all there is in your heart, take care, you will come out all wrong. I assure you that the king will make hash with you." — " You need not be afraid, Mr. Fox, I know what I have to do ; I thank you for your good advice ; I am a lawyer myself."

Compair Lapin had suspected that they would come to arrest him ; he had spoken so badly of the king and the government. It is for that he had put on his best coat, and a big gold chain around his neck. He had said to one of his neighbors with whom he was quite intimate, and also with his wife and daughter, and who was called Compair Bouki, when the latter asked him where he was going so finely dressed : " Yes, Compair Bouki, I shall soon go to see the king ; and as it is the coat that makes the man, this is why I dressed so well. It always produces a good effect on proud and foolish people." When the king was ready to begin the case of Compair Lapin, he said to the policemen : " Bring the prisoner here to be judged."

Then Compair Lapin advanced, and said : " O Lion, my dear Master, you sent for me ; here I am. What do you want ? "

The Lion said : " I have to condemn you, because you are always slandering me, and besides, you don't want to work to dig the well, which we are making to drink. Everybody is working except you, and when I sent Bourriquet to get you, you said to him that I was a scoundrel, and that you would whip me ! You will know that if your back has tasted of the whip, I have never been whipped ; even my late mother did not dare to touch me ! What do you have to say? You rascal with the long ears hanging down. I suppose they are so long, because the hounds have chased you so often. Speak right off, or I shall mash you, like a too ripe persimmon."

Compair Lapin kept quite cool ; he knew that all that was a big wind that would bring neither rain nor thunder. He rubbed his nose with both paws, then he shook his ears, he sneezed, and then he sat down and said : " The king is justice on earth — as God is

just in his holy Paradise! Great king, you who are more brave
than all of us together, you will hear the truth. When you sent
Bourriquet to get me, he who is more of a donkey than all the donkeys in the world, when he came to my house, I was sick. I told
him : ' you will tell the king that I am very sorry that I cannot come
now, but here is a fine gold chain, which you will present to the king
for me, and you will tell him that I have forty twelve other animals to
work in my place. Because that is too necessary a thing to get a well ;
it is life or death for us, and we cannot do without it. Tell him
also that there is but a great king like him to have such an idea, and
enough brains to save us all !' What do you think he answered me?
He replied that he did not care about a gold chain, that he did not
eat that. If I had given him a basket of corn or some hay, he would
have eaten it, but as to the chain, perhaps the king would hitch him
up to the plough with that same chain, and he would be sorry to
have brought it. When he went away, he said to me : ' Go on, papa,
I shall arrive before you, you will know that the ox which is ahead
always drinks clear water !' I suppose he meant that he would speak
before I should have the chance to be heard ! As I want the king to
believe that I am not telling stories, I have a witness who was there,
who heard all our conversation. If the king will have the kindness
to listen to his testimony, he will hear the same thing I have just
told him." Compair Lapin bowed to the king, and put the gold
chain around Lion's neck, and then he sat down on one side smiling,
he was so sure that his gift would produce a good effect and help
him to come out all right from his trouble. Now, Lion said to Mr.
Fox to speak quickly. " I know all that business, and if you
come here to lie, I 'll break your neck. You need not wag your tail
and make such grimaces, as if you were eating ants. Come on,
hurry ! I have no time." " Dear Master Lion," said the Fox, " I
shall tell you how all that happened : Compair Lapin, whom you see
here, is the best friend you have. The proof of it is that he brought
a big chain to make you a present. You will never see a Bourriquet
do that ; that is sure, because there is not in the world a greater
clown than those donkeys. Dan Rice took twenty-one years to train
a donkey ! He says that for $100,000 he would not undertake again
such a job. He would prefer to train fifty twelve thousand Lions,
because they would eat him up, or he would do something good with
them. Well, I must tell you, Mr. Lion, you, who are the king of all
animals, that same Bourriquet, whom you sent to represent you,
came to lie on you, and as to Compair Lapin, he is as white as snow!
Although Dr. Monkey has your confidence, it is he who is governing
secretly and advising all your people, and putting them in rebellion
against you, the king, to establish another government, where that

same Dr. Monkey and Bourriquet will govern in your place, when they will succeed in putting you out. That is what they have been trying to do for a long time, and that is what Compair Lapin and I wanted to tell you."

When the king heard that, he said : " That is all right ; I am glad you told me so. You can go with Compair Lapin, I acquit him." But while they were hearing the case, Dr. Monkey and Bourriquet thought that it was not healthy for them to remain there, so they escaped when they saw that the wrong side was being warmed up ; they vanished, and no one knew where they had gone, so well were they hidden. After that Compair Lapin and Mr. Fox both re-mained in the same parish where the king resided. Mr. Fox was his deputy or chief clerk, and the other was mate; that is to say, he commanded the others and made them work to finish digging the well with their paws. At last the well was completed ! All the ani-mals drank, and they became strong again. The lioness recovered her health also, and some time after that she gave birth to twelve little cubs as yellow as gold, and all as pretty as could be. The king was so glad that he pardoned all that were in the penitentiary, and he allowed the exiles to return. When he granted their pardon, he told them all to go and drink the water of the well. Then you may im-agine that Dr. Monkey with his accomplice Bourriquet came out of their hole to mingle with the others. But they began to spy and to watch all that was being done or said. One day they met Mr. Fox who was speaking of the government affairs in order to increase the tax. He and Compair Lapin found that there was not enough money in the treasury for them to become rich quickly. When Dr. Monkey saw them both together, he began to smile. He came near them, he bowed and said : " Let us forget what has passed, we must not be looking for those old papers. Let us be friends and live quietly like good neighbors." You might have thought they were the best friends when they parted. Dr. Monkey said to his partner Bourri-quet : " You see these two fellows Compair Lapin and Mr. Fox, they are d—— scoundrels. I must get the best of them, or they will beat me ; that is all I know ! " As Compair Lapin had said, when they judged him, that he never drank water, the king had told him : " Take care that you never try to drink water from this well ; I want to see if you say the truth, and I order every one to watch you."

You will not believe me when I tell you that it is true that rabbits never drink water, there is always enough water for them in the grass which they eat. But expressly because they had forbidden Compair Lapin to drink from that well, he wished to do it. All the other animals praised that water so highly : it was so clear, so good. That gave him such a thirst, that he felt at every moment as if he

had eaten well-peppered salt meat. He said to himself: "I don't
care a d—— I shall drink, and I shall see who is going to prevent me.
Besides, if they catch me, I shall always have the daughter of the
king to protect me. She will find some way of preventing them from
troubling me, for she has much influence with her father." He did
as he said; every evening he drank his fill. But at last he wanted
to drink in the daytime also. It was a strange well; its water was
not like any other water; it made people drunk like whiskey, only,
instead of making you sick after you were drunk, it made you much
stronger than before, and they were beginning to perceive that all
those who were old were growing young again. Even the vegetables
which you watered with it, if you cut them, the next day they would
grow as fine as the day before.

When Compair Lapin began to see the effect of that water, he
said: " I must have some for the day also, it does me a great deal of
good; and as I am much older than the daughter of the king, I must
become as young as she. Let me be, I shall arrange it. Don't you
say anything." Well, when it was dark, he took his little calabash,
which contained about two bottles of water, he went to the well, and
filled it up. But he was so careful that the guard, which they put
every evening near the well, saw nothing.

Dr. Monkey and Bourriquet watched all the time, because they
could not forget how Compair Lapin had treated them whilst he was
being judged. Therefore, they had sworn that they would catch
him. But in spite of all their efforts, they lost their trouble and
their time. At last, one day, Dr. Monkey went to see Bourriquet,
his comrade, and told him : " Come to my house, I have something
to show to you." He showed him Ti Bonhomme Godron (a man
made of tar), and said : " It is with that I want to catch the fellow ;
as this time I shall be able to prove that he is guilty, we shall have
all his money, which the king will confiscate to give us for discovering all his rascalities."

They took Ti Bonhomme Godron ; they put him in a little path,
where Compair Lapin was obliged to pass, very near the water, and
then they started ; they knew it was not necessary to watch ; Ti
Bonhomme Godron would attend to him without needing anybody's
help. I know not if Compair Lapin suspected something, but he
came quite late that evening. He never came at the same hour,
but he managed things so well that he always got his water, and no
one could catch him. When he arrived the evening they had placed
Bonhomme Godron there, he saw something black. He looked at it
for a long time, he had never seen anything like that before ! He
went back immediately, and went to bed. The next evening he came
again, advanced a little closer, looked for a long time, and shook his

head. At that moment, a frog jumped in the water : *tchoappe.* Compair Lapin flattened on the ground, as if crushed, and in two jumps he reached his house. He remained three days without returning, and Dr. Monkey and Bourriquet were beginning to despair, and to believe that it was true that Compair Lapin did not drink at all. But it was enough for this one that it was forbidden for him to be still more anxious to drink. " Oh ! well," said he ; " I don't care ! I have some money here, but the remainder is hidden in the briars. If they catch me, I shall pay the police, and they will let me go. Besides, I have the protection of the daughter of the king ; every night, she comes to see me. It would be very strange if she did nothing for me. Besides, I have always instructed the police to let go a man who had money, and I suppose that they will make no exception for me, for they would lose the money which I would give them."

This reassured him. He started in the evening ; it was a beautiful moonlight night, and every one was out late promenading. It was the end of spring : the honeysuckle perfumed the air, the mocking-bird was singing in the pecan-tree, there was a light breeze, which caused the leaves of the trees to dance, and the rustle prevented any one to hear him walk. Everybody was in bed ; only the dogs, from time to time, were barking at the big clouds, which were fleeing before the wind. " It is my turn now ; I, Compair Lapin, I am going to drink, but a drink that will count." He took his calabash. When he arrived at the place where Bonhomme Godron was, the old fellow was still there. It had been warm during the day, and the tar was soft. When Compair Lapin arrived there, he said : " Hum, hum, you have been long enough in my way. I do not come to drink ; that is a thing which I never do ; I want to take a bath to-night ; get away from here." " You don't want to answer ? I tell you that I want to take a bath, you black scoundrel." Bonhomme Godron did not reply ; that made Compair Lapin angry. He gave him a slap, his hand remained glued. " Let me go, or I shall strike you with the other hand." Bonhomme Godron did not reply. He struck him *cam* with the other hand ; it remained stuck also ! " I 'll kick you, d—— rascal, if you don't let me go." One foot remained stuck, and then the other one.

Then he said : " You are holding me that they might injure me, you want to try to rob me, but stop, you will see what I am going to do to you. Let me go, or I shall strike you with my head and break your mouth ! " As he said that, he struck, and a mule could not hit harder, he was so mad. His head, however, my dear friends, remained stuck also. He was caught, well caught. At daybreak, Dr. Monkey and Bourriquet arrived. When they saw Compair Lapin there, they laughed, they cursed him. They took a cart to bring him to prison, and all along the way they told the people how they had put a trap to catch the most famous rascal there was in the universe. It was the famous Compair Lapin who had so sullied the reputation of the king's daughter, that there was not a great prince who wanted to marry Miss Léonine, as Compair Lapin had spoken so much about his being her lover. Mr. Fox, who was passing, heard all the bad things which Dr. Monkey and Bourriquet were saying about Compair Lapin, and he replied : " Yes, it is true, there is nothing like a thief to catch another thief."

When they were taking Compair Lapin to prison, all who passed on the road threw bricks at him, and they made a true clown of him. When he arrived in the presence of the king, the latter said to him : " Now, I would like to hear what you can say to get out of this scrape." Compair Lapin replied : " When the tree falls, the goat climbs on it ! I know I can die but once, I don't care. If it is my money they want, I assure you that they will never see it. When I was free, never Bourriquet and Dr. Monkey tried to quarrel with me ; the wild hog knows on what tree he must rub himself. I assure you that they are famous rascals." — " You must not speak in that way before the king, but the king will try your case in a few minutes." — " What I say is well said ; I am ready to hear the judgment." — After the king and his friends had consulted together, they found Compair Lapin *guilty* and they condemned him to death. They ordered that he be put in prison until they could find an executioner willing to execute him. The king thought that he would get rid of a fellow who was too cunning for him, and then he would take vengeance on Compair Lapin, because he had injured Miss Léonine's character in such a manner that it was a scandal.

While Compair Lapin was in prison, he was thinking how he would manage to escape forever. He thought that he was in a worse plight than he had ever been before. He said to himself : " By Jove ! that is no child's play ; I think that I am gone up. Well, as I am tired, let me sleep a little : it will do me good." He lay down on the floor, and, soon after, he was snoring. He began to dream that the beautiful Léonine, the daughter of the king, was making a sign to him to tell him he need not be afraid, that she would fix everything all right. He awoke contented, and at daybreak the jailer opened the door of his prison and said to him : " They have found an executioner willing to execute you, but before that, they must cut off your ears ; it is Bourriquet who has offered his services to send you in the other world. Take courage, my old fellow, I am sorry for you, you are a good fellow, but you risked your life too often. You know that an ounce of prevention is better than a pound of cure ; now it is too late. Good-bye, comrade." At the same moment the sheriff came with his deputies to take him to the place of execution. — They arrived at the steep bank of a little river. There were tall trees, grass, and briars everywhere. They chose a clear space. When they arrived, there was a big crowd : gentlemen, ladies, many children. All had come to see how they were going to kill Compair Lapin. The king was there with all his family. Miss Léonine, the daughter of the king, was there also. Oh ! but she was so beautiful with her curls, which shone like gold in the sun. She had a muslin dress as white as snow with a blue sash, and a crown of roses on her head. The eyes of all were turned towards her ; she was so pretty that they forgot completely Compair Lapin, who was trembling like a leaf. Yes, indeed, he was sorry to leave such a large fortune and such a beautiful wife as the king's daughter. What pained him the most was to think that perhaps Dr. Monkey or Bourriquet would marry Miss Léonine as soon as he would be dead, because they both boasted that Compair Lapin was in their way. Without him, they said they would have succeeded long ago.

Now the king said : " Well, let us put an end to all this ; advance, Bourriquet, and read Compair Lapin his sentence." The king allowed him to choose his death, as he pleased : to be drowned in the river, burnt alive, or hung on a tree, or to have his neck cut with a sword. " Yes, yes," said Compair Lapin, "all that at once, or one after the other, if that pleases you so much that I should die, well, I am very glad. Only, I was afraid that you would throw me in those great thorns, that would tear my skin and I would suffer too much, and then, the snakes and the wasps would sting me. Oh ! no, not that, not that at all ! " Tell the king to do all except throwing me in those briars ; for the love of God, who is in Heaven, and who will judge you as you judge me ! " " Haw ! haw ! you are afraid of the thorns ? We want to see you suffer, suffer, you scoundrel." — They were making such a noise that the king said : " What is the matter ? " He came closer, accompanied by his daughter, Miss Léonine, who had come to see if Compair Lapin was going to die bravely ; that is to say, every one thought so, but she had come to encourage him and reassure him, because she had sent word to him secretly, while he was in prison, that even if the rope was around his neck, she, Miss Léonine, would arrive in time to take it off and save him, because she loved him more than anything in the world.

They related to the king and to Miss Léonine what Compair Lapin had said, and how much afraid he was to be thrown in the thorns and to suffer. Miss Léonine came forward and said : " Papa, I have a favor to ask you : I know that you hate Compair Lapin, and I also, because he has sullied my name. Well, I want to make you all see that what they said is not true. I want to see him suffer for all his stories ; we must get rid of him, and I ask you to throw him in the briars and let him rot there ; it is good enough for such a rascal." All clapped their hands, they were so glad. "Throw him in the briars; it is there indeed we must throw him," said the king ; "he must suffer. Quick ! Hurry !" — They took Compair Lapin by each limb, they swung him once ; poor devil, he was crying: "No, no, not in the briars, in fire, cut my neck, not in the briars." They said : "Twice" — *Vap !* they threw him in a great bunch of thorns.

As Compair Lapin fell in his native country, he sat down, he rubbed his nose, shook his ears, and then he said : "Thank you, all of you ; I thought you were stupid, but it is here my mother made me ; I am at home here, and not one of you can come here to catch me. Good-by, I know where I am going." Miss Léonine also was very glad ; she knew where she would meet Compair Lapin that very evening. That proves one thing to you, that Compair Lapin was a hypocrite and pleaded false things to know the truth. It proves another thing, that when a woman loves a man, she will do all he wishes, and the woman will do all in her power to save him, and in whatever place the man may be, the woman will go to meet him. This is why they say that what a woman wants, God wants also.

As I was there when all that happened, they sent me here to relate it to you. I have finished.

Compair Bouki and Compair Lapin. — No. 1.

One day, Compair Bouqui met Compair Lapin. "How," said he, "is that you? Don't you know that it is to-day that all persons are selling their mothers to have something to eat ?" — "Ah ! yes," said Compair Lapin, "I, also, am going to get my mother, and I shall sell her for a kettle of hominy and one of gombo." Now both of them started. Compair Bouqui tied his mother with a rope, and during that time Compair Lapin tied his with a cobweb. Before he entered the cart, he said : "Now, mamma, as soon as you will arrive near the briars you will jump down and run to the house." Compair Bouqui sold his mother, and returned in his cart with his kettle of hominy and his kettle of gombo. While he was on his way home, he saw a rabbit lying in the road, and a little further, another rabbit. He advanced a little more, and there was another rabbit. When he came to the third rabbit, he said : "It is not possible, those rabbits are dying of hunger instead of selling their mothers to get something to eat ; let me get down to catch them." He was not able to catch anything, because it was Compair Lapin who pretended to be dead, to make Compair Bouqui leave his cart. During that time, Compair Lapin ran to the cart of Compair Bouqui, stole his two kettles, cut the tail of his horse, planted it in the ground, and, taking the cart away, went to hide himself. Compair Bouqui came back to look for his cart, but he only saw the tail of his horse planted in the ground. He began to dig in the ground, as he thought that his horse and his cart had fallen in a hole, and he called for help. Tiger came out of the woods, and helped Compair Bouqui to dig. Compair Bouqui found Tiger so fat that he bit him on his back, and escaped. Tiger asked Compair Lapin what he could do to take vengeance on Compair Bouqui. Compair Lapin said : " We must give a grand ball, come this evening to my house." Tiger and Compair Lapin engaged good musicians and invited many persons. Compair Lapin came out on the gallery, and began to sing :

> " Come to the grand ball,
> Those that lost their wives,
> Beautiful negresses from Senegal."

Compair Bouqui, who heard that, ran to Compair Lapin and cried out : " It is my wife, it is not necessary to invite any more people." But Compair Lapin pretended not to hear, and he beat his drum, and sang : " Simion, carillon painpain, Simion, carillon painpain." Compair Bouqui entered Compair Lapin's cabin, and he took Tiger for a woman, because he had hidden his beard and dressed like a young lady. When the ball was over, Compair Bouqui remained alone with Tiger, who gave him a good beating and ran off with Compair Lapin. Now that is not all : Tiger and Compair Lapin did not know where Compair Bouqui was. When Compair Lapin came near his cabin, he cried out : " Good night, my cabin, good, night," and he said : " That is strange, my cabin, which always replies, says nothing to-day." Compair Bouqui, who was not at all cunning, answered : Good night, my master, good night." "Ah ! we have him," said Compair Lapin, " get some fire, we are going to give some smoke to Compair Bouqui, in this cabin." They burned poor Compair Bouqui, and Compair Lapin was so glad that he jumped like a kid and sang :

> " Aïe, aïe, aïe, Compair Lapin,
> He is a little animal that knows how to jump."

Compair Bouki and Compair Lapin. — No. 2.

One day, Compair Bouqui went to see Compair Lapin. When he entered the cabin, he saw a big pot, which was on the fire, and it smelt so good that Compair Bouqui could not stay quiet. When the food was cooked, Compair Bouqui had also his share and he found it so good that he kept on bothering Compair Lapin to know where he took such good meat. —" Pray, Compair Lapin, tell me where you find that meat." — " No, Compair Bouqui, you are too greedy." — " Compair Lapin, my poor children are dying of hunger, tell me where you find that meat." — " No, Compair Bouqui, you are too rascally."

At last, he bothered Compair Lapin so much, so much, that Compair Lapin said : " Listen, Compair Bouqui, I am going to tell you, but you must not tell any one, and you must do as I tell you. You know the king's ox, which is in the pasture, and which is so fat, well, you will take a bag and a knife, you will watch when he will open his mouth to eat, you will jump in his throat, and when you will arrive in his belly, you will begin to cut the meat to put in your bag. Now, be very careful not to cut near his heart, because you would kill him. When he will open his mouth again to eat, you will jump out and run home. Don't you let any one see you." The next morning, Compair Bouqui took his bag and his knife and ran into the pasture. When the king's ox opened his mouth to eat, he jumped into his belly, and he began to cut the meat and to put it into his bag. The more he cut, the closer he came to the heart of the ox. He saw that the meat was so fine and fat, that he said to himself : " What will it matter, if I cut a little piece, that will not kill him." He took his knife, he cut a piece, lo ! the ox of the king fell down dead, and Compair Bouqui could not come out of his belly.

All the people came to see what had happened, how the ox that was so fine had died like that. They said: "We must open him to see what was the matter with him." When they did that, what did they see? Compair Bouqui. "Ah! Compair Bouqui, it is you who killed the ox of the king, you wanted to steal meat, just wait, we are going to fix you."—They took Compair Bouqui, they opened his belly, they took out his bowels, they filled him with sand, and they closed the opening with a cork. When Compair Bouqui returned home he was very much ashamed. His children ran to see the good meat which he had brought.—"Papa, give us some meat."—"There is none, my children."—"Yes, papa, something smells good on you." The little ones advanced, and Compair Bouqui backed, backed. The children commenced to smell the cork; they found it smelt good, because there was honey on it. They began to suck the cork, to suck the cork. Lo! the cork came out; all the sand ran out, Compair Bouqui died on the spot. He was flat on the ground.

Compair Bouki and Compair Lapin. — No. 3.

One day the children of Compair Bouki met those of Compair Lapin, who had on fine Sunday dresses and new shoes. When the little Boukis returned home, they asked their father why he did not give them fine clothes like those of Compair Lapin's children. Compair Bouki went to see Compair Lapin, and asked him where he took the fine things he had given to his children. Compair Lapin did not want to reply, but Compair Bouki annoyed him so much that he said to him: "Go and cut wood in the forest; and when you will be tired, look in the centre of the forest, and you will see a big tree. Go to sleep under it, and when you will awake, say: 'Tree, how sweet you are!' The tree will say: 'If I were to open, what would you say?' You will reply: 'If you open, I shall be very glad.' When the tree will open, enter into it; it will close up, and you will see many pretty things. Take what you want, and tell the tree: 'Open!' when you will wish to depart." Compair Bouki did what Compair Lapin had said, but when he saw all there was in the tree, he wanted to take so many things that he forgot to say: "Tree, open!"

The tree belonged to some thieves, who hid their booty in it. They came back in the woods, and they found Compair Bouki, who was stealing their goods. ᷁ I need not tell you that they gave Compair Bouki such a beating that he could not move.

Compair Bouki and Compair Lapin. — No. 4.

Compair Bouki and Compair Lapin went together to pay a visit to some young ladies. While they were speaking, Compair Lapin said to the young ladies: "You see Compair Bouki; he is not a person, he is a horse which my father has left me." The young ladies said: "Oh! no, we cannot believe that." Now Compair Lapin returned home; and when came the day appointed for the visit to the young ladies, he dressed up fine, and covered his clothes with a hog's skin. When Compair Bouki came in, he said: "Are you ready, Compair?" Compair Lapin replied: "But no, don't you see how I am covered up? I feel cold, and I am suffering so much from my feet that I don't know how I am going to do to walk." Compair Bouki, who was always so stupid, said: "Mount on my back, and when you will be near the house of the young ladies, you will get down." Compair Lapin said: "I don't know if I shall be able to mount on your back, but I shall try." Without Compair Bouki's seeing it, Compair Lapin put on his spurs and mounted on Bouki's back. While he was on Compair Bouki's back, Compair Lapin was all the time moving. His friend asked him what was the matter. "I am suffering so much that I know not how to sit." Compair Lapin said that, but he was trying to shake off his hog's skin.

When they arrived near the house of the young ladies, Compair Lapin stuck Compair Bouki, with his spurs, and Compair Bouki started running. Compair Lapin jumped down, and went into the house of the young ladies, to whom he said: "You see that I was right when I told you that Compair Bouki was a horse which my father had left me."

Compair Bouki and Compair Lapin.— No. 5.

One day, quite early, Compair Lapin arose, and he felt hunger gaining upon him. He looked everywhere in the cabin; he found nothing to eat. He ran towards Compair Bouki. When he arrived, he saw Compair Bouki, who was gnawing a bone. — Eh! Compair Bouki, I had come to take breakfast with you; but I see that you don't have anything famous to give me. — Times are hard, Compair Lapin; there are no more rations in the cabin; only this bone left. Compair Lapin reflected a little. — Well! Compair Bouki, if you wish, we shall go hunting for the eggs of the tortoise. — Agreed upon! let us go right off. Compair Bouki took his basket and his hoe, and they started towards the bayou in the woods. — Compair Lapin, I don't often go hunting for tortoise eggs; I don't know well how to find them. — Don't trouble yourself, Compair Bouki, I find all the time a place where tortoises lay their eggs. You, you will dig them up.

When they arrived at the bayou, Compair Lapin walked slowly, looking well on this side and on that side. Soon he came to a dead stop. — Compair Bouki, the tortoise thinks she is cunning. She scratches the ground with her big paw, and she lays her eggs in a hole; then she puts a little sand on them, and then she scatters leaves on her nest. You see this hillock? Take off the leaves, and scratch with your hoe; sure you will find eggs. Compair Bouki did what Compair Lapin told him, and they saw a pile of eggs shining in that hole. — Compair Lapin, you are more cunning than I; I am very glad to have you for my friend. Compair Lapin shared the eggs; he gave half to Compair Bouki. — Compair Bouki, I am very hungry; I am going to eat my eggs immediately. — Do as you want, Compair Lapin; I shall take mine to my wife to have them cooked.

They went on a long time still, and they found many eggs. Compair Lapin always ate his; Compair Bouki did not like raw eggs; he put them all in his basket. — Compair Bouki, I am beginning to be tired; I believe it is time for us to return home. — I have enough eggs for to-day, Compair Lapin; let us go back. — As they were going towards the river, Compair Lapin said to himself: Compair Bouki does not know how to find tortoise eggs; it is I who found them; they ought all to belong to me. I must make some trick to gain them. — As they were nearly arrived at the river, Compair Lapin said: Compair Bouki, I forgot to take some eggs for my old mother. You would be very kind to lend me a dozen. I shall return them to you another time. — Compair Bouki gave a dozen, and they went each on his way. Compair Lapin went to put his dozen of eggs in his cabin, then he went to Compair Bouki's. When he came near the cabin of Compair Bouki he began to complain, and to hold his belly with both hands. Compair Bouki came out. — What is the matter with you, Compair Lapin? You don't look very well. — Oh! no, Compair Bouki, those eggs have poisoned me.

I beg of you; quick, run to gét the doctor. — I shall run as fast as I can, daddy. As soon as Compair Bouki started, Compair Lapin went to the kitchen and fell to eating tortoise eggs. — Thank you, great Lord, I shall eat my belly full to-day. The physician lives far, I have the time to eat all before they come.

When Compair Lapin had nearly finished eating the eggs, he heard Compair Bouki speaking outside. — Doctor Monkey, I am very glad that I met you on the road; my friend is very sick. — Compair Lapin did not lose any time; he opened the window and jumped out. Compair Bouki came into the cabin; he did not see Compair Lapin. He ran into the kitchen; the shells of the eggs were scattered all about. Compair Lapin was already in the fields. Compair Bouki tore his hair, he was so angry. He started to run after Compair Lapin. Compair Lapin had eaten so many eggs, that he was not able to run fast. When he saw Compair Bouki was pressing him too close, he hid in a hole in a tree.

Compair Bouki called Compair Torti, who was passing on the road. — Compair Torti, pray come to watch Compair Lapin, who stole all your eggs. I am going to get my axe to cut down this tree. — Go quickly, Compair Bouki ; I shall watch the rascal well. When Compair Bouki stàrted, Compair Lapin said : Compair Torti, look in this hole ; you will see if I have your eggs. Compair Torti lifted his head ; Compair Lapin sent some decayed wood in his eyes. Compair Torti went to wash his eyes in the bayou ; Compair Lapin ran off immediately. Compair Bouki came to cut the tree ; he saw that Compair Lapin had already run away. He was so angry he went to Compair Torti, on the bank of the bayou, and he cut off his tail with his axe. — It is for this reason that the tail of the tortoise is so short to this very day.

Compair Bouki and Compair Lapin. — No. 6.

One day, Compair Bouki, who was dying of hunger, went to see his old friend, Compair Lapin. He found him thinking of nothing, and occupied in cleaning some fish. Bouki asked where he had taken that. His old friend related his story to him. He told him : " You see, daddy, I went to watch for the fish cart on the road. I saw it coming ; I lay down in the road, as if I was dead. The master of the cart came down right off to pick me off. He shook me up a little ; and after that, he threw me in his cart, on a pile of fish. I did not move my feet, like Mr. Fox. I watched well the old master, until I saw he had forgotten me. I began quietly to throw all the fish in the road until we had nearly gone a mile further ; then, when I thought I had enough, I jumped down and picked up all the fish which I had thrown in the road. There were one hundred or a thousand — I did not count ; I was in such a hurry. I put them all by myself on my back, faster than I could ; and I came straight here to eat them." Compair Bouki reflected a long while ; he was a little afraid that if he tried to do the same thing, he would put himself again in trouble. Compair Lapin, who was looking at him with his good eyes, saw that his friend was reflecting too long. He told him : " Old friend, you are dying of hunger ; do like me ; go and watch for the cart on the road, steal as much as you can, and we shall have a grand festival."

Old Bouki, who was greedy, could not resist ; he started, he lay down on the road as if he was dead for true, he lifted his feet in the air to deceive people better. When the master of the cart came very near, he saw old Bouki, who was playing his tricks to catch him. He came down with a big plantation whip, and gave him a whipping which had red pepper, black pepper, and salt, it burned so much. Compair Bouki remained one month in his bed after that. He did not have a single feather left, and had colics to his very beak. They gave him a great deal of tafia to give him strength ; they put him in a large bath made with gombo, and they made him drink some laurel tea all the time after that. When Compair Bouki was cured, he swore, but too late, that Compair Lapin would never deceive him again.

> All the goats which are not rascals,
> Ought to fear the old rabbits.
>
> MAN HENRIETTE.

Ein Vié Zombi Malin. — The Cunning Old Wizard.

There was once a prince who was very rich. One day the princess, his daughter, lost a big diamond. While she was crying for her jewel, an old man came to the palace, and said that he was a wizard. The prince promised that he would give him anything he would ask, if he would say where was the diamond. The wizard only asked for three meals, and promised to find the jewel. They gave him an excellent breakfast, and when he had eaten all, he said : " One is taken." The servants of the prince began to tremble, because it was they who had stolen the diamond. After his dinner, the wizard said : " Two are taken." The servants trembled still more. After supper, the wizard said : " Three are taken." When they heard that, the three thieves fell on their knees before the wizard, and said that they would give back the diamond, if he promised to say nothing to their master.

Now the wizard took the diamond, rolled it up in a piece of bread, and threw it before a turkey in the yard. The turkey gobbled up the bread with the diamond. The wizard went to get the prince and his daughter, and told them that the diamond was in the turkey's stomach, and that they would find it, on killing the turkey. That was done, and the diamond was found. The prince was very glad, and said that the old man was the greatest wizard in the world. — At the court everybody was admiring the wizard, but a few young men were not sure that he was a true wizard, and they wanted to catch him. They caught a cricket in the grass, they put it in a box, and they asked the wizard to tell them what there was in the box. The old man did not know, and he said to himself : " Well, Cricket, you are caught." His name was Cricket, but the people there did not know that, and they thought that the wizard had guessed that there was a cricket in the box. Therefore, the old man passed for a great wizard, and they gave him many good things : and yet he was merely cunning, and had had luck.

Choal Djé (The Horse of God).

Choal Djé had a pond, and he allowed all the comrades to drink from it, except Compair Lapin and his comrades. One day he caught Compair Lapin near his pond. " If I catch you drinking from my pond, I shall make you pay a fine." Compair Lapin replied: " Well-ordained charity begins with one's self, and as you are the master I am not going to drink from your pond." But one day they killed a deer, and after having skinned it, they threw away the skin. Compair Lapin picked up the skin and passed his head in it; he then went to drink in Choal Djé's pond. When Choal Djé saw that, he advanced nearer and asked Compair Chévreil who it was that had marked him in that way. Compair Chévreil answered: " It is Compair Lapin who made the sign of the cross on me, and who put me in this condition, and if you don't let him drink in your pond, he will do the same thing with you." — " Well, you may tell Compair Lapin that he can come to drink in my pond with all his comrades. I don't want him to do the same thing with me." — Compair Lapin ran to his house, took off the skin, and came back with his comrades to drink in Choal Djé's pond. When Choal Djé saw him coming, he said to him: " Drink as much as you want, Compair Lapin, with your comrades." — Compair Lapin was always more cunning than everybody else.

Ein Fame ki tournin Macaque. — A Woman changed into a Monkey.

There was once a gentleman who had a field of peanuts. Every day he saw that some one was eating a row of peanuts. He asked his wife who was eating his peanuts. His wife said it was his brother who was eating them every day. He then caught hold of the little boy and gave him a good beating. The next day he saw another row of peanuts had been eaten. He seized the little boy and gave him another beating. The little boy said, "That is too much; my brother is always beating me; I must make him see that it is his wife who is eating his peanuts." The next day he did not carry his brother's dinner in the field, but he told him to come to the house, and he would show him who was eating his peanuts. When they came in, his wife approached to serve the dinner, and now the little boy began to sing : "Tou man, — tou mangé tou, tou man, tou mangé tou." The woman said : "Why are you singing that ? I don't want you to sing that, sing something else." — "No, that is what I want to sing." He continued to sing, and they saw the woman begin to scratch, begin to jump, and at last she became a monkey. She ran into the peanut field, and she ate a whole row. "You see," said the little boy, "that it is not I who eat your peanuts ; it is your wife who, every day, becomes a monkey." The gentleman advanced with a stick, but the monkey ran into the woods and climbed upon a tree.

The Talking Eggs.[1]

There was once a lady who had two daughters ; they were called Rose and Blanche. Rose was bad, and Blanche was good; but the mother liked Rose better, although she was bad, because she was her very picture. She would compel Blanche to do all the work, while Rose was seated in her rocking-chair. One day she sent Blanche to the well to get some water in a bucket. When Blanche arrived at the well, she saw an old woman, who said to her : "Pray, my little one, give me some water ; I am very thirsty." "Yes, aunt," said Blanche, "here is some water ;" and Blanche rinsed her bucket, and gave her good fresh water to drink. "Thank you, my child, you are a good girl ; God will bless you."

A few days after, the mother was so bad to Blanche that she ran away into the woods. She cried, and knew not where to go, because she was afraid to return home. She saw the same old woman, who was walking in front of her. "Ah ! my child, why are you crying ? What hurts you ?" "Ah, aunt, mamma has beaten me, and I am afraid to return to the cabin." "Well, my child, come with me ; I will give you supper and a bed ; but you must promise me not to laugh at anything which you will see." She took Blanche's hand, and they began to walk in the wood. As they advanced, the bushes of thorns opened before them, and closed behind their backs. A little further on, Blanche saw two axes, which were fighting ; she found that very strange, but she said nothing. They walked further, and behold ! it was two arms which were fighting ; a little further, two legs ; at last, she saw two heads which were fighting, and which said : "Blanche, good morning, my child ; God will help you." At last they arrived at the cabin of the old woman, who said to Blanche : "Make some fire, my child, to cook the supper ;" and she sat down near the fireplace, and took off her head. She placed it on her knees, and began to louse herself. Blanche found that very strange ;. she was afraid, but she said nothing. The old woman put back her head in its place and gave Blanche a large bone to put on the fire for their supper. Blanche put the bone in the pot. Lo ! in a moment the pot was full of good meat.

She gave Blanche a grain of rice to pound with the pestle, and thereupon the mortar became full of rice. After they had taken their supper, the old woman said to Blanche : "Pray, my child, scratch my back." Blanche scratched her back, but her hand was all cut, because the old woman's back was covered with broken glass. When she saw that Blanche's hand was bleeding, she only blew on it, and the hand was cured.

When Blanche got up the next morning, the old woman said to her : "You must go home now, but as you are a good girl I want to make you a present of the talking eggs. Go to the chicken-house ; all the eggs which say 'Take me,' you must take them ; all those which will say 'Do not take me,' you must not take. When you will be on the road, throw the eggs behind your back to break them."

As Blanche walked, she broke the eggs. Many pretty things came out of those eggs. It was now diamonds, now gold, a beautiful carriage, beautiful dresses. When she arrived at her mother's, she had so many fine things that the house was full of them. Therefore her mother was very glad to see her. The next day, she said to Rose : "You must go to the woods to look for this same old woman ; you must have fine dresses like Blanche."

Rose went to the woods, and she met the old woman, who told her to come to her cabin ; but when she saw the axes, the arms, the legs, the heads, fighting, and the old woman taking off her head to louse herself, she began to laugh and to ridicule everything she saw. Therefore the old woman said : "Ah ! my child, you are not a good girl ; God will punish you." The next day she said to Rose : "I don't want to send you back with nothing ; go to the chicken-house, and take the eggs which say 'Take me.'"

Rose went to the chicken-house. All the eggs began to say: "Take me," "Don't take me;" "Take me," "Don't take me." Rose was so bad that she said: "Ah, yes, you say 'Don't take me,' but you are precisely those I want." She took all the eggs which said "Don't take me," and she went away with them.

As she walked, she broke the eggs, and there came out a quantity of snakes, toads, frogs, which began to run after her. There were even a quantity of whips, which whipped her. Rose ran and shrieked. She arrived at her mother's so tired that she was not able to speak. When her mother saw all the beasts and the whips which were chasing her, she was so angry that she sent her away like a dog, and told her go to live in the woods.

Grease.

There was once a lady who had four daughters. They were so pretty that everybody wanted to marry them. They were called La Graisse, Dépomme, Banane, and Pacane. La Graisse was the prettiest, but she never went out in the sun, because they were afraid that she would melt. La Graisse used to go out every day in a beautiful golden carriage. The son of the king saw her every day, but La Graisse was so pretty and the carriage shone so much that it dazzled his eyes, and he had to rub them in order to be able to see. The king's son was in love with La Graisse. He ran to the mother to ask her to let him marry her; but the mother, who knew that La Graisse was the prettiest of her daughters, wanted to marry the others first. She called Dépomme: "Dépomme oh! orimomo, orimomo!" Dépomme came, but the gentleman looked at her well, and said that it was not the one he wanted; she would spoil too quickly. The mother called: "Banane oh! orimomo, orimomo!" Banane came. The gentleman did not want her; she would rot too quickly.

The mother called: "Pacane oh! orimomo, orimomo!" Pacane came. The gentleman said Pacane would become rancid. At last the mother called: "La Graisse oh! orimomo, orimomo!" La Graisse came. As soon as he saw her he took her, and led her to his beautiful house and married her.

The king's son went hunting every day. While he was not there, the servants tormented La Graisse. She was afraid to tell her husband, and she did all they wanted. One day the cook told her that she did not want to cook the dinner; that La Graisse had to do it herself. Poor La Graisse! she cried and cried, but they forced her to stay by the fire. But she was melting and melting: in the end, there was nothing but La Graisse (grease) everywhere; the kitchen was full of it.

The little bird of La Graisse saw that. It dipped its wings into the grease; it flew in the wood to the gentleman; it flapped its wings in his face. The gentleman saw the grease which was on the wings; he thought of his dear La Graisse; he galloped home; he found his wife all melted on the floor. He was so sorry that he picked up all the grease and put it in an old bath-tub, and when the grease was cold it became a woman again. But she was never as pretty as before; for the earth had mixed with the grease, and she was all yellow and dirty. Her husband did not love her any more, and sent her back to her mother.

The Golden Fish.

There was once a young girl who had a lover. It was a fine young man, a prince, but the father did not want him to court his daughter. He went to see an old wizard, who lived in the woods, and said to him : " I pray you, wizard, make that young man leave my daughter alone. I do not want them to marry."

One day the young girl and the young man were seated on the river bank; the wizard came and changed the young man into a fish, which jumped into the water.

The father thought that the young girl would forget the young man, now that he was a fish, and he did not watch her any more; but every day the young girl would sit on the river bank and sing : " Caliwa wa, caliwa co ; waco, moman dit oui; waco, popa dit non; caliwa wa, caliwa co."

As soon as she sang that the water opened, and a beautiful red fish, with a golden crown on his head, came near the young girl. He brought her cakes, oranges, apples, for her to eat.

The father perceived that the young girl went every day to the river bank. One day he watched her, and saw what she was doing. The next day he brought his gun with him; and when the girl sang, and the beautiful fish came, he killed it, and took it home to cook it.

The young girl was told to cook the fish. When she took it to cut it, the fish began to sing : " Cut me then, wa, wa; scrape me then, wa, wa; mix me then, wa, wa ; put some salt, wa, wa."

When the fish was cooked they placed it on the table. The young girl did not want to eat, and cried for her fish; but the father was so greedy and ate so much that his belly burst, and a quantity of little fishes came out and escaped to the water.

After the dinner the young girl went to sit down on the river bank, where they had thrown the scales of her fish. She wept so much that the earth opened, and she disappeared in the hole to go to meet her fish. When her mother came to look for her, she saw only one lock of her daughter's hair which was coming out of the earth.

" Give Me."

Once there was a lady who resided in a beautiful house. She had been married a long time, but had no children. One day that she was standing on her gallery, she saw an old woman who was passing with a basket of apples on her head. When the lady saw the beautiful apples she wished to eat one ; she called the old woman, and told her that she wanted to buy an apple. The old merchant-woman did not want to sell an apple ; but she gave one to the lady, and said : —

"I know that you wish to have a child ; eat this apple, and to-morrow you will be the mother of a beautiful boy."

The young woman took the apple, laughing, and pared it. She threw the peel in the yard, and ate the apple.

The old woman had not lied ; during the night the lady gave birth to a fine boy, and what is very strange is that a mare which was in the yard ate the apple-peels, and she had a foal during the night.

The lady was very glad to have a child ; and she said that as the little horse was born the same night as the little boy, it should be his property.

Both grew up together, and they loved each other very much. As the little horse was born through a miracle, he could be saddled and bridled without any one touching him. When the boy wanted to ride, he cried : " Saddle and bridle, my little horse!" and the horse came immediately, all ready to be mounted.

When the boy grew up, he was tired of remaining at his mother's, and set out to seek adventures. He said to no one where he was going, mounted his horse, and travelled for a long time, until he arrived in the country of a great king.

One evening he came to a beautiful house ; they told him that it was the residence of the king, and that he had a very pretty daughter.

The young man wanted to see the princess, therefore he descended from his horse and made him disappear ; for I ought to have told you that the horse could disappear whenever his master wished it, and he himself could change his clothes according to his desire, taking sometimes the clothes of a beggar, and sometimes the clothes of a prince.

On that day, he dressed like a beggar, and went towards the kitchen. He acted as if he could not speak well, and every time they spoke to him he answered but two words : " Give me." " You are hungry?" "Give me." — "You are thirsty?" "Give me." They called him *Give me*, and they allowed him to sleep in the kitchen, in the ashes. He helped the servants of the king, and they thought he was an idiot.

The whole week *Give me* remained in the kitchen, but when Sunday came, and every one had gone to mass, he put on his best clothes, ordered his horse to appear with saddle and bridle, and began to gallop all over the garden of the king. He broke the flower-pots, the young plants; nothing could stop him. On that very day the daughter of the king was sick, and she did not go to mass. She remained at home, and looked in the garden through the window. She saw *Give me,* and she found him very handsome.

Give me stopped galloping in the garden when he thought the mass was almost finished. He made his horse disappear, and went back to the kitchen with his beggar's clothes.

When the king came back he was furious to see the damage which had been done in his garden. He summoned his servants, but they said that *Give me* was the only person who had remained at home. The king questioned him, but he replied all the time, " *Give me.*"

The next Sunday the same thing happened again, and the daughter of the king remained at home to see *Give me.* The king was so angry that he said he would catch the rascal who was spoiling his garden. On the third Sunday he did not go to mass, but he hid himself in the house. He caught *Give me,* who was dressed like a prince and galloping in the garden on his horse.

The king was very much astonished, and he asked the handsome young man to relate his story.

Give me told him how he was born, and made his horse appear and disappear, and changed his clothes at his will.

He told the king that he was in love with his daughter, and asked her in marriage. The king said yes, and *Give me* married the princess, and sent for his mother.

They lived a long time, and were very happy, because it was a good old witch who had given *Give me's* mother the apple to eat.

APPENDIX ONE:
The Creole Dialect.

While speaking of the French language in Louisiana, it is necessary to say a few words about that very peculiar dialect, if it may be called so, spoken by the negroes in lower Louisiana. It is quite interesting to note how the ignorant and simple Africans have formed an idiom entirely by the sound, and we can understand, by studying the transformation of the French into the Creole dialect, the process by which Latin, spoken by the uncivilized Gauls, became our own French. However ridiculous the Creole dialect may appear, it is of importance to the student of philology; for its structure serves to strengthen the great laws of language, and its history tends to prove how dialects have sprung from one original language and spread all over the world.

To the negroes of Louisiana may be attributed the same characteristics that Prof. James A. Harrison recognizes in the American blacks of the South, that is to say, humor and a naïveté bordering on childishness, together with a great facility for imitating the sounds of nature and a wonderful aptitude for music. Their language partakes necessarily of their character, and is sometimes quaint, and always simple. Their plantation songs are quite poetical, and I may say, charming in their oddity.

Of course there is no established orthography for the Creole patois, and this obscure dialect of a Romance tongue is written, like the Spanish, without regard to etymology and simply by the sound, though the letters, in passing from the language into the dialect, have not kept their original value. It is this misconception in hearing that has given rise in the patois to the word-decay so important in the formation of dialects, but we may also observe in the language of the negroes a great many examples of abbreviations due entirely to the want of energy of the person speaking, a

153

principle well established by linguists, and of great value. The negro does not wish to say *embarrassé, embêter, appeler, entendre, vouloir, aujourd' hui, écorcher, là-dedans, capable,* but will say: *'bété, 'pélé, 'tendé, 'oulé, 'jordi, 'corché, ladan, capab',* cutting off as many letters and even syllables as possible, as we have done with the Latin for our French.

The process of agglutination is very frequent in the Creole patois, and we see such expressions as *in nomme* (un homme) and *dé nomme, in dézef* (un oeuf), *dé lacloche* (deux cloches), *troi dézo* (trois os), *in lari* (une rue), which may appear very strange, but are not more so than our *deux lierres* and *le lendemain.*

The genitive of the Old French exists purely in the Creole patois, and if the student of *la langue d' Oïl* finds it strange to see such expressions as " en son père verger," he will be quite astonished to hear the Louisiana negro say: *choal Jile mouri,* which might indicate that Jules was a horse, if we did not know that he was the owner of the animal. My friend, Dr. Alfred Mercier, even says that there is a dative in the patois, imported by the blacks from San Domingo, such as *zié à moin,* my eyes, *tchor à li,* his heart. I believe, however, that this mode of expression is very rare, and that the possessive adjectives are much more used: *mo zié, so tchor.*

PHONETICS.

With regard to the phonetics of the Creole dialect, we may say that the letters have not changed as much as in Negro-English.

Vowels.

a

is pronounced:
1. a in French: asteur, anon (allons).
2. o   "   moman, popa.

e

1. e mute in French: nomme, fame.
2. é   "   "   'pélé, kéke (quelque), téte.
3. i   "   "   piti, chimin, li (le).
4. in   "   "   donnin (donné).

i

as i in French: 'rivé (arrivé).

o

1. o in French, côté.
2. o in French word cotte: rose.
3. i in French: michié (monsieur).

u

1. i in French: lari, pini, vini, jige.
2. ou   "   la nouitte, tou souite.
3. oua "   mo *oua* ça (jai vu cela).

y

1. z in French: zié (yeux). **as consonant.**
2. y   "   bayou.   **as vowel.**

Diphthongs.

oi

1. é in French: frét (froid) drét (droit).
2. oi   "   dézoi (des oies).
3. oin   "   moin (moi).
4. o   "   zozo (oiseau).

ai

1. ai in French: lair (l'air).
2. in   " '   connin (connais).

eu

1. ai in French: bonair (bonheur), lonair (l'honneur).
2. é   "   vié (vieux).

ou

o in French: 'jordi (aujourd'hui).

au

au in French: au bor dolo (au bord de l'eau).

œ

é in French: ser (sœur).
o   "   tchor (cœur).

Of the nasal sounds, *an* and *in* 'are as in French; *on* is pronounced:

1. on in French: bonjou (bonjour), moune (monde).
2. o   "   mo, to, so (mon, ton son).

un is *in* in French, pronounced *inne,* when it represents the numeral adjective *un.*

CONSONANTS.

b

is as in French.

c

1. tch: tchor (cœur).
2. k in French: connin (connu).
3. s   "   cila (celui-là).

d

1. d in French: donnin (donné).
2. dj   **Djé (Dieu)**

f

is as in French.

g and j

often like z: manzé, (mangé), zonglé (jonglé).

h

is always mute, and consequently disappears in writing: **so** lonair (son honneur).

k, m, n, p

are as in French.

l

1. y: yé (les).
2. n: anon (allons) cf. Old French aner, whence aler and aller.

r

generally disappears, as pou for pour, nég' for nègre, vende for vendre, or comes before the vowel, as dromi for dormi.

s

1. s. in French: so.
2. ch   "   chongé (songé).

t

1. t in French: tombé.
2. k   "   to kenne (le tien).
3. tch   "   tchombo (tenu),
   and is always pronounced at the end of words.

q and x

are not necessary, as k takes the place of q, and the Creole patois being written phonetically does not need x, which represents cs or gs.

v
1. v in French: vini.
2. w in English: li oua (il a *vu*).

y
z in French (zié) (see vowels above).

z
is pronounced as in French, but is used to mark the plural, the
    sound of the plural s being represented by z: dé dézo
    (deux os).
ez disappears, as that sound is represented by é.

PARTS OF SPEECH.

THE ARTICLE.

Just as the French have simplified the Latin
pronoun ille, illa, illud into le, la, les, the negro
has formed his article by taking la for both genders singular: nomme la, fame la, and by changing les into yé for the plural, and joining it to the
singular la: nomme layé, fame layé.

> masculine singular: la
> feminine singular: la
> masculine and feminine plural: laye.

The partitive article does not exist in the patois,
as the words des or du are changed into dé and
di, and joined to the noun as one word: mo manzé
dipain é dipomme. De la disappears: mo boi
labière. If we wanted to use the word with an
article, we would say: labière la bon, divin la
mauvais.

> du becomes di
> des   "   dé
> de la disappears.

The indefinite article a or an is represented by
in, pronounced *inne* for masculine and feminine.
The article is the most extraordinary peculiarity
of the Creole dialect; the French article is always
joined to the noun and the article in the patois
added, even in nouns taken in a partitive sense.

The elided article l'is represented also by la for
masculine or feminine: nabe la (l'arbre); dolo la
(l'eau).

THE NOUN.

There is no distinction of gender in the patois. The article la serves for masculine and feminine singular, and yé for the plural, and the adjectives are therefore always invariable. The grammar of the noun is consequently very elementary. The only difficulty is to know how to form the noun, and that difficulty can be overcome by applying attentively the rules of phonetics given above, and by observing the invariable agglutination of the article to the noun.

A peculiar expression is that used for grande personne and enfant: *gran moune* and *piti moune*, personne not being considered.

THE ADJECTIVE.

The qualifying adjectives are all kept in the masculine, and we have such expressions as *bon michié la, bon michié layé; bon madame la, bon madame layé.*

POSSESSIVE ADJECTIVES.

masculine and feminine singular.
mo, to, so.
masculine and feminine plural.
mo, to, so, with yé placed after the noun: (mo piti yé).

DEMONSTRATIVE ADJECTIVES.

cila for masculine and feminine singular: nomme cila
fame cila
cila yé for " " plural: nomme cila yé
fame cila yé.

NUMERAL ADJECTIVES.

in, dé, troi, cate, etc., primié, déxiéme, etc.

INDEFINITE ADJECTIVES.

The indefinite adjectives are the same as in French, but pronounced differently: kéke (quelque), ki (quel), pligière (plusieurs), etc.

The comparison of adjectives is by pli (plus) and aussite (aussi), and of course there is no irregularity, and meilleur is always pli bon.

THE PRONOUN.

PERSONAL PRONOUNS.

First person.   Second person.

mo($^{le}_{me}$), moin (moi), nou.   to (tu and toi) toi, vou.

Third person.

li (le, lui and la), yé (les).

yé also represents ils, elles, eux, leur, se, en, y and soi.

INTERROGATIVE PRONOUNS.

Qui moune, qué, qui ça.

RELATIVE PRONOUNS

are not often used as "la chose que je t'ai dite," kichoge la mo té di toi. (Observe kichoge formed from quelque chose, and used as one word.)

DEMONSTRATIVE PRONOUNS.

masculine and feminine singular: cila, cila la.

"   "   plural: cila yé, cila layé.

"   "   singular: ça.

POSSESSIVE PRONOUNS.

In the possessive pronouns the t is changed into k. Cf. M. Müller's remark on the subject — "Science of Language," pages 181 and 182. Vol. II.

mo kenne   nou kenne
to kenne   vou kenne
so kenne   so kenne

INDEFINITE PRONOUNS.

The only point of interest about the indefinite pronouns is that our very convenient word *on* is changed into yé: yé di ça (on dit cela), and that rien becomes *arien*.

THE VERB.

In all the Romance languages the verbs are complicated and difficult. However, in that very remote Romance dialect, the Creole dialect, the verbs are very simple and easy. There is no distinction for the conjugations and hardly any for the tenses. The forms *apé* from après, *té* from été, *sra* and *srai* from serai, *malé* from allé being sufficient to indicate the present, the past, and the future.

COUPÉ (couper).

PRESENT INDICATIVE.

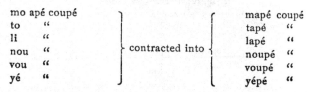

mo apé coupé		mapé coupé
to "		tapé "
li "		lapé "
nou "	contracted into	noupé "
vou "		voupé "
yé "		yépé "

IMPERFECT.

mo té apé coupé		motapé coupé
to " "		totapé "
li " "		litapé "
nou " "	contratced into	noutapé "
vou " "		voutapé "
yé " "		yétapé "

PAST DEFINITE, INDEFINITE, ANTERIOR, AND PLUPERFECT.

mo té coupé		mo coupé
to "		to "
li "		li "
nou "	contracted into	nou "
vou "		vou "
yé "		yó "

IMPERATIVE.

Coupé— anon coupé ——— couri coupé.

FUTURE.

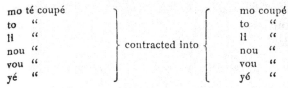

malé coupé—contracted into ma coupé
talé " " " ta "
li alé " " " la "
nou " "
vou " " } not contracted.
yé " "

FUTURE ANTERIOR.

mo sra coupé
to " "
li " "
nou " "
vou " "
yé " "

CONDITIONAL PRES. AND PAST.

mo	sré	coupé
to	"	"
li	"	"
nou	"	"
vou	"	"
yé	"	"

The subjunctive does not exist in the Creole patois. " Il faut que je coupe " is " I' fo mo coupé," the infinitive being used instead of the subjunctive.

All the verbs are conjugated on the model given above of couper. The auxiliaries change entirely, and *avoir* disappears, and is replaced by *gaingnin* from *gagner*. So the conjugation of avoir is:

mo apé gaingnin or mapé gaingnin
to   "   "   " tapé   "

etc., the same as for couper, substituting *gaingnin* to *coupé*.

The verb *être* only exists in the forms *té*, *sra*, *sré* used in compound tenses and in the expression *yé* of the present, from *est*, viz.: " Où êtes-vous?" *Où vou yé.* " Où sont-ils?" *Où yé yé?*

The passive is always replaced by the active form, and the present indicative of être aimé is:

			IMPERFECT INDICATIVE.		
(on) yé laimin moin			yé té laimin moin		
yé	"	toi	yé	"	toi
yé	"	li	yé	"	li
yé	"	nou	yé	"	nou
yé	"	vou	yé	"	vou
yé	"	yé	yé	"	yé.

Future—yé sra laimin moin, etc.
Conditional—yé sré laimin moin, etc.

IMPERSONAL VERBS.

They are also expressed by *yé*.

Present Ind.—yé négé.	Imperf. Ind.—yé té négé.
Future —yé sra négé.	Cond. —yé sré négé.

IRREGULAR VERBS.

Aller—is generally replaced by *couri* as " il est allé" *li couri*, except in *anon*.

envoyer—becomes voyé			sortir — becomes sorti		
dormir	"	dromi	ouvrir	"	ouvri
mentir	"	menti	courir	"	couri
venir	"	vini	mourir	"	mouri
boire	"	boi	coudre	"	coude
naître	"	nette	connaître	"	connin
prendre	"	prenne	vivre	"	vive
rire	"	ri	s'asseoir	"	assite
valoir	"	vau	voir	"	oua.
vouloir	"	oulé			

ADVERBS.

Contrary to all Romance languages, the Creole dialect does not form its adverbs of manner by the suffix *ment*, Latin *mente*. Instead of saying: " Il est mort bravement," the negro says: *li mouri ben brave* or *trè brave;* ben or trè indicating manner.

Adverbs of place—icite, là, ala (voilà), enhau, enba, dihor, divan.

Adverbs of time—dipi can, dimin, asteur, touzou, zamain, jordi.

Adverbs of quantity—in pé, boucou, etc.

Adverbs of interrogation—cofer, combien, etc

Adverb of doubt—pététe.

Adverbs of affirmation and of negation, as in French.

PREPOSITIONS.

The prepositions are almost the same as in French. The negro, however, never says *sur* or *sous,* but enhau and enba, viz.: " en hau la table, en ba la table." Pour becomes *pou.*

The principal conjunctions are: é, ou, ni, main (mais), pasqué (parce que), pisqué (puisque).

INTERJECTIONS.

As in all languages, any word may be used as an interjection in the dialect, to express a sudden emotion of the mind, but with the exception of the universal oh! and ah! Bon Djé (Bon Dieu!) is most used.

FORMS OF ADDRESS.

Michié, madame, mamzelle, maite, timaite, viémaite. Remark that *mamzelle* is used very often by the negroes, even while speaking of a married lady, in the same way that the French did, down to the seventeenth century, when not addressing a lady of noble birth, as "Mademoiselle Molière," the great Molière's wife.

Mr. Littré, in his "Histoire de la langue française," says that the Iliad can be translated more easily into Old French than into our modern language, and he gives the first book of Homer's poem written in the language of the thirteenth century. I believe that Old French, in its turn, can be translated very well into the Creole dialect, and I give below a few lines of "la Chanson de Roland" in our Louisiana patois.

OLD FRENCH.

Li quens Rollanz se jut desuz un pin,
envers Espaigne en ad turnet sun vis,
de plusurs choses a remembrer li prist:
de tantes terres cume li bers cunquist,
de dulce France, des humes de sun lign,
de Charlemagne sun seigneur kil nurrit,
ne poet muër nen plurt e ne suspirt.
mais lui meïsme ne volt metre en ubli,
claimet sa culpe, si prïet deu mercit:
veire paterne ki unkes ne mentis,
saint Lazarun de mort resurrexis,
e Danïel des lïuns guaresis,
guaris de mei l'anme de tuz perils
pur les pecchiez que en ma vie fis!
son destre guant à deu en purofrit,
sainz Gabrïels de sa main li ad pris
desur sun braz teneit le chief enclin,
juintes ses mains est alez à sa fin.
deus li tramist sun angle cherubin
e saint Michiel de la mer del peril.
ensemble od els sainz Gabriel i vint:
l'anme del cunte portent en pareïs

CREOLE DIALECT.

Conte Roland assite enba in pin,
côté l'Espagne li tournin so figuire,
li commencé pensé boucou kichoge:
tou laterre yé li prenne comme in brave,
la France si doux, nomme so famille,
é Charlemagne so maite, qui té nouri li
li pa capab' péché crié é soupiré.
main li vé pa blié li même,
li confessé so péché, mandè bon Djé pardon:
'mo bon popa qui jamin menti,
qui té ressuscité Saint Lazare
et sauvé Daniel dé lion layè,
sauvé mo zame dé tou danzer
pou péché qué dans mo la vie mo fai.
so dégant drét li ofri bon Djé,
saint Gabriel prenne li dans so la main
enhau so bra li tchombo so latéte,
so lamain yé jointe, é li mouri enfin.
bon Djé voyé so zange chérubin
é saint Michiel dè lamer péril,
avec yé saint Gabriel vini
é yé porté so zame dans paradis.

APPENDIX TWO:
Proverbs, Sayings, and Songs.

In 1885, MR. LAFCADIO HEARN, formerly of New Orleans, published 'Gombo Zhèbes,' a little dictionary of Creole proverbs, in which are to be found fifty-one proverbs in our Louisiana Creole dialect: In my commentaries on the popular tales, I have given quite a number of proverbs which are not in MR. HEARN's collection, and have explained their peculiar meaning. In those commentaries are also to be found the explanations of numerous idiomatic expressions of the Louisiana patois. Here are a few more proverbs and sayings which, I believe, have never been published. I am principally indebted for them to MR. DE MORUELLE and DR. ALFRED MERCIER.

Proverbs and Sayings.

Bon nageair, bon neyair. "On peut se noyer, même en sachant nager." The best swimmer is often drowned. This is very philosophical and means that he who knows the most, often does not succeed, if he is rash and overconfident. The proverb might be well applied to Napoleon.—*Chakenne halé so cordon so coté.* "Chacun essaie de tirer son épingle du jeu." In English, we might say : each one draws the blanket to himself. LAROCHEFOUCAULD would have liked this proverb, he who pretended that man was always actuated by selfishness.—*Malhor pou tou moune.* "Nul n'est à l'abri du malheur." No one is exempt from misfortune, or as MALHERBE says :

> " Le pauvre, en sa cabane où le chaume le couvre,
> Est sujet à ses lois,
> Et la garde qui veille aux barrières du Louvre
> N'én défend pas nos rois."

Camarde com chien avé chatte. "Ils s'accordent comme chien et chat." Adaptation of a French proverb ; they agree like cat and dog.—*Hibou trouvé yé piti joli.* Almost the same as in French. We are blind to our children's defects.—*Milate, cé la crasse blanc avé nég.* "Le mulâtre est le rebut du blanc et du nègre." A little too vulgar for literal translation, but expressing admirably the contempt of the full blooded negro for the mulatto.—*Cé jis la plime avé di l'encre li connin.* A peculiar and picturesque expression. "He knows nothing but pen and ink," that is to say, he is a book-worm.—*Dan tan gran gou, patate pa gagnin lapo.* When one is very hungry, one does not peal the sweet potato. It corresponds to the French proverb, "Ventre affamé n'a pas d'oreilles."—*Avan bouric té gagnin mal o zié, mouche té vive.* The fly lived before it needed to suck the sore eye of the donkey. This may be expressed in French : le soleil brille pour tout le monde, the sun shines for all ; or we may understand it to mean that no one is indispensable in this world.—*Mo lestoma cé pa gardemangé.* "Je dis ce que je pense." I say what I think. I keep nothing hidden in the sideboard.—*So lalangue pa gagnin dimanche.* His tongue knows no Sunday ; it never stops. *Moune layé oulé baingnin, é yé pa sélemen gagnin dolo pou boi.*

165

Those people want to bathe, and they don't even have water to drink. I saw in MR. HEARN'S 'Gombo Zhèbes' a proverb in the Martinique dialect which has the same meaning, although expressed differently: " Canna pa ni d'leau pou li baingnein é li trouvé pou li nagé."

Méfié fame-la, li pocrite com ein serpan dan zerbe. Beware of that woman, she is as hypocritical as a snake in the grass.—*Can vou jêne et joli, ça passé vite com la saison dé figue.* When you are young and pretty, it passes quickly like the season of the figs —*Camarade, jordi cé com dé melon, fo vou mangé cent pou trouvé ein bon.* Comrades, to-day is like melons, you must eat one hundred to find one good one.—*Metté mo nom drette là par terre.* Leave my name out of your disputes. Another example of the use of the favorite word *drette.*—*Mo té pa connin ki pou fé.* "Je ne savais que faire." I did not know what to do.—*Gnia plice moune icite passé laba.* There are more persons here than yonder.—*Marchan cibouye pa capab trompé marchan zognon.* "Fin contre fin."—*Ca so métié même.* He excels in this, that is his profession.—*Mo pa connin boucou, mé ça mo connin, mo connin ben.* The little I know, I know it well. Very emphatic.—*Ein supposé.* "Supposons," Let us suppose.—*Dein contini.* "Sans discontinuer." Without stopping.—*Li quiquiribou.* He is dead.—*Va pé cherché laguerre.* You are quarrelling me.

The following is a list of a few genuine Acadian words and sayings; they may be of interest to my friends who occupy themselves with Canadian French:

Aveugler, Arranger provisoirement; *Assire,* Asseoir; *Arrogan,* Ouragan; *Assolider,* Consolider; *Apotiquer,* Hypothéquer; *Anvaler,* Avaler; *Canthaliques,* Cantharides; *Cultivage,* Culture; *A la démain,* Pas à la main; *Dessaim,* Essaim; *Ecopeau,* Copeau; *Egouine,* Scie; *Ganuchettes,* Démangeaisons; *Imposer,* Empêcher; *Pointuchon,* Petite pointe; *Quimpailler,* Marcher longtemps; *Resipère,* Erysipèle; *Tragédie,* Chemin parcouru par un chevreuil; *Zibou,* Hibou; *Zaigrette,* Aigrette.

The following information from an old Acadian will, doubtless, be received most gratefully by our American astronomers: " La comète ne peut pas frapper la terre, parce que les comètes, ça tombe toujours dans la mer.—Here is also important news to geographers: " Quand *l'arrogan* a emporté la Guadeloupe, on n'a rien senti au bayou Lafourche."

Songs.

In the *Century Magazine* for 1886, MR. CABLE has published many creole songs. Most of them were well known to all Louisianians, and several are very pretty. There are, however, some inaccuracies in the text ; for instance, the following song on page 225 is French, and not written in the Patois, viz :

> Voyez ce mulet la, Miché Bainjo comme il est insolent.
> Chapeau sur côté, Miché Bainjo, La canne a la main.
> Miché Bainjo, Bottes qui fé crin, crin, Miché Bainjo.

It should be in patois ; Gardé milé la, Miché Bainjo, com li insolen. Chapo on (en ho) coté, Michié Bainjo, dicanne dan so lamain, Michié Bainjo, Botte kapé fé crin, crin, Michié Bainjo." The song, however, as I have heard it many times is thus :

> Gardé piti milate, ti banjo ! Badine dan lamain, ti banjo !
> Chapo en ho côté, ti banjo.

The word *banjo* is not a proper name but refers to the favorite musical instrument of the negroes.—On page 558, MR. CABLE speaks of the famous song about Mr. Préval, and says : "the number of stanzas has never been counted." It often happened that many stanzas were added to a song or to a poem, when it was very popular. The poems of Homer, among the ancients, is a good proof of this, and all students of Old French know the innumerable number of variants in the *laisses* of the *chansons de geste.* As to the song about Mr. Préval, the number of stanzas is well known, as the song has been published again and again, always in five foot verses. MR. CABLE, in his extract, has joined two verses into one, and destroyed the rhyme. Of course, in negro songs, the rhyme is far from being rich, and is generally a mere assonance as it is in la 'Chanson de Roland !' Sometimes there is no rhyme at all, but where there is one, it should be given.—It would be easy to correct the hundred and one errors in MR. CABLE's articles on the slave songs, but this would lead me too far ; my remarks are merely to show how difficult it is to write the creole patois, without having made a special study of it.

In the 'Guide to New Orleans,' a very interesting book published in 1885 by MR. W. H. COLEMAN, we find also several pretty negro songs, but so completely disfigured by errors in the text that it is difficult for a stranger to understand them. The real negro songs, that is to say, composed by the negroes, have hardly any rhyme, and still less rhythm. They are words with a pleasing cadence and harmony so as to be easily sung. Many are as satirical as the *soties* of the Middle Ages, some are love songs, some have reference to local customs, while others

have very little meaning, if any at all. Here is one which seems
to be a satire, a personal vengeance :

Mo cher zami, malé di zote tou
Pou zote tou connin, pou zote répété
Cé moin ki fé chanchon la
Cé moin ki fé chanchon la.
Malé fé zote tou dansé bambonla.

Si zote oua Sabin can li galopé,
Li semblé lapin ki dan démélé*
Adié, adié, michié la poltron†
Li bon pou metté pou gardé cochon.

Pou fé rodomon
Li crié si fort
Yé té cré cé lion
Ki té dan bois-fort.

So colère tingné‡
Li couri caché
Dan pié latanié.

Can li révini coté so cabane
Li quitté Lainé pou li bate so fame.
Scié, Rosalie, scié ; Rosalie scié
Li oule to la po pou li fé soulié.

This is a pretty song, and quite expressive : Sabin must have
been a cowardly and braggadocio mulatto. The rhythm is
comparatively very good.

The following is an amusing popular refrain :

Morceau cassave dan bouillon posson
Cé kichoge ki dou, cé kichoge ki bon
Tourné co-dinde, tourné co-dinde, tourné co-dinde,
Cé macaque ki apé joué violon.

Last summer, I wrote, under dictation of an old negro of St.
Charles Parish, several songs which, I believe, have never been
published. Here are a few which refer to plantation life and to
the work done there :

No. 1.

Michié Mogène
Lévé bo matin,**
Sellé so choual
Couri dan déser.††
Li gardé louvrage
Louvrage pa vancé
Tou mo zami tendé ! ‡‡
Vini oua, malhor gagnin moin.

Démélé, the same as *zéronce*.   †The feminine used emphatically for the masculine.
‡*S'éteignit*, was extinguished.
**Bon matin*, early.   ††*Champ*, field.   ‡‡*entendez*, listen.

Tous les ans, yé mandé bras nouveau,
Tous les ans, yé mandé chargemen,
Tous les ans, yé mandé rendemen.
Tou mo zami, tendé!
Vini oua, malhor gagnin moin.

No. 2.

Si vou contan colomme* cila-la,
Cé ein colomme ki philosophe.
Piti maite, mandé Michié
Si li contan colomme cila-la.

Ya pa midi,
Ya pa dimanche,
Ya pa la nouitte.
Piti maite, mandé Michié
Si li contan colomme cila-la.†

Lannée cila, malé *marron*,‡
Malé mandé Copal so la clé.
Piti maite mandé Michié
Si li contan colomme cila-la.

No. 3.

Ramassé dicanne à riban
 Tombé, ramassé.
Ramassé dicanne vié madame
 Tombé, ramassè.

No. 4.

Vié Michié, ah! bon Djié.
Vou palé don moin tan pou mangé } *(bis)*
Donnin tan choual pou mangé,
Donnin tan béf pou mangé,
Poussé mouton Missippi.
Palé don moin tan pou mangé.

Moulin, yé poussé charrette,
Charrette, yé poussé marreuse,**
Marreuse, yé poussé couteau,
Ménin vou dicanne dan moulin,
Vié Michié, ah! bon Djié.
Vou palé don moin tan pou mangé.

The following songs, also given by the old St. Charles negro, are about miscellaneous subjects:

Économe, overseer. †There was no noon, there was no Sunday, there was no night for this overseer, work all the time. ‡Run away slave. **The woman who tied the canes in bundles.

No. 1.

Michié Mazureau
Ki dan so bireau,
Li semblé crapo
Ki dan baille dolo.
Dansé Calinda
Boumboum, boumboum. } *(bis)*

Mamzelle Amélie
Li couri dan bal
Li mété *cantché**
Li di cé savate
Dansé Calinda
Boumboum, boumboum. } *(bis)*

A dix zére di soir,
Soyain† moin don do!
Moman moin mandé
Coté ma palé
Dansé Calinda, etc.

Mo gagnin piquan dan mo doi;
Mo mandé Layotte ein lépingle.
La réponse Layotte li fé moin
Li pa bon pou chien tendé.
Pencor oua pareille belle Layotte.
Mo dija roulé tou la cote
Pencor oua pareille belle Layotte. } *(bis)*

No. 3.

Joli son la plairi, (b*is*)
Mo répond mo ségré. (secret)
Mo polé tendé langue méricain. (*bis*)
Mo di vou mo piti maite,
Yen a batimen on la mer, (*bis*)
Kapé chargé nég méricain.

No. 4.

Maringouin quitté chivreil la plain,
Li vini pren *rivole‡* on moin.
Gournouille sorti dan fossé,
Vini tchombo moin dan collé;
Mandé moin la rison,
Cofer mo frappé maringonin.
Mo frappé mo l'epole,
Mo frappé mo lestoma
Mo di, "maringonin cé cila
Ki vini pren rivole on moin.
Maringouin, gouin, gouin, gouin,
Li quitté chivreil la plairi,
Li vini pren rivole on moin.

---

*Shoe made of raw hide.   †Rub my back.   ‡Vengeance, *revanche.*

As I have already said, the negroes sometimes sing for hours a mere refrain, such as this, which is exceedingly popular :

> Mapé couri dan bal,
>> Dan bal, dan bal,
> Mapé couri dan bal,
>> Dan bal, à soir.

Here is a pretty little song :

> Si to lainmin li, li va lainmin toi. (*bis*).
> Oh ! non, cher moman, mo pa connin li,
> Mo pa lainmin li, vé pa connin li,
> Moin mo pa compran so langage à li.

> Si to lainmin li, la fé to bonair. (*bis*)
> Oh ! non, cher moman, mo pa oulé marié,
> Michié layé, cé mo pli gran terrair. (*bis*)

The above songs are genuine folk-lore, being popular songs composed by negroes. The following song, composed evidently during the war, is very interesting. It was communicated to me by Dr. Parra, of New Orleans. I am in doubt whether it is of negro composition :

Capitaine Caillou.

> Can moin Caillou parti marron l'Afrique
> Pou té vini cherché la liberté,
> Yé té di moin, dan pays l'Amérique,
> Négue té joui dé la légalité.

> Can mo rivé dan pays l'Amérique,
> Mo nec tendé yapé tiré canon.
> L'odér la poude fé moin trapé frisson
> Confédéré fé moin gagnin colique.

> A Port Hudson, yankee fé moin couri
> Race noire planté drapeau l'Union.
> Confédéré ki na pa peur mouri
> Va pluché nou com yé pluché zonion.

> Capitaine Caillou frappé par la mitraille,
> Dan la plaine yé laissé li pourri.
> Yankee layé, cé pa gran choge ki vaille
> Yé fé tué négue sans tiré gran profi.

> Can yé vini cherché so la dépouille,
> Yé nec trouvé ké dézo milé
> Ki té mélé avé la po grounouille
> Dan bourbié et pi dan rigolé.

L'abbé Lemaitre di nou dan so l'église
Confédéré va dansé Calinda
Aforce nég béte, yé cré tou so bétise
Méprisé li, li cé ein naposta.

Can vouzote va oua l'ami Fernandez
Di li fo prié pou l'âme à Caillou.
Di li méfié gros jige Bermudez
Ki fé sermen neyé li dan bayou.

The following song was given me by Miss MARIE J. AUGUS-
TIN as being a genuine Louisiana negro song :

Aïe! Toucoutou
Yo connin vou,
Vou cé youne morico
Ya pa savon
Ki acé bon
Pou blanchi vou la po!

Coman va fé vaillan djabaille,
Vou ki lainmin brillé,
Kan blanc la yo va donnin bal,
Vou pa capabe allé
　Aïe! Toucoutou, &c.

Kan tou milate a fréquenté
La cou michié Lidor,
Dézo pourri va pa gagné
Pou von donnin Médor!
　Aïe! Toucoutou.

Many gentlemen in Louisiana have written pretty Creole
songs. The best were by MAJOR JOHN AUGUSTIN; they were
published in the New Orleans *Times-Democrat.* The following
song is quite graceful :

CHANSON CRÉOLE.

En ho zarbe dan manche,
Zozo chanté dan branche,
　Et li contan
　Plis passé blan
Qui toujour fé dimanche.

Mo t'apé coupé canne,
Tou chagrin dan savanne;
　O ven di nor
　To soufflé for
Pou pov 'nég' dan cabanne!

Zozo chanté z'amour à li
Dan ciel cléré soleil siperbe
Et ven pli dou caressé z'herbe
Qué chanson pape ou bengali.

Mangeur poulé vini sur brise,
Dan bec li pran joli zozo ;
Coeur moin gonflé, mo songé Lise,
Ça blan té vand, lot' bor do lo.

En ho z'arbe dan manche
Na pu zozo dan branche,
　Na pu z'amour
　Ni rien di tou
Pou pov nèg fé dimanche ;

Mo rété coupé canne,
Mo rentré dan cabanne ;
　O ven di nor,
　C'été la Mor
To souflé dan savanne.

Father ADRIEN ROUQUETTE (Chatah-Ima), our distinguished Louisiana poet, wrote a charming poem in the patois, "Zozo Mokeur."

The largest collection of articles and poems written in the Creole patois by white men, is to be found in *le Carillon*, a weekly journal published in New Orleans in 1874 and 1875, by DR. J. M. DUREL,. The files of this paper were kindly placed at my disposal by my friend, MR. CHARLES DUREL, and I have read with great pleasure all the contributions written in patois. They are not only interesting for the study of the dialect, but as a souvenir of the troublous times of the White League in Lousiana, the articles and poems referring generally to the events of the day, and satirizing most bitterly and wittily the radical administration of MR. KELLOGG.

APPENDIX THREE:
Customs and Superstitions in Louisiana.

In order to understand fully the customs of a past age and of plantation life before the war, we must bear in mind that the planters lived in the greatest opulence and possessed many slaves. These were, as a rule, well treated by their masters, and, in spite of their slavery, they were contented and happy. Not having any of the responsibilities of life, they were less serious than the present freedmen, and more inclined to take advantage of all opportunities to amuse themselves.

New Year's Day on the plantations was an occasion of great merriment and pleasure for the slaves. Its observance gave rise to scenes so characteristic of old times that I shall endeavor to describe them.

At daylight, on the 1st of January, the rejoicing began on the plantation; everything was in an uproar, and all the negroes, old and young, were running about, shaking hands and exchanging wishes for the new year. The servants employed at the house came to awaken the master and mistress and the children. The nurses came to our beds to present their *souhaits*. To the boys it was always, "Mo souhaité ké vou bon garçon, fé plein l'argent é ké vou bienhéreux;" to the girls, "Mo souhaité ké vou bon fïe, ké vou gagnin ein mari riche é plein piti."

Even the very old and infirm, who had not left the hospital for months, came to the house with the rest of *l'atelier* for their gifts. These they were sure to get, each person receiving a piece of an ox killed expressly for them, several pounds of flour, and a new tin pan and spoon. The men received, besides, a new jean or cottonade suit of clothes, and the women a dress and a most gaudy headkerchief or *tignon*, the redder the better. Each woman that had had a child during the year received two dresses instead of one. After the *souhaits* were presented to the masters, and the gifts were made, the dancing and singing began. The scene was indeed striking, interesting, and weird. Two or three hundred men and women were there in front of the house, wild with joy and most boisterous, although always respectful.

Their musical instruments were, first, a barrel with one end covered with an ox-hide, — this was the drum; then two sticks and the jawbone of a mule, with the teeth still on it, — this was the violin. The principal musician bestrode the barrel and began to beat on the hide, singing as loud as he could. He beat with his hands, with his feet, and sometimes, when quite carried away by his enthusiasm, with his head also. The second musician took the sticks and beat on the wood of the barrel, while the third made a dreadful music by

175

rattling the teeth of the jawbone with a stick. Five or six men stood around the musicians and sang without stopping. All this produced a most strange and savage music, but, withal, not disagreeable, as the negroes have a very good ear for music, and keep a pleasant rhythm in their songs. These dancing - songs generally consisted of one phrase, repeated for hours on the same air.

In the dance called *carabiné*, and which was quite graceful, the man took his *danseuse* by the hand, and made her turn around very rapidly for more than an hour, the woman waving a red handkerchief over her head, and every one singing, —

> " Madame Gobar, en sortant di bal,
> Madame Gobar, tiyon li tombé."

The other dance, called *pilé Chactas*, was not as graceful as the *carabiné*, but was more strange. The woman had to dance almost without moving her feet. It was the man who did all the work : turning around her, kneeling down, making the most grotesque and extraordinary faces, writhing like a serpent, while the woman was almost immovable. After a little while, however, she began to get excited, and untying her neckerchief, she waved it around gracefully, and finally ended by wiping off the perspiration from the face of her *danseur*, and also from the faces of the musicians who played the barrel and the jawbone, an act which must have been gratefully received by those sweltering individuals.

The ball, for such it was, lasted for several hours, and was a great amusement to us children. It must have been less entertaining to our parents, but they never interfered, as they considered that, by a well-established custom, New Year's Day was one of mirth and pleasure for the childlike slaves. Very different is this scene from those described in " Uncle Tom's Cabin," for the slaves were certainly not unhappy on the plantations. The proof of this is, that, although our equals politically and citizens of the United States, they often refer to the time of slavery, and speak willingly of those bygone days.

Another custom which was quite interesting was the cutting of the last cane for grinding. When the hands had reached the last rows left standing, the foreman (*commandeur*) chose the tallest cane, and the best laborer (*le meilleur couteau*) came to the cane chosen, which was the only one in the field left uncut. Then the whole gang congregated around the spot, with the overseer and foreman, and the latter, taking a blue ribbon, tied it to the cane, and, brandishing his knife in the air, sang to the cane as if it were a person, and danced around it several times before cutting it. When this was done, all the laborers, men, women, and children, mounted in the empty carts, carrying the last cane in triumph, waving colored handkerchiefs in the air, and singing as loud as they could. The procession went to the house of the master, who gave a drink to every negro, and the day ended with a ball, amid general rejoicing.

Shooting at the *papegai* was another great popular amusement. A rude bird representing a rooster was made of wood, and was placed on a high pole to be shot at. A calf or an ox was killed, and every part of the wooden bird represented a similar portion of the animal. All who wanted to shoot had to pay a certain amount for each chance. This sport is still a favorite one in the country, both with the whites and the blacks, but not as much so as before the war.

The negroes, as all ignorant people, are very superstitious. The celebrated sect of the Voudoux, of which so much has been said, was the best proof of the credulity and superstition of the blacks, as well as of the barbarity of their nature.

The idea of incantation and of charms for good or evil is as old as the world. In Virgil's eighth eclogue we all remember the words of Alphesibœus : —

> " Terna tibi hæc primum triplici diversa colore
> Licia circumdo, terque hæc altaria circum
> Effigiem duco; numero deus impare gaudet."

In the Middle Ages astrology was considered a science, and sorcery was admitted. It is well known that when John the Fearless of Burgundy killed Louis of Orleans, the celebrated theologian Jean Petit proved to the poor Charles VI. that John had rendered him a great service in killing his brother, as the latter had conjured the two devils, Hermas and Astramon, to harm the king, and they would have caused his death had not the Duke of Burgundy, like a devoted subject, saved his liege lord.

The religion of the Voudoux was based on sorcery, and, being practised by very ignorant people, was, of course, most immoral and hideous. It is, fortunately, fast disappearing, the negroes becoming more civilized. The dances of the Voudoux have often been described, and were, according to the accounts, perfect bacchanalia. They usually took place at some retired spot on the banks of Lake Pontchartrain or of Bayou St. John.

Although this sect is nearly extinct, the negroes are still very much afraid of their witchcraft. The Voudoux, however, do not always succeed in their enchantments, as is evidenced by the following amusing incident. One of my friends, returning home from his work quite late one evening, saw on a doorstep two little candles, lit, and between them four nickels, placed as a cross. Feeling quite anxious as to the dreadful fate which was to befall the inhabitants of the house, the gentleman blew out the candles, threw them in the gutter, put the nickels in his pocket, and walked off with the proud satisfaction of having saved a whole family from great calamities. This is how the Creoles fear the Voudoux!

The negroes are also very much afraid of the will-o'-the-wisp, or *ignis fatuus.* They believe that on a dark night it leads its victim, who is obliged to follow, either in the river, where he is drowned, or in bushes of thorns, which tear him to pieces, the Jack-a-lantern exclaiming all the time, "*Aïe, aïe, mo gagnin toi,*" — "Aïe, aïe, I have you."

The old negro who was speaking to me of the *ignis fatuus* told me that he was born with a caul, and that he saw ghosts on All Saints' Day. He also added he often saw a woman without a head, and he had the gift of prophecy.

There are a great many superstitions among the common people in Louisiana, but as I believe that they are general to all countries, I shall not mention them all. Here are a few : —

1. A person must come out of a room by the same door through which he came in; otherwise there will be a misfortune.

2. Put nails in shape of a cross in the nest of a goose, that thunder should not spoil the eggs and prevent them from hatching.

3. When a woman whistles, it makes the Virgin Mary weep.

4. When little children in their sleep put their arms on their heads, we must put them down, for they are calling misfortune on their heads.

5. When the palate falls, we must tie very tight a lock of hair in the middle of the head, and the palate will resume its natural position.

6. A dog that howls at night announces the death of some one.

7. A horse that neighs where there is a dead body announces the death of some one.

8. When a hearse stops before your door it is a sign of misfortune.

9. To kneel on the threshold is an omen of misfortune.

10. When one eats a sweet potato one must eat first a piece of the peel in order that the potato should not be too heavy on the stomach.

11. If in walking your right ankle turns, you will have a pleasant surprise; if it is the left ankle, a disappointment.

12. If your right ear is hot, some one is speaking well of you; if it is the left ear, some one is speaking badly of you.

13. To pass a child through a window makes a thief of him.

14. To pass over a child lying down will prevent him from growing.

15. You must always burn and not throw away your hair, because the birds will pick it up to make their nest, and that will make you crazy.

16. If you make a child who stammers eat in the same dish as a little dog, that will cure the child.

17. If your nose itches an old bachelor is going to kiss you, and a young man is crazy to do so.

18. If you strike your "crazy bone," you will be disappointed

19. If a child teething looks at himself in a mirror, his teething will be painful.

20. To pass in front of a carriage at a funeral is a bad omen.

21. When a fly bothers you it is a sign that you are going to receive a letter.

22. When a snake is cut to pieces, its friends come to get it to put the pieces together.

23. When in taking leave four persons cross hands it is a sign of marriage.

24. To dream of death is a sign of marriage; to dream of a marriage is a sign of death.

25. It is a sign of misfortune to pass the loaf of bread turned down.

26. When you cut a banana you cut the cross of Christ.

27. If you have a sore on the tip of the tongue, it is a sign that you have lied.

28. If you forget what you were going to say, it is a sign that you were going to lie.

29. If you sweep the feet of a child with a broom, it will make him walk early.

30. To turn a chair on one leg is a bad omen.

31. If scissors fall down with one point in the floor you will receive a visit, and it will come in the direction in which the other point lies.

32. If you plant lettuce on Good Friday it will not grow.

33. If you plough on Good Friday the ground will bleed.

34. If you carry an Irish potato in your pocket it will cure your rheumatism.

35. To cure a wart take a green pea, cut it, rub it on the wart, then take the pea and wrap it in a piece of paper and throw it away. The person who will pick it up will get the wart.

36. To open an umbrella in the house chases away the lovers.

37. To put an umbrella on the bed causes disputes.

38. To throw black pepper on a table is a sign of marriage.

39. It chases chicken lice from a chicken house to put in it the head of a crocodile.

40. It cures rheumatism to tie an eel's skin on the leg or the arm.

41. You must watch for a full moon if you want to make soap.

42. It makes the hair healthier to cut the ends of it at the time of the new moon.

43. If you cut your nails on Monday you will secure a present during the week.

44. If you wear green garters you will often receive presents.

45. If you walk on the tail of a cat you will not marry during the year.

46. It is a sign of misfortune to stumble in a graveyard.

47. It is a sign of misfortune to light a candle in a room when there is already another light.

48. It is a sign of good luck to meet a person who squints.

49. It is a sign that you will hear good news if you see a white butterfly.

50. If a girl wears on her left leg a yellow garter which has been worn by a bride she will marry during the year.

The crows, coming to eat pecans, cry : " Paul, Paul, *a ti gra?* *a ti gra?* *Necque* [only] *la po, necque la po.*"

When roosters crow, the negroes pretend that the big ones say, "Piti coq bon pou fé bouillon," and the little ones reply, " Popa aussite."

The following is a game for winning pecans : One person holds several pecans in his hand, and says, " Ti zozo dan boi." The other replies, " Tiré li." " Combien coups ? " "*Dé, trois, cate,*" etc. If the player has guessed right, he wins the pecans ; otherwise he must give the same number of nuts to his adversary.

In the Attakapas, an Acadian once told me the following riddle, which I had found ridiculous : " Quel est l'animal qui a quatre tirants, deux vire-chiens, et un vire-mouches ? " " Une vache."

I was lately quite astonished to find in M. Rolland's " Faune Populaire de la France," vol. v. p. 113, almost the same *devinette,* namely : —

> Cuatro andantes
> Cuatro mamantes
> Un quita — moscas
>
> Y dos apuntantes
> — Vaca.
> Espagnol, Demofilo, Adivinanzas, p. 286.

> Dos punxents
> Dos lluents
> Cuatre tups, tups
> Y un ventador de mosques
> — Le bou.
> Iles Baléares, Demofilo, p. 363.

Alcée Fortier.

APPENDIX FOUR:
Etude sur la Langue Créole en Louisiane.

by Dr. Alfred Mercier

[2011 Editor's Note]
The following essay was originally printed in the *Comptes-Rendus de l'Athénée Louisianais* (July 1, 1880). It was considered to be the first proper study of the subject of Louisiana Creole grammar, laying the ground work for the more extensive work in the field done later by Fortier and others. Dr. Mercier was a prolific author of poetry, literary criticism, articles on various scientific subjects such as lightning and earthquakes, and novels, one of which, *L'Habitation St. Ybars* (1881), features so many Creole expressions and bits of conversation that, although it is a work of fiction, to this day it is continually cited in linguistic studies of the Creole language. Dr. Mercier also published several translations of fables into Creole dialect in the *Comptes-Rendus*, "Fables d'Esope traduites en patois créole," (May 1890) and "La cigale et la fourmi" (May 1896).

Etude sur la Langue Créole en Louisiane.

I

Reportons-nous, par la pensée, au temps de la traite des noirs; assistons au débarquement de ces esclaves, qui vont être employés les uns aux travaux des champs, les autres à ceux du foyer domestique. Les voici en contact avec une autre race, dans un milieu tout différent de celui où ils sont nés et où ils ont grandi. Ils ne savent ni lire ni écrire; ils parlent une langue qu'ils ont apprise d'instinct. Les mots sont pour eux simplement des sons; chaque son arrivant à leur cerveau, par l'intermédiaire de l'oreille, y peint une image à laquelle se rattache une suite de pensées.

Il nous est assez difficile, à nous hommes civilisés, habitués dès notre enfance à lire et à écrire, de nous mettre à la place d'êtres humains pour qui les caractères de l'écriture sont comme s'ils n'existaient pas, et pour qui le langage est une sorte de musique articulée. C'est cependant ce qu'il faut faire, si nous voulons comprendre comment le nègre inculte, mis en présence du blanc, devine d'abord, en l'entendant parler, ce qu'il veut de lui, et comment ensuite il compose, avec la langue de son maître, une langue à son usage personnel.

Le nègre introduit en Louisiane a formé, avec le français que parlaient ses maîtres, un patois qui se parle encore dans la partie franco-louisianaise de notre population. Le maître, pour être compris de l'esclave, parla lui aussi le-langage inventé par celui-ci; l'enfant blanc, confié aux soins de la négresse, apprit à parler comme sa gardienne. Tous les petits blancs d'origine française, en Louisiane, ont parlé ce patois concurremment avec le français; il y en a même parmi nous qui ont fait usage exclusivement du dialecte des nègres, jusqu'à l'âge de dix ou douze ans; je suis un de ceux-là: je me souviens de la récompense qui me fut accordée, le jour où je m'engageai envers mes parents à ne leur parler désormais que le français.

Le patois des nègres, le créole, comme on dit, est encore très répandu en Louisiane; il y a tout un quartier de la Nouvelle-Orléans où l'on s'en sert, dans l'intimité, en s'adressant aux domestiques et aux enfants. Du reste, quiconque parle ici le créole sait aussi s'exprimer en bon français; il n'est pas de petit nègre ou de petite négresse, dans les rues les plus retirées, qui ne se fasse un point d'honneur, si vous l'interrogez en français, de vous répondre dans le langage que vous lui parlez.

Il m'a semblé intéressant d'étudier le créole dans sa formation grammaticale. Il y a là, si je ne me trompe, au point de vue de la psychologie et de la philologie, de curieuses recherches à faire. Il y a d'abord un fait important à constater; c'est la rapidité avec laquelle le nègre, importé en Louisiane, oublie sa langue natale. Il y a pour cela deux raisons; la première, c'est que l'esclave pour comprendre son maitre et pour en être compris, est obligé de se faire le plus tôt possible au langage dont celui-ci se sert; la seconde, c'est que son idiome africain n'étant pas une langue écrite, il n'a pas, pour conserver la tradition, la ressource du livre. Une langue dans laquelle on ne lit ni n'écrit, s'altère et s'oublie rapidement. Nous avons, en ce moment même, un exemple frappant de ce fait, dans ce qui se passe chez nos franco-louisianais, qui, ne lisant et n'écrivant plus le français, se contentent de le parler; il est facile de prévoir, à la difficulté qu'ils éprouvent à s'énoncer, que bientôt ils ne sauront même plus le parler. Quant à l'Africain, son langage indigène a si bien disparu qu'il n'en reste plus de trace; à peine pourrait-on, en cherchant bien dans le patois créole, trouver six ou huit mots d'origine africaine.

Il va sans dire qu'il n'y a pas d'orthographe dans la langue créole; il n'y a que des sons. En nous appliquant à rendre ces sons, nous emploierons aussi peu de lettres que possible, laissant entièrement de côté toute considération d'étymologie.

C'est certainement chose curieuse que d'assister aux opérations intellectuelles, par lesquelles le sauvage de la côte d'Afrique, transporté sur un autre continent, se compose une grammaire avec les mots étrangers qui frappent son oreille. Nous nous servons à dessein du mot grammaire; oui, le nègre s'en est fait une; les mots qu'il entendait sortir de la bouche des blancs, se sont combinés dans son cerveau de manière à y créer toutes les parties du discours nécessaires à l'expression de sa pensée. En premier lieu, il compose son verbe. Pour son présent de l'indicatif, quand celui-ci indique une manière d'être fixe, il se sert du pronom et de l'adjectif qui qualifie la manière d'être. Ainsi, pour exprimer l'état du contentement, il dit: *Mo contan,* je suis content, pour *moi être content;* il supprime l'infinitif.

A proprement parler, il n'existe qu'un verbe, le verbe substantif *être;* les autres ne sont que des attributs. Par exemple, quand nous disons: *Je lis;* c'est comme si nous disions: *Je suis lisant.* Ce participe présent *lisant* est en réalité un adjectif; cela est si vrai qu'en latin il se décline *legens, legentis, legentem,* comme les adjectifs de la troisième déclinaison *sapiens, sapientis, sapientem.*

Le présent de l'indicatif annonce que l'action exprimée par le verbe, est en train de se faire. Vous vous présentez à la porte d'une maison, et vous dites à la négresse qui vient vous ouvrir que vous désirez parler à son maître; elle vous répond qu'il dîne, c'est-à-dire qu'il est dînant: pour faire son participe présent, elle prend le pronon *lui* qu'elle prononce *li*, elle le met devant la préposition *après*, *apé*; de ces deux mots elle en fait un, *lapé*, qu'elle fait suivre de l'infinitif dîner, *lapé dinin*, il est après dîner.

Cette préposition après, *apé*, joue un grand rôle dans le dialecte créole. Autrefois, en France, on l'employait dans le sens que lui donnent nos nègres; *être après faire quelque chose*, est même une locution qu'on retrouve encore, croyons-nous, dans le Languedoc. Il est probable que les colons de la Louisiane, au dix-huitième siècle et au commencement du dix-neuvième, en faisaient usage.

Ainsi, pour exprimer une manière d'être actuelle, on emploie en créole le mot qui caractérise cette manière d'être et on le fait précéder du pronom:

Mo	Je suis	
To	Tu es	*malade,*
Li	Il est	
Nou	Nous sommes	
Vou	Vous êtes	*malades.*
Yé	Ils sont	

Pour rendre une action en voie d'accomplissement, on a recours au pronom. joint à la préposition *apé* que l'on fait suivre de l'infinitif, *moi après*, *mo apé*, lequel *mo apé* se contracte en *mapé*. De même *to apé* se contracte en *tapé*; *li apé* en *lapé*; *nou apé* en *napé*; *vou apé* en *vapé*; *yé apé* en *yapé*:

Mapé	
Tapé	
Lapé	
Napé	dinin.
Vapé	
Yapé	

Je suis	
Tu es	
Il est	
Nous sommes	après dîner.
Vous êtes	
Ils sont	

Comme on le voit, des pronoms *moi, toi, lui, nous vous, ils* ou *eux (yé)*, il ne reste plus, dans le créole, par suite de la contraction, que la lettre initiale, ou plutôt le son initial que cette première lettre représente; car, encore une fois, rappelons-nous que le dialecte dont il s'agit ici, sort de la bouche de gens pour qui les lettres n'existent pas.

Quand le blanc parle de choses qui se rapportent à un temps écoulé, le son *tè* est celui qui frappe le plus souvent l'oreille de l'Africain: *j'étais, tu étais, il était, ils étaient*. Le nègre saisit ce son *tè*; pour lui il figure le passé. L'accolant aux pronoms, il forme son imparfait de l'indicatif du verbe être:

Moté	J'étais
Toté	Tu étais
Lité	Il était
Nouté	Nous étions
Vouté	Vous étiez
Yété	Ils étaient.

On voit déjà comment dans l'esprit du nègre réduit aux seules ressources de l'audition, la langue raffinée de l'homme civilisé tend à se simplifier.

Pour son parfait, il emploie l'infinitif précédé du nom ou du pronom; exemple: "La nuit vint, il soupa; *la nouite vini, li soupé.*" Ce *vini* et ce *soupé* s'appliquent aux trois personnes du singulier et du pluriel; ils restent invariables. Cela est logique. En effet, dès que l'on a des pronoms pour signifier à quelle per-

sonne du singulier ou du pluriel est le verbe, pour quoi faire varier la terminaison de celui-ci? Dans le latin le pronom étant supprimé, on comprend la nécessité de changer le son selon la personne qui accomplit l'action indiquée par le verbe; ainsi, dans *amo, amas, amamus, amatis, o* est le son qui appartient à la première personne du singulier, *as* à la seconde, *us* à la première personne du pluriel, *is* à la deuxième. Mais en français, le pronom suffisant pour indiquer à quelle personne est le verbe, c'est faire en quelque sorte un pléonasme que de faire varier la terminaison de ce verbe.

Le nègre entend dire au blanc qui attend quelqu'un: "Il va venir"; aussitôt il s'empare de ce son *va*, pour en faire le signe du futur. Pour dire, par exemple, que ce gros bateau à vapeur ne pourra pas descendre, quand l'eau *sera* basse, il s'exprime ainsi: "*Gro stimbotte-la pa capab décende can lo va basse.*" A ce son *va* il accole l'infinitif du verbe, pour déterminer de quelle espèce est l'action qui sera faite, et le pronom indique à quelle personne est le sujet. Ainsi, *va chanté* annonce qu'on chantera. Qui chantera? le pronom répond à cette question:

Mo	
To	
Li	
Nou	va chanté.
Vou	
Yé	

Telle est la forme primitive du futur créole; il ne tarde pas à subir deux changements. D'abord, le son *va* s'agglutine au pronom, et l'on a *mova, tova, liva, nouva, vouva, yéva* chanté; ensuite, par une contraction dans laquelle les sons *ov, iv, ouv, év*, disparaissent, la lettre initiale du pronom s'unit au son radical *a* et nous avons:

Ma	
Ta	
La	
Na	chanté.
Va	
Ya	

La condensation ne s'arrête pas là; dans certaines circonstances la consonne s'évanouit de *na*, *va* et *ya*; la voyelle *a* reste seule pour représenter le futur. Voulons-nous dire en créole que le temps est beau aujourd'hui, et que les oiseaux chanteront plus qu'hier? nous parlerons de la façon suivante: "*Tan bel zordi, zozo A chanté plice pacé ier.*" Dans un conte, dont nous parlerons plus tard, Mlle Calinda dit à M. Chevreuil et à M. Tortue: "Vous tirerez une course de quarante arpents." Comme elle parle créole, elle s'exprime ainsi: "*Ouzote* (vous autres) A *galopé* (galoperez) *dice foi cate narpan.*"

Yéva et *vouva* se réduisant à la simple voyelle *a*, cela peut paraître extraordinaire; mais les diminutions de ce genre ne sont pas rares dans l'histoire des langues, surtout quand un mot passe d'une langue dans une autre. Dans le latin nous voyons l'impératif *ito* va, se contracter en *i*. Un mot grec de quatre syllabes, *episcopos*, évêque, se rapetisse à mesure qu'il marche vers le Nord; arrivé en Scandinavie, il est réduit à l'état de monosyllabe, *ops*.

En créole, pour l'impératif on se sert de l'infinitif précédé du nom ou du pronom: "Que Jules vienne avec vous, *Jule vini avé vou*; viens demain, *to vini dimin.*"

L'infinitif employé comme impératif n'appartient pas exclusivement au créole; on le rencontre dans la langue grecque, les poèmes d'Homère en offrent de fréquents exemples. Nous-mêmes, en français, nous donnons des ordres au moyen de l'infinitif; les médecins emploient volontiers, dans leurs ordonnances, cette forme de langage.

La première personne du pluriel à l'impératif créole, offre une particularité assez curieuse. Ici, le nègre appelle à son secours l'impératif du verbe aller, qu'il prononce *anon;* "Traversons cette rue, *anon traversé larue cila.*" Il eût été bien embarrassé s'il lui avait fallu dire à l'impératif *buvons, dormons, cousons;* il échappe à la difficulté grâce à son invariable *anon* qu'il joint à l'infinitif, *anon boi,* buvons; *anon dromi,* dormons; *anon coudé,* cousons.

Comme on peut le voir déjà, pour cet Africain inculte, que l'on peut comparer à un grand enfant obligé d'apprendre oralement une langue étrangère, l'infinitif est l'ancre de salut; il y revient toujours. Nous allons le voir s'y cramponner encore pour fabriquer son conditionnel. Souvent son oreille est frappée d'un certain son, quand son maitre parle d'une chose qui serait ou se ferait moyennant une condition: il lui entend dire que s'il avait plu davantage, la canne à sucre *serait* plus avancée; que s'il faisait beau, il *chasserait.* Ce son *srè* étant pour lui le signe du conditionnel, il s'en empare; il le met entre le nom ou le pronom et l'infinitif, et cette combinaison ingénieuse va lui suffire pour exprimer sa pensée, dans les circonstances où l'accomplissement d'un fait dépend de l'existence d'un autre fait. Pour dire qu'il fumerait s'il avait du tabac, il parlera ainsi: *Mo sré fumin si mo sré gagnin taba.*" Veut-il faire entendre que s'il faisait plus froid, les bécassines seraient déjà arrivées? Il dira: " *Si sré fé pli frette, bécassine sré dija rivé.*"

Le conditionnel passé marque qu'une chose aurait été faite dans un temps passé, si la condition dont elle dépend avait été remplie. Ceci est passablement compliqué, et l'on se demande si cette fois le nègre, qui ne sait seulement pas ce que c'est que son verbe, pourra se tirer d'affaire. Il y parvient néanmoins. Pour cela il combine le son qui représente le passé, *té,* avec celui qui représente le conditionnel, *srè.* Il veut nous apprendre qu'hier il serait allé à la chasse, s'il n'avait pas fait si chaud; il dira: " *Ier mo TÉ SRÉ couri à la chache si TÉ SRÉ pa fé si tan cho.*"

Notre présent de l'indicatif, dans certains cas de généralisation, embrasse à la fois les trois temps, le passé, le présent, le futur. On demande à quelqu'un quels sont ses moyens d'existence, il répond: "Je coupe du bois "; cela veut dire qu'il coupait du bois hier, qu'il en coupe aujourd'hui, qu'il en coupera demain. Le nègre connait cette nuance. Vous lui adressez la question: "Que faites-vous pour vivre? il répond: *Mo coupé di boi,*" moi couper du bois.

Quelquefois le participe présent est précédé de la préposition *en* exprimée ou sous-entendue; alors on l'appel *gérondif.* Le gérondif existe dans le créole; mais il se manifeste sous une autre forme qu'en français. Ici, comme toujours, le nègre appelle à son secours son grand sauveur, l'infinitif, qu'il fait précéder de la préposition *après, apé.* Il veut dire à un enfant qu'*en* jouant longtemps au soleil il prendra la

fièvre; il parle ainsi: *Ta pranne la fièvre apé joué lontan dan soleil.*"

Le français, en se créolisant, tend à la simplification, et acquiert quelquefois une concision qui lui donne de la force ou de la grâce. Dans mainte circonstance le verbe *être* ou le verbe *avoir* disparait. *Li vaillan,* il est vaillant; *li pa peur,* il n'a pas peur. Les particules négatives surabondent dans le français; c'est un des défauts de la langue. Voyez, dans cette petite phrase *il n'a pas peur,* il y a deux négations *ne* et *pas.* Le créole n'en a qu'une, et il dit en trois mots, *li pa peur,* une chose pour laquelle il faut cinq mots en français. Mais la différence sera bien plus sensible, si l'on compare les deux phrases suivantes:

"Je commence à être fatigué; je crois qu'il est temps de nous en retourner." Quatorze mots.

"Mo comancé lasse; mo cré tan nou tournin." Huit mots.

La suppression de la préposition *a* et de la conjonction *que* donne de l'agilité à la phrase créole: "Je vais dire *à* Madame *que* vous *êtes* là; *ma lé di Madame vou la.*"

II.

Il y a de nombreux points de similitude entre le créole et le français primitif. Cela devait être; de même qu'il y a nécessairement entre deux enfants du même âge des ressemblances physiologiques et intellectuelles, de même il y a des analogies naturelles entre deux langues au sortir du berceau. Le créole nait du français comme celui-ci nait du latin. Comment faisait-on dans le français du douzième siècle, pour rendre le génitif latin; par exemple, pour dire la fille *du* roi, *filia regis?* On n'employait pas l'article *du;* on disait simplement *la fille le roi.* Nous ne parlons pas autrement en créole: "Quelle est cette belle maison? c'est la maison *du* docteur Clark. *Ki bel mézon la? cé mézon docter Clark.*"

M. Littré, dans son Histoire de la langue française, cite ces deux vers du douzième siècle:

Adelbred out avant un fiz
De la fille cunte Théodriz; .

Adelbred eut auparavant un fils de la fille *du* comte Théodriz. Nous dirions de même en créole, sans l'article du: " *Adelbred divan té gagnin ain fi avé fie conte Téodriz.*"

Dans le français primitif on voit l'article s'agglutiner au nom et former avec lui un seul mot. "Le mot lierre, dit M. Littré, vient du latin *hedera* au féminin; il reste féminin en provençal *edra,* en espagnol *yedra,* en portugais *hera,* en italien *edera. Edre* est devenu, dans la langue postérieure, *herre* ou *hiere* qui a été conservé dans plusieurs patois; puis l'article s'y est agglutiné et a formé le lierre; c'est au seizième siècle que l'agglutination s'est faite."

Nous faisons donc un pléonasme, quand nous disons le lierre; rigoureusement parlant, il faudrait dire l'ierre. La même remarque peut s'appliquer aux mots *luette* et *lendemain.* Autrefois on disait *uette,* une *uette,* du latin *uva; endemain,* un *endemain,* du latin *indè manè.* Pour être correct il faudrait donc dire *l'uette, l'endemain,* avec une apostrophe.

Les agglutinations de l'article et du nom fourmillent dans le créole; *ain larue,* une rue; *mo labou-*

che, ma bouche. On demande à un nègre si c'est le second coup de cloche, ou la seconde cloche qui sonne pour le dîner : " *Oui*, répond-il, *cé segon lacloche.* " Une cuisinière demande à sa maîtresse quelle soupe elle veut aujourd'hui, la soupe au bœuf ou la soupe aux écrevisses : " *Ki lasoupe vou oulé ? lasoupe bef ou lasoupe cribiche ?* "

L'agglutination, dans certains cas, se fait entre l'article au pluriel et le nom au singulier ; pour *un* os on dit *ain dézo*, pour un œuf *ain dézef*. On dira en parlant au singulier : " *Dézo mo bra apé fé moin mal ;* l'os de mon bras me fait mal. *Vou poul té pondi ain dézef dan mo jardin*, votre poule a pondu un œuf dans mon jardin."

En passant d'une langue à une autre, ou d'un idiome à son patois, un mot change la place d'une de ses lettres ; le dissyllabe grec *nevron*, en se latinisant fait passer son *r* du second au premier rang *nervus*; dans le Berry on dit *fromi* pour *fourmi*, et dans la vallée de l'Epte, en Normandie, *flaibe* pour *faible.* Le même fait s'observe dans le créole : *Can mo rivé li té encore apé* DROMI, quand j'arrivai il dormait encore; *Mamzel apé coude on la* GARLIE, Mademoiselle coud sur la galerie.

III

Il y a, dans le créole, des locutions qui paraissent bizarres ; on se demande, par exemple, d'où peut venir celle-ci : " *Li parti couri*, " il partit courir, pour *il* s'en alla. Est-elle sortie spontanément de la bouche du nègre ? c'est fort possible. En tout cas, on sera peut-être surpris de voir que cette façon de parler se trouve presque mot pour mot dans Homère. Elle devait être familière aux Grecs du temps de la guerre de Troie ; on la rencontre fréquemment dans l'Iliade et l'Odyssée. Entre autres vers où elle se trouve, citons celui-ci :

Bê dè théein pará te klisías kai nêas 'Achaiôn ;

Mot à mot : *dè* donc, *bé* il partit (il s'en alla), *théein* courir, *pará te klisías* et vers les tentes, *kai nêas* et les navires, *'Achaiôn* des Grecs ; il partit courir vers les tentes et les navires des Grecs. Ce vers se traduit admirablement en créole :

" *Li parti couri coté tente é batiman Grecs.*"

Dans le dialecte louisianais on se sert aussi du datif pour exprimer la possession : *ziés à moin*, mes yeux ; *tchor à li*, mon cœur. Nous devons cette manière de parler aux émigrés de St-Domingue. Ce datif marquant la possession est souvent usité par Homère. Thétis, en parlant à Achille, ne dit pas *mon enfant*, mais *enfant à moi*, '*ô moi téknon émòn*, ô *mon enfant à moi*, comme une négresse dirait *ô cher piti à moin.* Quand Homère nous montre Junon emportée par la colère, il ne dit pas que la déesse ne put retenir *sa colère*, mais bien que *le cœur à Junon ne retint pas la colère*, 'Ére ouk 'ékade sthêthos chólon ; en créole *tchor à Junon pa tchombo colère.*

Le parler créole suffit aux besoins ordinaires de la vie ; il se prête au récit, il excelle dans le conte. On traduirait facilement en langage nègre des passages entiers de l'Iliade et de l'Odyssée. Cela n'a rien de surprenant. Comme on a pu le voir d'après le peu qui a été dit plus haut, le créole et le français primitif se ressemblent ; or, M. Littré a prouvé, par un exemple

célèbre dans les annales de la philologie, que la vieille langue de France était la meilleure pour reproduire le vieux poète grec. On mettrait en créole, avec une facilité encore plus grande, les fables de La Fontaine; cela même a été fait, je crois, pour un certain nombre d'entre elles, en créole de St-Domingue ou de la Martinique. La simplicité du récit, dans ces petits poèmes, et la naïveté du style, s'adapteraient heureusement à notre dialecte, qui, né d'hier, garde encore les caractères propres à l'enfance.

Dès que la pensée s'élève dans la sphère de l'abstraction, le parler créole ne peut plus la suivre ; on dirait que la présence de la métaphysique le frappe subitement de paralysie.

Il y a une différence sensible entre le langage créole de la campagne et celui de la ville ; ce dernier se rapproche davantage du français, surtout quand la personne qui le parle sait lire et écrire. Le créole des champs est plus naïf ; il a gardé la couleur primitive ; c'est à lui que nous demanderons un modèle, en finissant, pour justifier ce que nous avons dit au cours de cette étude.

La lettre *r* disparaît souvent dans le créole ; on a *pou* à la place de pour, *apé* pour après, *di* pour dire, *cate* pour quatre, etc. Le son de l'*u* est remplacé par celui de l'*i*; on a *torti* pour tortue, *jige* pour juge. Le pronom personnel *tu* a disparu entièrement, il est remplacé par *to* et *toi*. Ces remarques ne doivent pas nous étonner ; on sait quelle peine la langue de l'enfant éprouve souvent à exécuter le roulement qu'exige la lettre *r* ; il y a des peuplades qui ne le prononcent pas; la tribu de nos Chactas lui substitue la lettre *l*. Quant à l'*u*, dont le son nous paraît si simple, à nous qui parlons le français, vous savez quel temps il faut aux Anglais et aux Italiens pour s'en rendre maîtres. Le son *ou* paraît plus naturel que *u* ; les Africains prononcent la nuit la *nouite*, tout de suite *tou souite.* Le son *eu* se rapprochant d'*u*, il le change en *air* ; il dit *lonair* pour l'honneur. Le *j* et le *g* dans les mots en *ja*, *jou*, *gé*, le gênent, ils les transforme en *z* ; il dira *zalon* pour jalon, *touzou* pour toujours, *manzé* pour mangé. Le pronom personnel *je* n'existe pas pour lui, il le remplace par *mo*. Quand un mot lui paraît trop long, il l'ampute sans façon ; d'embarrassé il fait *baracé*, d'appelé *pélé*, d'oublié *blié.*

Nous allons maintenant donner un conte nègre. Il ne reproduit pas seulement, avec fidélité, le langage créole, il donne aussi une idée du genre d'esprit qui caractérise l'Africain. Il s'agit du mariage de Mlle Calinda. Courtisée par compère Chevreuil et compère Tortue, elle hésite ; elle ne sait auquel donner la préférence : compère Chevreuil est plus vaillant, mais compère Tortue a si bon cœur! Enfin elle déclare qu'elle prendra pour mari celui qui sera vainqueur à la course. Compère Tortue ne se déconcerte pas; il se rappelle que, dans un combat de vitesse, son grand-père l'emporta sur compère Lapin. Il va donc consulter un vieux crocodile, qui était si malin qu'on l'avait surnommé l'avocat. Le conseil que donne le vieux crocodile, prouve combien il est passé maître dans l'art de tirer les gens d'embarras. C'est là que l'on voit l'intention du conteur ; sous un air de grosse bonhomie il raille avec finesse l'habileté inventive de Messieurs les avocats. Grâce à l'ingénieux avis du vieux crocodile, compère Tortue épouse Mlle Calinda.

CONTE NÈGRE.

MARIAGE MLLE CALINDA.

Dan tan lé zote foi, compair Chivreil avé compair Torti té tou lé dé apé fé lamou à Mamzel Calinda.

Mamzel Calinda té linmin mié compair Chivreil, cofair li pli vaïan; mé li té linmin compair Torti oucite, li si tan gagnin bon tchor!

Popa Mamzel Calinda di li:

"Mo fie, li tan to maïé; fo to soizi cila to oulé."

Landimin, compair Chivreil avé compair Torti rivé tou yé dé coté Mamzel Calinda.

Mamzel Calinda qui té zonglé tou la nouite, di yé:

"Michié Chivreil avé Michié Torti, mo popa oulé mo maïé. Mo pa oulé di ain dan ouzote non. Ouzote a galopé ain la course dice foi cate narpan; cila qui sorti divan, ma maïé avé li. Apé dimin dimance, ouzote a galopé."

Yé parti couri, compair Chivreil so tchor contan; compair Torti apé zonglé li-minme:

"Dan tan pacé, mo gran popa bate compair Lapin pou galopé. Pa conin coman ma fé pou bate compair Chivreil."

Dan tan cila, navé ain vié, vié cocodri ki té gagnin plice pacé cincante di zan. Li té si malin, yé té pélé li compair Zavoca.

La nouite vini, compair Torti couri trouvé compair Zavoca, é conté li coman li baracé pou so lacourse.

Compair Zavoca di compair Torti:

"Mo ben oulé idé toi, mo gaçon; nou proce minme famie; la tair avé do lo minme kichoge pou nizote. Ma zonglé zafair cila. To vini dimin bon matin; ma di toi ki pou fé."

Compair Torti couri coucé; mé li pas dromi boucou, li té si tan tracassé. Bon matin li parti couri coté compair Zavoca.

Compair Zavoca dija diboute apé boi so café.

"Bouzou, Michié Zavoca."

"Bouzou, mo gaçon. Zafair cila donne moin boucou traca; min mo cré ta bate compair Chivreil, si to fé mékié ma di toi.

"Vouzote a pranne jige jordi pou misiré chimin au ra bayou; chac cate narpan mété zalon. Compair Chivreil a galopé on la té; toi, ta galopé dans dolo. To ben compranne ça mo di toi?

"O oui, compair Zavoca, mo ben couté tou ça vapé di.

"A soua, can la nouite vini, ta couri pranne nef dan to zami, é ta caché aine dan zerb au ra chakène zalon yé. Toi, ta couri caché au ra la mison Mamzel Calinda. To ben compranne ça mo di toi?

"O oui, compair Zavoca, mo tou compranne mékié ça vou di.

"Eben! couri paré pou sové lonair nou nachion."

Compair Torti couri coté compair Chivreil, é ranzé tou kichoge compair Zavoca di li. Compair Chivreil si tan sire gagnin la course, li di oui tou ça compair Torti oulé. Landimin bon matin, tou zabitan semblé pou oua gran la course.

Can lhair rivé, compair Chivreil avé compair Torti tou lé dé paré. Jige la crié: "Go!" é yé parti galopé.

Tan compair Chivreil rivé coté primié zalon, li hélé:

"Halo! compair Torti.

"Mo la, compair Chivreil."

Tan yé rivé dézième zalon, compair Chivreil sifflé: "Fioute!" Compair Torti réponne: "Croak!"

Troisième zalon bouté, compair Torti tink à tink avé compair Chivreil.

"Diabe! Torti la galopé pli vite pacé stimbotte; fo mo grouyé mo cor."

Tan compair Chivreil rivé coté névième zalon, li oua compair Torti apé patchiou dan dolo. Li mété tou so laforce dihior pou aïen; avan li rivé coté bite, li tendé tou moune apé hélé: "Houra! houra! pou compair Torti."

Tan li rivé, li oua compair Torti on la garlie apé brassé Mamzel Calinda. Ça fé li si tan mal, li sapé dan boi.

Compair Torti maïé avé Mamzel Calinda samedi capé vini, é tou moune manzé, boi, jika yé tchiak.

LE MARIAGE DE MLLE CALINDA.

Dans le temps d'autrefois, compère Chevreuil avec compère Tortue étaient tous les deux après faire l'amour à Mlle Calinda.

Mlle Calinda aimait mieux compère Chevreuil, comme le plus vaillant; mais elle aimait compère Tortue aussi, il avait si tant bon cœur!

Le père de Mlle Calinda lui dit:

"Ma fille, il est temps de te marier; il faut choisir celui que tu veux."

Le lendemain, compère Chevreuil avec compère Tortue arrivèrent tous les deux près de Mlle Calinda.

Mlle Calinda qui avait réfléchi toute la nuit, leur dit:

"M. Chevreuil avec M. Tortue, mon père veut que je me marie. Je ne veux pas dire à l'un de vous autres non. Vous autres galoperez une course dix fois quatre arpens; celui-là qui arrivera devant, je me marierai avec lui. Après-demain dimanche, vous galoperez."

Ils partirent s'en aller, compère Chevreuil son cœur content; compère Tortue en réfléchissant en lui-même:

"Dans le temps passé, mon grand-père battit compère Lapin au galoper. Je ne sais comment je ferai pour battre compère Chevreuil."

Dans ce temps-là, il y avait un vieux, vieux crocodile qui avait plus de cinquante dix ans. Il était si malin qu'on l'appelait compère Avocat.

La nuit vint, compère Tortue courut trouver compère Avocat, et lui raconta comme il était embarrassé pour sa course. Compère Avocat dit à compère Tortue:

"Je veux bien t'aider, mon garçon; nous sommes proche même famille; la terre avec l'eau sont la même chose pour nous autres. Je réfléchirai sur cette affaire-là. Viens demain matin; je te dirai ce qu'il y a à faire."

Compère Tortue courut se coucher; mais il ne dormit pas beaucoup, il était si tant tracassé! Le matin il partit courir du côté de compère Avocat.

Compère Avocat était déjà debout, après prendre son café.

"Bonjour, Monsieur Avocat.

"Bonjour, mon garçon. Cette affaire tu m'a donné beaucoup de tracas; mais je crois que tu battras compère Chevreuil, si tu fais le métier que je te dirai.

" Vous prendrez juge aujourd'hui pour mesurer le chemin au ras du bayou ; chaque quatre arpens, mettez un jalon ; compère Chevreuil galopera sur la terre ; toi, tu galoperas dans l'eau. Tu comprends bien ce que je te dis ?

" Oh ! oui, compère Avocat, j'écoute bien tout ce que vous êtes après dire.

" Le soir, quand la nuit viendra tu iras prendre neuf de tes amis, et tu en cacheras un au ras de chacun de ces jalons. Toi, tu iras te cacher au ras de la maison de Mlle Calinda. Tu comprends bien ce que je te dis ?

" Oh ! oui, compère Avocat, je comprends bien tout le métier que vous me dites.

" Eh bien ! va te préparer pour sauver l'honneur de notre nation."

Compère Tortue alla vers compère Chevreuil, et arrangea tout ce que lui avait dit compère Avocat. Compère Chevreuil était si sûr de gagner la course, qu'il dit oui à tout ce que voulait Compère Tortue. Le lendemain, de bon matin, tous les habitants s'assemblèrent pour voir la grande course.

Quand l'heure arriva, Compère Chevreuil et Compère Tortue étaient tous les deux prêts. Le juge cria : " Allez ! " et ils partirent à galoper.

Quand compère Chevreuil arriva au premier jalon, il appela :

" Hé ! compère Tortue.

" Je suis là, compère Chevreuil."

Quand ils arrivèrent au deuxième jalon, compère Chevreuil siffla :

" Fioute ! "

Compère Tortue répondit :

" Croack ! "

Le troisième jalon atteint, compère Tortue était toujours tingue à tingue avec compère Chevreuil.

" Diable ! cette tortue-là galope plus vite qu'un bateau à vapeur ; il faut que je remue mon corps."

Quand compère Chevreuil arriva au neuvième jalon, il vit compère Tortue qui plongeait dans l'eau. Il mit toute sa force dehors pour rien ; avant qu'il arrivât au but, il entendit tout le monde crier :

" Hourra ! hourra ! pour compère Tortue."

Quand il arriva, il vit compère Tortue sur la galerie, embrassant Mlle Calinda. Ça lui fit tant de mal, qu'il s'échappa dans le bois.

Compère Tortue se maria avec Mlle Calinda, le samedi suivant, et tout le monde mangea et but si bien qu'on se grisa.

DR. ALFRED MERCIER.

NOTES AND COMMENTARY

PART I. ANIMAL TALES.

I. *The Elephant and the Whale.* — This tale is evidently of African origin; in "Fables Sénégalaises, recueillies de l'ouolof et mises en vers français, par le baron Roger, Firmin Didot, 1828" (lent me by Professor Gerber), we see in Fable II., "Le Chacal, l'Eléphant et l'Hippopotame," nearly the same plot as in the Louisiana tale: the jackal borrows an ox from the elephant, and promises one as large as the elephant in return. He does likewise with the hippopotamus. He gives the end of a rope to each one, and says: "Your ox is at the end, pull." They pull, and not being able to move one another, go and see what it is, and meet.

In Baron Roger's Fable III., "Le lapin qui se revêt de la peau d'une gazelle," the same stratagem is used by the rabbit as at the end of the "Elephant and the Whale." In Ouolof *Bouki* means the hyena, and is always a dupe, as the *Compair Bouki* of our Louisiana tale.

Informant, Dorlis Aguillard, colored man, 157 Thalia Street, New Orleans.

II. *Compair Taureau and Jean Malin.* — The motives in this story are to be found in many folk-lore tales, but our Louisiana tale is, nevertheless, interesting, and is full of *local color;* for instance, when the boy states that "he was born when the peach-trees were in bloom, the year the snow fell;" snow is so seldom seen in Louisiana that the date of a snowstorm is as easy to remember as the day of the battle of New Orleans, "la guerre Jackson," say the old negroes.

Jean Malin and Jean Sotte are as famous in folk-lore tales as Compair Lapin and Compair Bouki.

Informant, Dorlis Aguillard, 157 Thalia Street, New Orleans.

III. *Compair Lapin and the Earthworm.* — The beginning of this story is graceful and poetic, and proves that negroes observe and love nature. The poor little earthworm, helpless, while all other animals are joyous and moving about, appeals to the Devil, and tacitly sells himself to him. The elephant, carrying the trunk of the tree, and the rabbit, sitting on a branch among the leaves, and pretending to work, is a common incident in folk-lore.

Informant, Dorlis Aguillard, 157 Thalia Street, New Orleans.

IV. *Compair Lapin and Compair l'Ours.* — This is a variant of the well-known story of the keg of butter (see No. XIII., "Compair Lapin's Godchild"). The incident of the boat stage and the way Rabbit escapes are curious and original. I have not seen them in any other folk-tale.

Informant, Julia, little negress, 7 Prytania Street, New Orleans.

V. *The Irishman and the Frogs.* — This story is much better in the original dialect than in English, and is based on a play of words. "Brum" for "rum," and "jou" for French "genou," knee.

Informant, Julia, 7 Prytania Street, New Orleans.

V. *Compair Lapin and Madame Carencro.* — We like to find a reason for everything which appears strange to us in nature; and primitive people, especially, are very ingenious in discovering what they consider to be the cause of an anomaly in animals and plants.   They explain just as well how the tortoise lost his tail as how Madame Carencro became bald.

Informant, Julia, 7 Prytania Street, New Orleans.

VII. *Compair Lapin and Mr. Turkey.* — In this story Compair Lapin is not as cunning as usual, and we can hardly believe that he acted as foolishly as Compair Bouki would have done.   The tale is genuine negro folk-lore, as is evidenced by the exact knowledge of the habit of turkeys sleeping on their perches.

Informant, Julia, 7 Prytania Street, New Orleans.

VIII. *Compair Bouki and the Monkeys.* — The monkey, in our Louisiana stories, is often a dupe.   He is, however, more cunning than Bouki, whose stratagems always fail in the end.   Here we have words supposed to indicate the language of the monkeys and of Bouki, and it is interesting to see a negro imitate an animal in his stories.

Informant, an old negro at *la Vacherie*, St. James Parish.

IX. *Mr. Monkey, the Bridegroom.* — Mr. Monkey here shares the fate of poor Bouki, who is so often deceived by his friend, Compair Lapin.   Mr. Monkey is not happier in his love affairs than Mr. Bull in No. II.

Informant, Méranthe, colored nurse, Hospital Street, New Orleans.

X. *The Tortoise.* — This is an amusing story, and it shows that the tortoise deserves to share with the fox and the rabbit the reputation of being the most cunning animals.   Here the tortoise deceives the boy with as much ease as it deceived the deer in the celebrated race for the hand of Mamzelle Calinda.

Informant, Julia, 7 Prytania Street, New Orleans.

XI. *Compair Bouki, Compair Lapin, and the Birds' Eggs.* — The way Bouki finds out what Lapin is cooking in his kettle, and the scraping off the pieces from his teeth by his mother, are typical of the negro mind, rude, but at the same time droll and cunning.   When the birds ask Bouki if he has eaten their eggs, he is proud of what he has done, and acknowledges it with blind conceit and foolish boldness.

Informant, Julia, 7 Prytania Street, New Orleans.

XII. *The Dog and the Tiger.* — Here we have an explanation of why dogs are not afraid of wild beasts, and the story belongs to the class of No. VI., " Compair Lapin and Madame Carencro."   The killing of the deer and the reply to the lion prove that it is not only at present that the " reason of the strongest is always the best."

Informant, old negro at *la Vacherie*.

XIII. *Compair Lapin's Godchild.* — In M. Cosquin's " Contes populaires de Lorraine," we see No. 54, " Le Loup et le Renard," in which the incident of the butter is nearly the same as in our Louisiana story.   The end, however, of our No. XIII. is like that of the " Tar Baby," and not like that of the French tale from Lorraine.   In his notes, M. Cosquin mentions a large number of variants in different countries, which correspond very closely with the Louisiana tale, the names of the children being nearly identical.   Our No. IV., " Compair Lapin and Compair l'Ours," is also a variant of our No. XIII.

Informant, old negro from *la Vacherie*.

XIV. *Miss Mockingbird, Mr. Mockingbird, and Mr. Owl.* — The stratagem by which Miss Mockingbird keeps alive the lover whom she prefers is interesting, and we pity the poor deluded owl.   To appreciate this story one must hear it recited, or rather sung.

Informant, old negro from *la Vacherie*.

XV. *Marriage of Compair Lapin.* — This story may be said to be a continuation of " Ti Bonhomme Godron " (" The Tar Baby "), published by me in my

"Bits of Louisiana Folk-Lore" (1888), and reproduced in the appendix to this book. The number of characters introduced, and the various incidents, render the "Marriage of Compair Lapin" the most interesting in my collection. The incident about Jupiter and the dogs, although a little coarse, is amusing and quaint, and the stratagem by which King Lion is defeated is ingenious and worthy of Compair Lapin's fertile brain. Master Fox appears in the tale, but he is no match for Compair Lapin, whom he finds to be no Isengrimus, the Wolf.

Informant, Dorlis Aguillard, 157 Thalia Street, New Orleans.

PART II. MÄRCHEN.

XVI. *King Peacock.* — This story is pretty and naïve. The daughter submits so gently to her fate that we are glad to hear King Peacock ask her in marriage. She accepts him on the spot, and her dream is realized. The incident of the red seeds is common to a number of tales.

Informant, old negro from *la Vacherie.*

XVII. *The Singing Bones.* — This is a variant of a story found everywhere.

Informant, old negress, 77 Esplanade Avenue.

XVIII. *Jean Sotte.* — This story might have been included among the animal tales, as Compair Lapin is one of the personages, and gives such good advice to Jean Sotte. The riddle is a reminiscence of classic mythology ; and Jean Sotte's reply about bull's milk, although a little coarse, is very appropriate and reminds us of a peculiar custom referred to in "Aucassin et Nicoléte."

Informant, Dorlis Aguillard, 127 Thalia Street.

XIX. *The Devil's Marriage.* — The incident of the obstacles thrown in the way of the pursuer are common to many stories. M. Cosquin gives "Le Sifflet Enchanté," "L'Oiseau Vert," "La Chatte Blanche," "Le Prince et son Cheval," in which are found some of the incidents of the "Devil's marriage." The warning of the old woman to take dirty eggs and not clean ones belongs essentially to folk-lore, and the women hanging in the closet is a motive of the Blue Beard type. Climbing up the pole to catch the pumpkin has a local color peculiar to Louisiana, and the ingratitude to the old horse is another incident often found in folk-tales.

Informant, old negro at *la Vacherie.*

XX. *The Little Finger.* — This story gives the tradition of the negroes about the way they left Africa, and about life in that country. The little bird, Nita, must be their African mocking-bird, and the part it plays in the tale is graceful and poetic. The real folk-lore incident is the little finger left unburied and calling for help; this is of the type of the singing bones. The whole story shows the lively imagination and somewhat poetic fancy of the negroes.

Informant, Dorlis Aguillard, 127 Thalia Street.

XXI. *The Statue of St. Anthony.* — This is a pretty and naïve tale. We take an interest in the faith of the young girl in St. Anthony, and we are glad to see that the statue at last granted her prayer.

Informant, Félicie, colored woman who had lived for some time in Mexico.

XXII. *The Little Boys and the Giants.* — We have here a variant of the "Petit Poucet" story. The incident of the pebble changed into a rock is common to folk-tales.

Informant, old negress, 77 Esplanade Avenue.

XXIII. *The Men who became Birds.* — This is a variant of one of the tales in the "Seven Wise Men." The *local color* is the girl changed into a negress.

Informant, old negress, 77 Esplanade Avenue.

XXIV. *The Good Little Servant.* — This is a story of the type of the good servant and the bad servant. The incident of the master and the whips hidden in a basket and brought into the ballroom is amusing.

Informant, Julia, 7 Prytania Street.

XXV. *The Basket of Flowers.* — The incident in this story common to folk-tales is the object stolen by a bird and found in the hollow of a tree.

Informant, old negress, 77 Esplanade Avenue.

XXVI. *John Green Peas.* — The incidents of the goose laying gold coin and of the shepherd taking John's place in the bag are to be found in numberless folk-tales. M. Cosquin has of this type the following stories: " René et son Seigneur," " Richedeau," " Le Roi et ses Fils," " L'Homme au Pois."

Informant, Félicie, colored woman.

XXVII. *A Poor Little Boy.* — This story is of the type of the deceitful wife, and has a moral end.

Informant, Julia, 7 Prytania Street.

XXVIII. —*PITI BONHOMME GODRON.*

This tale was written in 1884 by MR. ZÉNON DE MORUELLE, of Waterloo, La., and communicated to me by my friend, DR. ALFRED MERCIER. It is a genuine negro story, and illustrates admirably the peculiarities of speech and the quaint and some-times witty ideas of our Louisiana negroes. With the author's permission, I now reproduce it from the manuscript, slightly modifying some expressions which appeared to me a little too realistic, and changing the orthography to make it accord with my own ideas of the phonetics of the Creole patois, cf. TRANS-ACTIONS of the MOD. LANG. ASSO., 1884–5., page 103.

Page 98, Note 1:—*Piti Bonhomme Godron.*—In French, this ex-pression might be translated: " la Petite Sentinelle de Goudron," as the little black fellow placed by the well is really a sentinel, being left alone to guard the precious water.

This tale is exceedingly popular among our negroes, and is related with many variants. In one of them Compair Lapin is caught while stealing vegetables, and in *Mélusine* for 1877 is another short variant taken from a Louisiana newspaper. In neither story, however, is the proverbial cunning of *Brer Rab-bit* as well exemplified as in MR. DE MORUELLE'S, tale. Here also, we see a real intrigue, naïve and rude, but interesting, and such as an uncultured narrator, with a vivid imagination, may have invented.

Piti.—Note here how the mute *e* is rarely kept in Creole : it is either changed into *i*, as from *petit* to *piti*; or more generally it takes the sound of *e fermé* as *ké* for *que*, *lé* for *le*, thus losing one of the chief characteristics of the French language, the mute *e*, and rendering our Louisiana patois more akin to the other Romance languages, in this respect, than to French. This pronunciation of the *e* as *é* reminds us of the Gascon dialect.

The *e* mute of the French, in words ending in -*ne* sometimes becomes nasal in Creole; as *donnin*, *boucanin*, from *donne*, *boucane*. The nouns, however, ending in -*ne* keep the French sound ; as *plaine*, *savane*, *laine*. The negroes always dropping as many syllables as possible, the word *piti* is generally pro-nounced *ti*.

P. 98, N. 2 :—*Bounefoi, Bonnefoi ; Lapin, Lapin !* The negro narrator begins his story with the words : " bonne foi, bonne foi !"
good faith, good faith ! which signify that what is going to be
said is strictly true, and no one must doubt it. The auditors, in
their turn, reply : Lapin, Lapin! implying that they are not
dupes, and are like the rabbit, which is the emblem of cunning,
while *compair Bouki*, (the goat), is the incarnation of stupidity
and credulity.

Often also, the narrator says ; "Tim, tim," and all reply
" bois sec, baton cassé dan . . . . . macaque."

— N. 3 :—*Mo va or mo alé*, the future in patois, contracted into m?
and malé, viz :

Mo va raconté				Ma raconté	
to	"			ta	"
li	"	contracted into		la	"
nou	"			*na raconté*	
vou	"			va	"
yé	"			ya	"

In his article on " the Creole Slave Dances " in the *Century*
for 1886, MR. CABLE quotes GOTTSCHALK's celebrated "Quand
patate la cuite na va mangé li !" and says : "still the dance
rages on, all to that one nonsense line meaning only, ' When
that 'tater's cooked don't you eat it up !'" This is an entire
misconstruction of the word *na* in the patois. It does not mean
' not ' but is the future. The line is, therefore, far from being
nonsensical.

— N. 4 :—*Vouzote—Vous autres*, pronounced as one word, with the
r omitted. The process of agglutination is exceedingly common in the patois of the negroes ; *lari, dézef, déra, dolo.*

— N. 5 :—*ein kichoge*—peculiar expression for *une (quelque) chose.*

— N. 6 :— *ben drolle.* — Adverbs of manner not formed by suffix
-*ment*, but by *ben* or *trè*; *trè* is very rare.

— N. 7 :—*Ki té rivé yen a lontan—qui était arrivé il y a longtemps.*
The past tenses of the Indicative are always formed by *té* from
été; except the imperfect which takes *té apé, été après*, to indicate progressive action. For the sake of concision, the *té* of
the Preterit, etc., is often omitted, viz : mo té rivé, contracted
into mo rivé ; mo té apé rivé, contracted into mo tapè rivé etc.,
yen a. The verb avoir is rare in the patois ; *gagnin* from *gagner* being used instead of *avoir*, verb transitive ; avoir, auxili-
ary, disappears.

— N. 8 :—*moune*—monde.— The word *moune* always used for *personne*, substantive : gran moune, piti moune. Personne, pronoun, remains : personne pa vini.

— N. 9 :—*Com ça.*—While relating a story, the negro continually
repeats this expression, stopping a moment, as if to recollect
what he had to say : li di com ça, li fé com ça.

P. 98, N. 10 :—*tchué.*—The French *t* becomes *tch* : *tchué (tué)*, *tchui,* (*cui*), *tchombo* (*tenu*) ; or *k* : *to kenne* (le tien). *Yé sré manzé—sré* and *sra* used for conditional and future anterior. *Yé.* Observe the use of *yé* as personal pronoun, subject, and direct and indirect object ; indefinite pronoun ; definite article.

— N. 11 :—*Manzé*—the *g* often softened into *z.*

— N. 12 :—*la sícheresse pou pini yé.*—It is very curious to contrast the theogony of the negroes with ours. As the drouth was often so severe in Africa, the natives thought that the end of the world would come in that way, by the want of water. They do not seem to have any tradition of the Deluge.

— N. 13 :—*Lair té boucanin.*—The word *boucane* for *fumée* used in Louisiana to designate principally the smoke from the chimneys of the sugar-houses : *la sucrerie boucane* means that the grinding season (*la roulaison*) has begun.

The description of the drouth is quite pretty : *kéke nétoile té tombé en ho la terre.* A few stars fell on the earth—*nétoile*, the *n* belongs to the word, dé nétoile, troi nétoile (deux étoiles, trois étoiles) en ho la terre.—A funny expression is, *tombé en haut la terre ;* we might have expected *tombé en bas.*

— N. 14 :—*bo matin*—De bonne heure—early.

— N. 15 :—*navigué*—for running about, a word used also in French by the common people, and here most picturesque, to navigate during a dreadful drouth, when the water had turned into vapor.

— N. 16 :—*Michié Macaque, li té batar sorcier, batar voudou.* Dr. Monkey is the Tartuffe of the story, and we are as well pleased to see his hypocrisy punished, as when Molière's false bigot is arrested by order of the king. The word *batar* here does not mean bastard, but half wizard, half voudou. The words sorcier and voudou are not synonymous. The *sorcier* or *zombi* is invested with supernatural powers, that is to say, he can predict the future, but he is not, like the *voudou*, a kind of high priest of an occult and wicked religion.

P. 99, N. 17 :—*grand parlair, ti faisair.*—A French proverb adopted by the negroes. We shall see later on that they have many proverbs, which might well be adopted by the French.

— N. 18 :—*so prière à li*—His prayer. An example of the dative said to be imported from San Domingo, and I believe, quite rare in Louisiana. Here is a stanza of a celebrated San Domingo song, in which we see three examples of the dative :

> Lisett to quitté la plaine,
>   Mo perdi bonheur *à moué* ;
> *Ziés à moué* semblé fontaine,
>   Dépi mo pas miré toué.
> Jour-là quand mo coupé canne,
>   Mo songé zamour *à moué* ;
> La nuit quand mo dans cabane,
>   Dans droumi mo tchombo toué.

P. 99, N. 19 :—*Michié Rénard*—The part which Mr. Fox plays in this story is quite interesting. He shares with Brer Rabbit the honor of being the great trickster, and seems here to have recovered the cunning and rascality of the Renart of the thirteenth century. In our Louisiana tales, compair Lapin, as in Uncle Remus, is the great deceiver, while compair Bouki is always imposed upon, as was poor Isengrin, the wolf. Sometimes, we see compair Torti, the tortoise, take the place of compair Lapin as the smart fellow, cf. DR. MERCIER'S tale, Athénée Louisianais, Vol. I.

The Mr. Fox of this story is something of a *libre penseur*, and had he lived in the Middle Ages, would not have had the honor of being represented in stone among the ornaments of the great cathedrals. He deserves to live in the nineteenth century, he is such a shrewd and practical lawyer.

— N. 20 :—*Tapé vini fé to vantor ici.*—You are coming to play your braggart here—The negroes are, very keen in perceiving the ridicules of men and satirize very sharply the braggadocio and the *rodomont*. They call the latter : *ti coq jinga*, a young rooster always crowing and ready to fight, but which flees at the first blow.

— N. 21 :—*cocodri*—the crocodile, a favorite of the negroes, who eat his tail with great relish. Sometimes, a negro will lie on his back in the sun for hours, and when asked what he is doing there, he will say : Mapé chauffé dans soleil com cocodri.

— N. 22 :—*I fo mo di vouzote.*—The paragraph beginning with these words is curious, as showing the great difference between men and beasts. When all men came together to build the tower of Babel, they could accomplish nothing, owing to the confusion of tongues. Here, all animals understood each other and succeeded in their undertaking. Hence, Boileau was right, when he said :

> De tous les animaux qui s'él. vent dans l'air,
> Qui marchent sur la terre, ou nagent dans la mer,
> De Paris au Pérou, du Japon jusqú à Rome
> Le plus sot animal, à mon avis, c'est l'homme.

P. 100, N. 23 :—*Lion ki té lé roi.*—Lion the king is quite *un piètre sire* and may be compared to many a king in the *chansons de geste* of Charlemagne's cycle, when the great barons began to despise the feeble successors of the great emperor, and the trouvères gave a finer part in their works to the lords than to the king.

— N. 24 :—*ein gros popa* tambour.—An amusing and very common superlative among tne negroes, and used with any word : *ein gros popa nabe, ein gros popa récolte.* Observe the *a* changed into *o* in *popa* and *moman.*

— N. 25 :—*cè ein vaillant ti bougre.*—A fine little fellow. The word *bougre* although not elegant is energetic, and is generally used by the negroes instead of the milder word *nomme.*

P. 100, N. 26 .—*ta vini drèt*—you will come right off. A good example of the laconism of the patois; three short words used, and the meaning is complete.

— N. 27 :—*Bourriquet*—the donkey, takes the place here of Compair Bouki for stupidity. He and Dr. Monkey are a fine pair. His joy on being considered an important personage is comical, and his way of saluting the company is amusing, and the comparison about tearing *la cotonnade*, (home-made nankeen) has a strong *couleur locale.*

— N. 28 ·—*Mo fout pa mal toi avè lé roi*—The word *fout,* although far from elegant, is so often used by the negroes that I see no harm in leaving it here. It is as if we wanted to omit *damn* from the vocabulary of the English speaking negro.

— N. 29:—*Lapin pa jamin fè piti sans zoreille.*—A proverb, corresponding to *tel père, tel fils.*—Compair Lapin in this reply to Bourriquet speaks like a hero, he is not afraid, he is not one of La Foutaine's rabbits, he will make king Lion and all his court trot under his whip.

P. 101, N. 30 :—*pɔu sire*—It is quite strange how the negro patois, formed from the French, has abandoned the sound of the French *u.* This peculiar sound was probably too difficult to them, as it is to many of our pupils, and they changed our *u* to *i* or to *ou*; *sûr* became *sire,* *la nuit* became *la nouite.*

— N. 31:—*li pa gagnin maite, jis Bon Djiè.* To understand the boldness of Compair Lapin in daring to say that he has no other master than God, we must remember that the story is supposed to be related during the time of slavery; hence the horror of Bourriquet and the anger of the King.

— N. 32 :—*Bon Djiè.*—Like the little children, the negroes always say *Bon Djiè,* the *Good God,* using the adjective where we would merely say: *Dieu.*

— N. 33:—*ma montré vouzote coman cabri porté la tchiè.* — A proverb—I shall show you who I am—"Je vous ferai voir de quel bois je me chauffe." The proverb in the patois is quite characteristic : the goat carrying his tail high in the air indicates a proud and independent nature. Such a dreadful threat was not out of place in order to prevent the tiger and the bear from eating Compair Lapin. King Lion never ate another animal, *he* was too kind a sovereign, but he knew the voracious habits of his great lords and wanted to punish his subjects himself; remember Louis XI at Plessis-lez-Tours.

— N. 34.—*yé vini bitté en ho Compair Lapin.*—They stumbled upon Compair Lapin who was eating a root. The picture is here a real *pastorale*: Tiger and bear roaming over hills and valleys and suddenly falling upon their victim, who is innocently engaged at his meal, and drinking from the root of a cockle bur, which proved that he did not need the well of the King. We take an interest in him here as being persecuted.

P. 101, N. 35 :—*Zerbe coquin*—a most unpleasant weed which grows but too luxuriantly in Louisiana and stops not only thieves, but honest men also, as I have often found out, to my great discomfort.

— N. 36 :—*ein ti chanson li té fé en ho lé roi.*—Compair Lapin's sarcastic nature shows itself in the little song which he sings here about the king. Lion is nothing but a George Dandin, a fool who is making other fools work for him, but the Rabbit, *he* does not care any more for the king than a dog cares for Sunday, and that surely is the climax to his contempt.—*Mo fout ben lé roi com chien fout ben dimanche*, a negro proverb which is quite expressive.

P. 102, N. 37 :—*Ravé pas gagnin raison divan poule.* La raison du plus fort est toujours la meilleure. A proverb which I have heard hundreds of times, and which it would be very appropriate to place at the end of La Fontaine's fable "le Loup et l'Agneau;" it illustrates admirably the helplessness of the weak in presence of the strong.

— N. 38 :—*vou gagnin la bouche doux.* Your mouth is sweet. It is not by his eloquence, by his golden words that *Compair Lapin* will win his case, he is not a St Jean Bouche-d'or, but his hypocritical words will catch his hearers, as honey catches flies.

— N. 39 :—*Béf dan poto pas pair couto*—I am resigned to my fate. This proverb is very true. While tied to be killed, the ox seems the emblem of resignation, and only shows his agony by his great rolling eyes. In his reply to Dr. Monkey's taunts, Brer Rabbit proves himself to be another Sancho Panza. He always has a proverb applicable to his situation. Here are three more of them :

— N. 40 :—*Mo pencore rendi au boute quarante narpent.*" "Je ne suis pas encore à bout de force." This expression comes from the fact that it is impossible to attempt to run a race of forty arpents without being worn out long before reaching the goal. Lapin means by that that he has not given up all hope, in spite of his feigned resignation.

— N. 41 :—*pét éte to minme avan lontan ta batte les taons*—A very strange proverb which may be translated : Perhaps, before long, you yourself will be in misery, that is to say, will have nothing to do but to chase away bugs and insects. The French expression *être le dindon de la farce* is curiously rendered by the negro : *la farce a resté pou toi.*

— N. 42 :— *Chaque chien gagnin so jou.* Every dog has his day. Dr. Monkey need not fear, he will be caught one day. Our friend Rabbit is surely a great philosopher and could have governed an island as well as Don Quijote's celebrated esquireu,

— N. 43 :—*ein gros diboi*—A large tree. Observe how very *débonnaire* King Lion is; his throne is not of gold, but an uprooted tree is a good seat for him. We might imagine seeing St.

Louis under his oak at Vincennes, were it not for the bribe
which Lion receives most unblushingly from compair Lapin.

P. 102, N. 44 :—*A la gaillard la.*—There is the fellow, *ala* from *voilà.*

— N. 45 :—*Cofer*—an example of agglutination from *pourquoi faire.*

— N. 46 :—*fé li bande complimen avé kèke piti cado.*—Compliment
him as highly as you can, and add a few presents. The expression *bande compliment* has struck me as being well chosen :
an armed band of compliments taking the king by storm.

— N. 47 :—*té gagnin doutance*—I have heard this word *doutance* for
doute, not only among the negroes, but also among the
Acadians. Also, the word *paré* for *prêt.*

P. 103, N. 48 :—*cé la plime ki fé zozo*—A proverb. One goes everywhere with fine clothes. The contrary of the English saying :
"all is not gold that glitters" and of the French proverb :
"l'habit ne fait pas le moine." I fear that in our days "cé la
plime ki fé zozo" is too often correct. I like that word *zozo*
very much, it is childlike and simple, like the former slaves.

— N. 49:—*to trop connin batte to la djole en ho moin.*—You know
too well how to beat your jaw about me. Observe the
term *en ho*, universally used for *sur*, and often contracted into
the simple word *on:* "*li tombé on moin,*" etc. The whole
discourse of the King is full of idioms. The reference to the

— N. 50:—hound (chien taïaut), and especially the comparison "*ma
crasé toi com ein plaquemine ki ben mir,*" I shall mash you
like a very ripe persimmon, have a real country air and prove
that our narrator was no city man.

— N. 51 :—*cété ein gros divent ki pa mènin la pli ni tonnair.*—
Another genuine negro comparison. King Lion was nothing
but a bag of wind, but while speaking to him, Compair Lapin
raises him to the skies. It is always the story of Célimène and
Arsinoé in "le Misanthrope," Act III, scenes 3 and 4.

— N. 52:—*vou ki brave passé nouzote.*—The word passé for *more* is
often used in the patois: In the proverb "prend gar vo mié
passé pardon," and in the song "Tafia doux passé siro,"
whiskey is sweeter than syrup.

— N. 53:—*ma gagé quarante donze lote zanimo.*—I shall engage
forty twelve other animals. A strange way of counting of the
negroes, but very common. The English speaking pupils find
our French *sixty ten* just as strange. The *quatre-vingts* and
quinze-vingts, borrowed from the Gauls, may also be compared to the *quarante douze* of the negroes.

— N. 54:—*si to té donnin li ein la manne maï.*—What could Bourriquet have done with a gold chain? Corn or hay was much
better for him :

> " Mais le moindre grain de mil
> Serait bien mieux mon affaire."

— N. 55:—*Béf ki divan toujou boi dolo clair.*—"Le premier arrivé

est le mieux servi:" indeed, the ox which arrives the first at
the brook will drink clear water, whilst the others will find it
muddy. These negro proverbs deserve really to be kept and
explained, they are certainly very expressive.

P. 104, N. 56:—*mo lé* from mo oulé—I wish—*je veux*.

— N. 57:—*la tendé pareil com ça mo sorti di li*—He will hear the
same thing which I have just told him. *la tendé*; future of
tendé (entendre)—*pareil com ça* a peculiar expression, borrowed from bad French, just as *mo sorti* for *je viens de*.

— 58:—*Dan Rice*—Never was a man more popular with the negroes
and the children than DAN RICE, and allusions to his circus are
frequent in Louisiana, where BARNUM is hardly known.

— 59:—*li papé récommencé ein pareil job*—papé contracted from pa
apé (pas après recommencer) *job*, an English word used by
every one in Louisiana and adopted as French : il a un bon *job* ;
c'est un *jobber*.

— N. 60:—*pasqué*—parce que—because.

— N. 61:—*vini menti en ho vous.*—A favorite negro expression ;
observe the various uses of *en ho*.

   Kapé gouvernin- kapé from *qui est après*; another example of
the laconism of the patois.

— N. 62:—*Ouchon*—A word created to represent the noise made by
Dr. Monkey and Bourriquet when they ran off; an onomatopoeia.

— N. 63:—*yé fout yé can raide.*—They vanished, they disappeared.
The energy of the expression cannot be rendered in English
nor in French. I suppose that *can* means here *le camp*, a local
word for *quarters*, and that *fout can* signifies to run away from
the quarters, probably an allusion to the *nègres marrons*.

— N. 64:—*maite d'équipage.*—The word *équipage* does not not refer
here to the crew of a ship, but to the place in the sugar-house
where are the kettles, the names of which are: *la grande, la
propre, le flambeau, le sirop*, and *la batterie*, where the syrup
becomes *la cuite*, which, when cool turns to sugar. *Maître
d'équipage* is, therefore, the man who superintends the work
done at *l'équipage*.

P. 105, N. 65:—*Cé pá la peine nou couri cherché tou vié papier layé*—
It is useless to look for all these old papers, let by gones be by-
gones. A good proverb in the mouth of the hypocritical Dr.
Monkey, who with his foolish friend Bourriquet, was trying
already to catch Compair Lapin at fault.

— N. 66:—*palé cré*—pas alé cré, the future. You will not believe.
Here, we are told that rabbits never drink ; but it is still the
story of the forbidden fruit, Compair Lapin will drink because
it is forbidden to him ; there must have been also an Adam
among his ancestors.

— N. 67:—*la viande salé ki té ben pimenté.*—Well peppered salt
meat. The negroes in Louisiana are very fond of pepper, and
salt meat being given them as rations, the above comparison is

very natural. I have often heard negro mothers say to their children : *Toi, cé piment, to fronté com di pice.* You are as bad as red pepper, you are as insolent as fleas.

P. 105, N. 68 :—*protection f ie lé roi.*—A true genitive, as in Old French.

P. 106, N. 69 :—*Tou ça yé ki té vié té apé vini jéne encor. ça yé*—demonstrative pronoun, the forms of which are : *cila, cila la, cila yé, cila layé, ça* and *ça yé.* All who drank from the well became young again ; we see by this how the negroes adapt history and legend to their tales. Here is the famous well that PONCE DE LEON searched in vain, and which was to make him once more a young and elegant knight. Observe, however, what has been added by the narrator of our story : vegetables cut the day before would grow again if sprinkled with the marvellous water. This imagination of the people is what renders popular tales interesting, it is to see what changes are made in different countries in tales, which are probably everywhere the same in the main plot.

— N. 70.—*so piti calebasse.*—The *calebasse*, the *gourd*, when filled with dry peas was called *chichicois*, and was one of the many strange musical instruments of the negroes.

— N. 71 :—*li soucouyé so la tête.*—*Soucouyé* represents more forcibly than *secouer* what Compair Lapin did on seeing the black fellow by the well, we almost think that we hear the noise of Rabbit's big ears flapping against his head, in his surprise and embarrassment.

— N. 72 :—*so la tête.*—It is strange that the Creole patois has kept the article with the possessive adjective, when it is not done in modern French and rarely in Old French.

— N. 73:—*grounouille.*—A frog; often pronunced by metathesis gournouille. The bull-frog is called *ouararon* on account of its peculiar cry. When it is about to rain the negroes sing : "Crapo dansé, grounouille chanté,moman Miranda dan bayou."

— N. 74 :—*Tchoappe*—a word like Onchon used as an onomatopoeia.

P. 107, N. 75 :—*la restan.*—It is curious to observe how the gender of a French word changes in its passage into the patois.

— N. 76:—*gran zéronce.*—A word to be seen frequently in our tales, and referring principally to the blackberry bushes with which our Louisiana forests are so extensively covered. The *zéronce* are not to be invaded with impunity, as many a hunter has found out, on coming out of them with his clothes torn and his hands bleeding. We must remember, however, that they are the home of our friend Rabbit, who seems invulnerable to their thorns.

— N. 77:—*li lainmin moin com cochon láinmin la boue.*—He loves me as the hog loves mud, a comparison not elegant, but very correct and exceedingly popular.

— N. 78:—*Chèvrefeille té bomé láir.*—The description of this spring evening is quite poetical, but the *couleur locale* is well kept, especially in this passage:

P. 107, N. 79.:—*chien ki tapé japé apré gro niage ki té apé galpé divan divent.* —The dogs which were barking at the large clouds which were running ahead of the wind.

— N. 80:—*mo lé baingnin asoir.*—I want to take a bath this evening. The address of Compair Lapin to Ti Bonhomme Godron is amusing. He pretends at first that he does not want to drink the water, but only comes to bathe in the well, then he gets angry, loses his usual cunning and gets caught.

P. 108, N. 81:—*li té sali so répitation hors service.*—A good expression, her reputation was soiled out of service, as Compair Lapin had spread everywhere *paillé* (*éparpillé*) that he was Miss Léonine's lover.

— N. 82:—*can di boi tombé, cabri mouté*—Proverb—Quand on est ruiné, chacun vous tourne le dos. When the tree is down, be it the tallest oak tree, the goat can despise it and climb on it ; it is always the famous *coup de pied de l'âne* to the dying lion.

— N. 83:—*Cochon marron connin où yé frotté.* —Another form of this proverb is: cochon marron pa frotté apé gorofié, The word gorofié, says MR. DE MORUELLE, comes by corruption from *gare-aux-pieds.* It is a tree with long and hard thorns, which the wild hog takes good care not to touch. The proverb might be translated thus: "le lâche ne s'attaque jamais au brave," the coward never attacks the brave man. Dr. Monkey and Bourriquet would never have dared to insult our brave *Compair Lapin,* when he was in liberty.

— N. 84:—*Ça mo di, li ben di*—What I have said is well said. A sentence of great concision and force. Lapin is quite sure that he is right: *Magister dixit.*

— N. 85:—*ein fie ki té mince com ein dicanne é ki tournin gros com ein bari farine.*—A most singular and amusing comparison, a little coarse, but characteristic and expressive.

— N. 86:—*cé pa baptême catin.*—A proverb. That is very serious, it is not the baptism of a doll—catin for *poupée* is very common.

P. 109, N. 87:—*dromi*—for dormi.—There is a pretty negro *dicton* beginning with this word : *dromi trompé moin,* sleep has deceived me, I awoke too late.

— N. 88:—*A la barre jou*—At dawn, that is to say, when the first streak of day is seen.

— N. 89:—*Oh! mé li té bel.*—The description of Miss Léonine's *toilette* is admirable, it shows the *good* taste of the negroes ; a dress of white muslin, with a blue ribbon, and a wreath of roses on her head, in the hottest sun, at noon, and yet all eyes were riveted on her, *braqué enho li.*

— N. 90:—*Oui, oua!*—an exclamation. Yes, indeed!

—N. 91:—*ki té apé tremblé com ein feille liard.*—Poor Compair

P. 109, N. 92 :—*Lapin*, his bravery has abandoned him. How is he to get out of this bad scrape?

— N. 93 :—*donnin li so choix pou choisi so la mort.*—Gave him his choice to choose his death. A funny pleonasm, which reminds us of our French *monter en haut* and *descendre en bas.*

— N. 94 :—*tou ça ensemb.*—All these at the same time. Compair Lapin chooses to be killed in three different ways at the same time, rather than be thrown in the thorns (*grand zéronce*).

P. 110, N. 95 :—*Ça ça yé.*—A very concise expression. "What is the matter?

— N. 96 :—*Mamzelle Léonine vancé.*—Miss Léonine plays here an interesting part; she pretends to hate Compair Lapin, and begs that he be thrown in the thorns. It is, of course, to save him.

— N. 97 :—*cé là minme mo moman té fé moin*—A common *dicton* in the Creole patois. "I am at home here, that is my country." In French, we sometimes say: "Je suis sur mon fumier." Compair Lapin was indeed at home and saved.

— N. 98 :—*Nimporte kichoge ein fame oulé*, Bon Djié aussite. An interesting translation of the famous saying: "ce que femme veut, Dieu le veut."

P. 111, N. 99 :—*Com mo té la can tou ça rivé.*—Of course, the narrator was always an eye witness of all he relates; is not his motto, *Bonne foi, Bonne foi?*

— N. 100 :—*Mo fini.*—The end—" Finis coronat opus."

Compair Bouki é Compair Lapin.

The stories about Compair Bouki and Compair Lapin are probably the most amusing of all our popular tales; they are innumerable, and in all of them, the rabbit is victorious, playing, as I have already said, the part of Renart in the story of the thirteenth century. 'Jean Sot é Jean l'Esprit' are tales of the same kind, in which, of course, Jean Sot is Bouki and l'Esprit is Lapin. I give several Bouki and Lapin stories, numbering them 1, 2, 3, 4, 5, and 6.

XXIX.—*Compair Bouki è Compair Lapin.*—No. 1.

Page III, Note 1:—*Compair.*—The real orthography of this word is probably *compè* with the *r* omitted, but I have adopted the spelling of the tales already published, such as DR. MERCIER'S 'Mamzelle Calinda.'

— N. 2:—*ma vende li pou ein chaudière di gri è ein chaudière gombo.*—I shall sell her for a pot of hominy and one of gombo. The idea is very amusing and quaint, but however absurd, Lapin knew the astounding stupidity of Bouki.

— N. 3:—*Compair Lapin marré so kenne avé ein fil zaraigné.*—Observe the cunning of Rabbit: Bouki has tied his mother with a big rope, but Lapin ties his with a cobweb, that she might run away in the *zéronce.*

P. 112, N. 4:—*Coupé la tchê so choal, planté li dan la terre.*—This stratagem of Compair Lapin is quite funny. Having stolen Bouki's cart, he cut the horse's tail and stuck it in the ground, so that his foolish friend might believe that the horse and cart had fallen in a hole.

— N. 5:—*Vini dan gran bal.*—Compair Bouki was apparently a *vert-galant*, as he claims for his wife the beautiful negress from Senegal mentioned by Compair Lapin. He is, however, punished for his intended infidelity to Madame Bouki, and meets Tiger dressed as a woman, who gives him a good beating.

— N. 6:—*Simion carillon painpain.* These words have no meaning, and are merely sung for imitative harmony.

— N. 7:—*Aïe, aïe, aïe, compair Lapin.*—A most popular refrain among the negroes, and sung when there is lively dancing.

XXX.—*Compair Bouki è Compair Lapin.*—No. 2.

P. 113, N. 1:—This story was written for me by my sister, MRS. N. LEBEUF, of Jefferson Parish, who has kindly helped me very much in my collection of tales.

— N. 2:—*vou va sotté dan so lagorge.*—The plot of this tale was probably taken from one of GRIMM'S 'Märchen,' but the conclusion is of real negro invention.

— N. 3:—*yé bourré li avé di sabe, è ye metté ein bouchon pou fermin trou la.* They stuffed him with sand and put a cork to stop the opening.

P. 114, N. 4:—*yavé di miel en ho la.*—There was honey on the cork, and Bouki's children licking it the cork came out and poor Bouki died flat on the ground. Quite a peculiar patricide!

XXXI.—*Compair Bouki è Compair Lapin.*—No. 3.

P. 114, N. 1 :—This story seems to be based upon the celebrated tale, "Alibaba and the Forty Thieves," in the "Arabian Nights ;" it is, however, interesting to see how it is related by the negroes ; for instance, in the Oriental story, the mere "Sésame ouvre-toi," is sufficient to obtain an entrance into the cavern. In the negro story, there is a conversation between Bouki and the tree.

— N. 2 : — *Bouki.*—"*Nabe com to dou!*" "Tree, how sweet you are!" The Tree.—"Si mo té ouvri, ça to sré di?" "If I opened, what would you say ?" Bouki.—"Mo sré ben conten." "I should be very glad."—This last answer is delightfully *naïve* and worthy of our friend Bouki.

XXXII.—*Compair Bouki è Compair Lapin.*—No. 4.

— N. 1 :—This story is very short, but is nevertheless amusing. It was probably the worst trick that Lapin ever played his friend. What ! to make the grave Bouki pass for a horse, mount on his back, spur him on, and make him gallop, in the presence of the *mamzelle* whom he was courting ! That was too bad ; *c'était le comble!*

P. 115, N. 2 :—*nec apé grouillé.*—A peculiar expression. "Ne faisait que grouiller."

XXXIII.—*Compair Bouki è Compair Lapin.*—No. 5.

— N. 1 :—The manuscript of this tale was given to me by DR. MERCIER, for whom it had been written by a colored man ; a copy of it was sent by the DOCTOR, with a translation in French, to M. EUGÈNE ROLLAND, and published by him in Volume V, of 'Faune Populaire de la France." I reproduce it here in order that my collection of Bouki and Lapin tales may be complete. It is one of our best Louisiana Stories.

— N. 2 :—*na pi rantion dan cabane.*—Ration, an allusion to the pork and corn meal given to the field hands every Saturday on plantations. In this sentence *na* has a negative meaning, but *n* is the negative, and *a* is the verb.

— N. 3 :—*na couri tou souite.*—Another example of the future in the Creole patois ; there is no negative here. The meaning is : we shall go immediately.

P. 116, N. 4 :—*Compair Torti lèvé so la tête.*—The tortoise, who is generally as cunning as the rabbit, was as foolish here as Compair Bouki. As his stupidity had cost him his tail, he probably became cunning from that time ; there is nothing like experience in this world !

XXXVI.—*Compair Bouki è Compair Lapin.*—No. 6.

P. 117, N. 1 :—This tale was taken from *le Diamant,* a periodical published in New Orleans for a few months this year, by MR. A. MEYNIER. The plot is evidently borrowed from 'le Roman de Renart.'

P. 117, N. 2:—*Li trouvé li apé zonglé arien*—A happy expression, "reflecting about nothing." This rabbit was not like that of La Fontaine.

— N. 3:—*su chimin, su mo do.*—This is not good patois, it should be : *en ho chimin, en ho mo do.*

P. 118, N. 4:—*ein gro couarte l'habitation.*—A terrible whip, twisted in four.

— N. 5:—*ein fouet ki té gagnin piment, di poivre é di sel.*—"A whipping seasoned with red pepper, black pepper, and salt." Poor Bouki was sadly used up. Let him hereafter beware of

— N. 6:—Compair Lapin, that is what Man Henriette says, and I cheerfully add my advice to hers in bidding him good-bye.

XXXV.—*Ein vié Zombi Malin.*

— N. 1:—This story was communicated to me by a gentleman who had heard it related a hundred times to his children by their old negro nurse. I thought it was a genuine Louisiana story, and was, therefore, much surprised to find the almost identical tale in M. ROLLAND's 'Faune Populaire de la France,' Vol. III, about the grillon, called *grillet* in Bouches-du-Rhône and in Switzerland. I give, nevertheless, the Louisiana version of the story, in our Creole patois.

XXXVI.—*Choal Djié.*

P. 119, N. 1:—A name given by the negroes to an insect which we call in French *prie-Dieu.*

— N. 2:—*Cé Compair Lapin ki fé signe la croi on moin.*—That gentle sign of the cross, which left a bloody mark, is an answer worthy of Compair Lapin. We see that our friend Rabbit is still at his old tricks. In bidding him good-bye, it is with the hope that he will mend his evil ways, for he may meet with another *Ti Bonhomme Godron* and not find Miss Léonine to help him out of his bad scrape.

XXXVII.—*Ein Fame ki tournin Macaque.*

P. 120, N. 1:—This is a tale which I wrote almost under the dictation of a negro woman ; it is far from being witty, but is interesting as being a real folk-lore story. I may add here that it is quite a treat to hear a negro relate a tale. He not only speaks, but actually acts, making vehement gestures and often singing a refrain or an air of his own composition.

Fin.

Printed in the USA
CPSIA information can be obtained
at www.ICGtesting.com
CBHW030453281023
1539CB00005B/9